ANVIL BOOKS

MY FIGHT FOR IRISH FREEDOM

DAN BREEN

DAN BREEN

MY FIGHT
FOR IRISH FREEDOM

ANVIL BOOKS

MY FIGHT
FOR IRISH FREEDOM

An Anvil Book.

Published in the
Republic of Ireland
by Anvil Books Ltd.,
Tralee, Co. Kerry.

First published by the Talbot Press, 1924
Published by Anvil Books, 1964
Reprinted 1968
Reprinted 1970
Reprinted 1973.
© Copyright Dan Breen.

Made and printed in the Republic of Ireland
by The Kerryman Ltd., Tralee, Co. Kerry.
Set in 8/10 Imperial Roman.

To

SEÁN TREACY

J. J. HOGAN

AND

SÉAMUS ROBINSON

CONTENTS

ILLUSTRATIONS

(Between pages 48 and 49)

The Happy Warrior.

Sir John French, the Lord Lieutenant; Martin Savage; section of the memorial at Solohead Cross.

Group comprising Séamus Robinson, Seán Treacy, Dan Breen, Michael Brennan and Seán Hogan; group comprising Mick McDonnell, Tom Kehoe, Jim Slattery, Vincent Byrne and Paddy Daly.

Maurice Crowe, Con Moloney, and Seán Fitzpatrick; group of Fourth and Fifth Battalion officers, Third Tipperary Brigade.

General Lucas and I.R.A. guards; British military outside Mountjoy jail.

Sir Hamar Greenwood and Auxiliaries in Dublin; Black-and-Tans in County Limerick.

Crowds outside Mountjoy jail; Fifth Battalion Column, Third Tipperary Brigade.

Wedding of Dan Breen and Brighid Malone; guests at the wedding.

(Between pages 144 and 145)

Shooting of Sean Treacy and others—eight pictures.

The Murder Gang.

The guard room in Dublin Castle where I.R.A. leaders were murdered on Bloody Sunday.

Michael Sadlier, Dinny Lacey and Dinny Sadlier; scene near Dublin Castle on the morning of the Truce.

Paddy Dalton and Martin ("Sparkie") Breen; lying-in-state of General Liam Lynch.

FOREWORD

EARLY IN MARCH 1922 Dan Breen was staying at the presbytery of his fellow-countyman, Father Dan Kelly, at Menlo Park, San Francisco, when he received a cablegram urgently requesting him to return home. The threat of civil war loomed over Ireland. Dan had a premonition, fortunately not realised, that he was going back to meet his death. He was impelled to write what we might term an *apologia pro vita sua*. On the train journey from San Francisco to New York, interrupted with stop-offs to see his friends at Chicago and Philadelphia, he jotted down a rough draft of his early life, his upbringing, his patriotic yearnings, and his part in Ireland's fight for freedom. It is obvious from the comparatively meagre details about the Civil War, which he later added as a postscript, that his heart was not in this conflict. He protested that he was born to be a soldier and not a politician, but he hoped, desperately, that a super-statesman would arise who would command the confidence of the Treaty and anti-Treaty elements and unite them once more in the fight against Britain, the old enemy. But alas his hope proved vain. He was caught up willy-nilly in the toils of the internecine struggle and he emerged broken-hearted.

The highlights of Dan's story are undoubtedly the rescue of Seán Hogan at Knocklong and the affray at "Fernside." In both of those engagements all the odds were against his survival, and yet he lived to tell the story. The fact that it was written at white heat in such a short space of time gives a swiftness, almost a breathlessness of movement to the narration that has been rarely achieved by any writer. At times the very sound of his words echoes the excitement of the situation which he is describing. To give one example: "There was a crash of glass at the front of the house and the hall-door was burst open. From the stairs came the sound of rushing footsteps.

" We sprang out of bed. Simultaneously we gripped our revolvers. Fingers were groping on our door. I held my breath. Seán pressed my arm and whispered, ' Good-bye, Dan, until we meet above.'

" Crack ! Crack ! The bullets came whizzing through the door. Crack ! Crack ! My German Mauser pistol was replying.

" There was no light save the flash of shots. Outside a voice was shouting . . . . ."

The reader is reminded of the suspense maintained in *The Three Musketeers*, or perhaps still more forcibly of that picaresque Australian classic, *Robbery Under Arms*.

The difficulty of writing under such conditions, without an opportunity of referring to notes or works of reference, provides an excuse for a jumbling of sequence and for an occasional flight of fancy which is in accordance with the accepted tradition of the Shanachie. Dan makes no claim to be a *literatus* but he has the genius of the born story-teller.

EDITOR—ANVIL BOOKS

CHAPTER ONE

CHILDHOOD AND EARLY MANHOOD

I WAS BORN ON 11 AUGUST 1894 in my father's cottage at Grange, one mile south of Donohill, Co. Tipperary. I received the name Daniel at my christening, which took place two days later at Solohead parish church. My parents were Daniel Breen and Honora Moore. My mother was a native of Reenavana, Doon, Co. Limerick. The children born to them in order of seniority were Laurence, Mary, John, Winifred, Catherine, Patrick, Dan and Laurence (Junior). The firstborn, Laurence, died when I was about four years old. He was eighteen at the time of his death. He and two other lads of about the same age had spent some hours fishing the Multeen brook on a night of dense fog. All three of them contracted pneumonia and died a couple of weeks later. A superstitious old woman spread the tale that the young fellows had watched a hurling match between two teams of fairies in the rath field and thereby forfeited their lives.

My father died from blood-poisoning at the age of sixty. A thorn pierced his finger when he was scarting a fence. The wound turned septic and he was laid up for more than one year before his death. He was a pleasant-looking, bearded man of middle height. I was about six years old at the time of his death and I have only a faint recollection of him. I remember one sunny day when he took me by the hand and led me through the fields. When I got tired he lifted me on to his shoulders and brought me home pick-a-back. I have a distinct memory of the coffin being brought into the room in which he was waked. The womenfolk set up such a keening that Martin Breen, my father's cousin, ordered them to go down to the kitchen.

My father's death must have been a great blow to my mother, who had to provide for a houseful of children, the youngest of whom was still in the cradle. My mother was a midwife and managed to make ends meet even though

11

she was hard pressed at times. Her meagre earnings were supplemented by Mary and John. Mary was hired as a general-servant in a neighbour's house at a wage of six pounds a year. John went to work for a farmer. They brought home every penny that they earned.

Even though I was very young at the time of the Boer War, I can still remember the neighbours sitting round the fire, listening to someone reading aloud the news from *The Irish People*. I recall their exultation over the victories gained by the Boer Generals, Cronje and de Wit, and how thrilled they were by the British defeat at Spion Kop.

I remember the last eviction which took place one mile from Grange. Michael Dwyer Bán, a relative of ours, was ejected from his home and died on the roadside. This event left an indelible impression on my mind.

The Land Act of 1903, which enabled tenants to purchase their holdings, brought great joy to the farmers. They seemed to have entered an utopia where the threat of famine no longer existed. In a short time, however, they began to complain of the high rent, £2 to £2-5-0 an acre. I often heard my godfather, Long Jim Ryan, and my uncle, Lar Breen, talking about this high rent and also the poor price paid for milk delivered to the new Cleeve's factory. They considered that threepence a gallon was not an economic return. I did not know the meaning of the word " economic " but I received the impression that everything was not tinted with a colour of rose. Their chief grievance was that no " back-milk " was given to the suppliers.

Our family barely existed above the hair-line of poverty. Most of the neighbours were in a similar plight. Potatoes and milk were our staple diet. On special occasions we had a meal of salted pork but the luxury of fresh meat was altogether beyond our reach.

I went to Garryshane school at the age of four. Even though the building was situated in the village of Donohill, the national school had to get its title from the name of the field on which it was built. The Protestants objected to the school being called " Donohill National School." They claimed exclusive right to the prefix " Donohill " because it was the official name of their parish.

The school was a drab two-storey building with no play-ground for the pupils. The girls occupied the upper floor, the boys the ground floor. The principal of the boys' school was James Power, a kinsman of the Breens. He

died about the time that I was in the fourth class. Charlie
Walshe, a Kerryman, was appointed to act as substitute
teacher pending the appointment of a new principal. He
was better known in later years as Cormac Breathnach,
Lord Mayor of Dublin. Charlie had been engaged by the
Gaelic League to teach Irish in the rural areas. He did
relief-work in several national schools of our district. It
may be of interest to learn that he also taught Seán Treacy,
Dinny Lacey, Packy Deere, Seán Hogan and a lot of my
pals who are now dead. Some of those lads did not belong
to our parish, but all of them lived within a two-mile radius.
He did not confine his history lesson to the official textbook.
He gave us the naked facts about the English conquest of
Ireland, and the manner in which our country was held in
bondage. We learned about the Penal Laws, the systematic
ruining of Irish trade, the elimination of our native language.
He told us also of the ruthless manner in which Irish
rebellions had been crushed. By the time that we had
passed from his class, we were no longer content to grow
up "happy English children," as envisaged by the Board of
Education. To the end of his days Charlie was in the habit
of boasting of his rebel past-pupils.

When I reached my fourteenth year, my schooldays
came to an end. I had to go out and earn my bread. Father
Martin Ryan, our Parish Priest, gave me my first job on the
renovation of our old school. Laurence Dwyer was foreman
and carpenter, Pat O'Neill did the plastering, Mylie Carew
and I did the rough labour. Father Ryan paid me nine
shillings a week, no mean sum in the eyes of a young
gossoon. I was a proud boy on that first Saturday night
when I handed my pay-packet to my mother. When the
renovation of the school had been completed, I worked for
farmers in the district.

In the spring of 1913 I got a job as linesman on the
Great Southern Railway. My wages were eighteen shillings
a week, plus a living-out allowance of nine shillings. My
work took me to Mallow, Cork and Dublin, because the
maintenance-gangs had to move from place to place as their
services were required. Even in Dublin lodging-houses we
got the best of grub at nine shillings a week.

My work as linesman on the railway made me familiar
with its network and this knowledge served me well in later
years when I was an outlaw. I was employed at the laying
of the yard at Inchicore when the Great Strike of 1913

occurred. I walked round the streets of Dublin after the day's work had finished and saw the police wielding their batons in frenzied charges, felling strikers and sightseers indiscriminately.

CHAPTER TWO

IRISH POLITICS

EVERY SCHOOLBOY KNOWS the circumstances that agitated Irish politics in the years that immediately preceded the Great War, 1914-1918. At the risk of being accounted tedious, I wish to recapitulate the salient events that followed in quick succession from the spring of 1912 to the autumn of 1914.

The Home Rule Bill of 1912 was introduced by the British Prime Minister, Mr. Herbert H. Asquith (later Earl of Oxford and Asquith) on 11 April of that year. Under the Bill the Irish Parliament was to have no influence on foreign affairs, no part in the fixing or collection of customs and excise, very little control over finance and no control of police for six years.

Compared with previous abortive Home Rule Bills of 1886 and 1893, the 1912 measure promised Ireland less immediate financial autonomy, but it gave control of the police at an earlier date. As regards representation in the British Parliament at Westminster, under the Union she had 103 representatives, she would have none at all under the Bill of 1886; eighty under the Bill of 1893, and forty-two under the Bill of 1912.

This 1912 brand of Home Rule was known to our crowd as the " gas and water " measure.

The 1912 Bill passed through the House of Commons by substantial majorities, the most vital amendment moved by Sir Edward Carson, to exclude from its scope the whole of Ulster being defeated by 294 votes to 197. Having been rejected by the House of Lords, however, the Bill could not become law because of their veto and was set for a period of suspended animation until the summer of 1914. By that time the situation had been changed completely by Ulster's expressed determination to resist the measure by force of arms. Of course, it was bluff. " One of the most

gigantic political bluffs in all history," was how it was later
described by J. W. Gerard, the American Ambassador in
Berlin, in his book *My Years in Germany*. But meantime
the sabre-rattling went on.

As early as 11 September, Sir Edward Carson (one-time
Dublin barrister and Unionist M.P. for Trinity College;
Solicitor-General in the Tory Government from 1899 to
1905) appeared on the Ulster scene as leader of the campaign
against Home Rule. Parades of the Ulster Volunteers were
reviewed by the leaders of the Unionist party.

On Saturday, 28 September 1912 (afterwards called
" Ulster Day ") a " Solemn League and Covenant " against
Home Rule was opened for signature and was eventually
signed by 471,414 Ulster men and women over the age of
sixteen.

Some fanatics even signed in their own blood. Carson
was the first to sign; and drilling of the Ulster Volunteers
began.

As an earnest of their determination to resist Home Rule,
the Ulster Unionists mobilized between eighty and ninety
thousand Ulster (Orange) Volunteers at Balmoral, a suburb
of Belfast, on 9 April 1912. They were reviewed on the
Show Ground by Bonar Law, leader of the British Conservative
(Unionist) party, and other frock-coated warriors, before a
crowd of Covenanters estimated at a hundred thousand. A
quarter of a century earlier Lord Randolph Churchill had set
the tenor for these activities in an inflammatory anti-Home
Rule speech in the Ulster Hall, Belfast, when Gladstone's first
Home Rule Bill was introduced.

A little later, in a letter to a correspondent, Lord Randolph
coined the famous phrase : " Ulster will fight and Ulster
will be right."

Bonar Law had with him that day at Balmoral about
seventy members of the British Parliament, from English,
Scottish and Welsh constituencies. " I have only one word
more to say," he told another gathering of Orange Covenanters,
at Larne, also on 9 April, " and that is that if this Home
Rule Bill should by any chance be forced through, then God
help Ulster, but heaven help the Government that tries to
enforce it."

Since 1886 the emphasis in the Conservative party had
been laid on unionism rather than conservatism, and the
party was more often referred to as the Unionist party than
as the Conservative party.

Asquith introduced his Home Rule Bill for Ireland on 11 April 1912. Bonar Law, speaking for the British Unionists of whom he was the leader, and Carson, speaking for the Irish Unionists, threatened physical resistance to the Act, if and when it passed into law. " The Government last night declared war against Ulster," said Carson in the Albert Hall, on 12 June. " We will accept the declaration of war. We are not altogether unprepared."

The 17th September 1913 marked the beginning of a fortnight of reviews of Ulster Volunteers by Carson and Lieutenant-General Sir George Richardson, their Commander, an Englishman who had been proved in battle against defenceless Indians. A week later, on 24 September, arrangements were announced for the constitution of an Ulster Provisional Government with a central authority of seventy-five members, a military council, and a guarantee fund of a £ million. The Ulster Volunteers were told by political leaders, amongst them being the heads of the British Conservative party, that rebellion against Home Rule for Ireland " was a sacred duty." Drilling went on, arms were landed, the aid of the German Kaiser invoked, and the British Crown defied. The Protestant Church of Ulster gave its blessing to these threats of violence. It was all part of the great bluff. But it worked.

The British Government took no action, but gave signs of being intimidated. There was talk of compromise, and of plans to partition Ireland.

The lesson of the Northern diehards was not lost on the South. If the Ulster Volunteers can arm to fight Home Rule, it was asked, why not another openly armed and trained Volunteer force in the South, with a vastly different objective ? And so on 25 November 1913 at the Rotunda Rink, Dublin, the Irish Volunteers were inaugurated. The associations which had the national interest at heart were invited to send delegates to the general meeting under the presidency of John (Eoin) McNeill, Professor of Early and Medieval History in University College, Dublin, and Vice-President of the Gaelic League. It was not a sectional organisation, and it attracted many who were identified with the Home Rule movement, which was supported by the majority in nationalist Ireland. In the beginning John Redmond and the other leaders of the Irish Parliamentary Party held aloof, and the Lord Mayor of Dublin, Lorcan Sherlock, had refused the use of the Mansion House for the inaugural meeting.

The Provisional Committee of the Irish Volunteers numbered thirty, of whom sixteen were members of the Irish Republican Brotherhood. There was no official president, though Professor McNeill usually presided at the meetings.

Redmond, having first tried to discourage the growth of the Irish Volunteers, later became alarmed by their increasing strength, and eventually he tried to gain control of the organisation. Although he failed to achieve this objective, he did succeed in compelling the Provisional Committee to add twenty-five persons nominated by himself to their committee, in June 1914; he had fixed on twenty-five because he thought there were only twenty-five members on the original committee.

In order to prevent a split in the Volunteers, the Provisional Committee submitted to Redmond's demand, for he had threatened that unless his nominees were co-opted on the Provisional Committee, he would instruct his followers to break away from the central organisation and set up their own county committees.

Whilst the leaders of the Irish Parliamentary party had at first ignored the Volunteers, many supporters of the party had joined the movement.

These latest developments were followed by a big increase in the number of paper volunteers, with a view to strengthening the position of the party in the movement; the vast majority of these new recruits had no intention of fighting for Irish freedom. As a result, the efficiency of the Volunteers was impaired by the latest acquisitions.

Ten days after the inauguration of the Irish Volunteers in Dublin the British Government, on 5 December, issued a proclamation in the *London Gazette*, prohibiting the importation of arms into Ireland. For at least twelve months previously Carson's Ulster Volunteers had been receiving substantial supplies of arms and ammunition, paid for with Tory gold, with the openly defiant purpose of opposing the application of the Home Rule measure to Ulster.

"Ulster Unionists," declared the *Irish Times* in its issue of 6 December 1913, "are convinced that the action of the Government has come too late, and that there are now sufficient arms in Ulster to offer effective resistance to any attempt that might be made to force Home Rule on Ulster." Two days later the same newspaper added: "The recent Government Proclamation puts an end to the arming of the Irish Volunteers." Thus the *Irish Times* summed up accurately the real purpose of the British Proclamation.

Meanwhile, the importation of arms and ammunition by the Ulster Orangemen continued without hindrance, and to increase those armaments, plans were made to raid certain British arms depots in Ulster. On 19 March 1914 Government orders were issued to Sir Arthur Paget, Commander of the British forces in Ireland, for the movement of troops to safeguard these depots. Next day Paget asked the officers of his command for an undertaking that, if called upon, they would serve in Ulster; if they refused to obey this order, they would be obliged to resign. General Sir Hubert Gough, commanding the Third Cavalry Brigade at the Curragh Camp, flatly refused to give the undertaking and handed in his resignation. He was supported by fifty-seven other British officers, who likewise tendered their resignations. On 21 March General Gough and his officers having received a " satisfactory guarantee " from the Government, withdrew their resignations. This incident became known as " the mutiny at the Curragh." In point of fact, there was no mutiny at the Curragh, but there may have been one at the War Office where that arch enemy of Irish freedom, Sir Henry Wilson, was intriguing more or less successfully against Home Rule. The Curragh officers had merely said that they would prefer to be dismissed from the army rather than proceed against Ulster.

On 24-25 April 1914 a notable gun running took place at Larne. A consignment of 35,000 German Mauser rifles, with 2,500,000 rounds of ammunition, was landed by the Ulstermen without opposition from British forces. The password was " Gough " !

On 26 July the yacht, *Asgard*, manned by Erskine Childers and his wife, two West of Ireland fishermen, and Miss Mary Spring-Rice sailed into Howth harbour with a cargo of nine hundred second-hand Mauser rifles and 26,000 rounds of ammunition, and delivery was taken by about 800 Irish Volunteers, who then marched to Dublin with the empty guns on their shoulders. They were forcibly intercepted at Clontarf by some D.M.P. men under the command of William V. Harrel (the Assistant Commissioner of the Dublin Metropolitan Police) and a company of the King's Own Scottish Borderers, led by Major Haig, who seized a few of the rifles in the scuffle that followed.

As the military paraded through the city on their return to barracks, they were hooted by citizens and pelted with stones. At Bachelor's Walk the soldiers fired on the unarmed crowd, killing three and wounding thirty-seven others. Harrel was afterwards censured for having exceeded his authority in calling out the military, and he was dismissed. The King's Own Scottish Borderers became known as the Kings Own Scottish Murderers.

A second consignment of 600 rifles and 20,000 rounds of ammunition was landed from the yacht *Chotah*, at Kilcoole, Co. Wicklow, on 1 August without incident. Thomas Myles and James Creed Meridith were the navigators of the *Chotah*, and Sean Fitzgibbon and Sean T. O'Kelly (later President of Ireland) were in charge of the Volunteer party who took delivery.

On 4 August 1914 Britain declared war on the Central Powers. On 18 September the Home Rule Act was given the Royal Assent. A special Bill was passed by which the operation of the Act was suspended for an indefinite period. Even though Home Rule had been placed on the Statute Book, it was not to come into force until a year after the war had ended: as a pledge had been given that Ulster would not be " coerced," Carson's campaign was crowned with success.

A new and unexpected development followed the entry of Britain into the Great War. The Home Rule Bill was being held up by the veto of the Lords, and Redmond was under pressure to accept an amending bill that embodied partition. The outbreak of war had given him an unique opportunity to enforce his full demands for Home Rule. All nationalist Ireland, including even the separatists, were prepared to support Redmond in a strong stand. He had all the cards in his hands.

He dashed the hopes of all his supporters by throwing in his hand. On 3 August 1914 Sir Edward Grey, the Foreign Secretary, had told the House of Commons that Britain would enter the war in alliance with France; Redmond, without even consulting his own party, pledged before the assembly that Ireland would give unconditional support to Britain in the prosecution of the war.

He went even further. He agreed to the suspension of Home Rule until the end of the war, when it was to be subject to the Amending Act that embodied everything demanded by Carson and his Covenanters. And later he even set up in Ireland as a recruiting agent for the British army, and told the young men that it was their duty to go out to France and fight for Britain "and the freedom of small nations."

"Get me 5,000 men and I will say 'thank you,'" said Lord Kitchener, Secretary for War, to Redmond. "Get me 10,000 and I will take off my hat to you." Kitchener, who despised the Irish people, was born at Crotta, Lixnaw, in County Kerry.

One wonders how such a campaign had any chance of succeeding with the people. Yet it did meet with a very large measure of success, mainly because the whole force of the Parliamentary party, the Daily Press and almost every provincial newspaper was behind it. The country was soon flooded with pro-British propaganda, stories of German atrocities, lies and fallacious arguments. Most of the Irish people were carried off their feet by this campaign; all the leaders in whom they had trusted seemed to speak with one voice.

Whatever nationalist feelings Redmond may have entertained as a young man had been well and truly watered down over the years in the House of Commons, in which so much of his life and that of his colleagues of the Irish party had been spent.

Those who believed in complete separation from Britain and to whom the idea of partition was anathema had to take action. On 24 September 1914 a manifesto signed by twenty members of the original Provisional Committee was issued from Volunteer Headquarters in Dublin, declaring Redmond's nominees expelled from the Committee. The Volunteers were thus split into two groups, one known as the "Irish Volunteers," under McNeill, and the other the "National Volunteers," under the chairmanship of Redmond. About ninety per cent of the Volunteers followed Redmond. The wheat had been separated from the chaff, and the stage set for the fight for Irish Freedom.

Incidentally, the idea of dividing Ireland was the brain-child of a British Liberal M.P., one T. G. R. Agar-Robartes. He wanted four of the nine counties of Ulster excluded from the jurisdiction of a Dublin Parliament. "Orange bitters and Irish whiskey will not mix," he had observed laconically in June 1912.

Sickened to death by all this British duplicity, cant and humbug, by all the sham talk about a Home Rule Bill that gave only a vestige of self-government to my country, I made up my mind to join the Irish Republican Brotherhood.

CHAPTER THREE

SWORN IN BY SEÁN TREACY

I WAS SWORN IN by Seán Treacy. I was Seán's most intimate friend and we shared all our secrets. I am concerned that full justice has not been done to his memory.

Seán was still in swaddling clothes when his father, Denis Treacy, died. His mother took the little lad and moved to Lackenacreena near Hollyford. When her brother, Jim Allis, got married, Mrs. Treacy changed residence once more. She and her son, now aged eleven, went to live with her sister, Maryanne Allis.

Seán attended the Christian Brothers' school at Tipperary, and was marked down as a very promising pupil who showed a special proficiency in the Irish language. He was an eager student of the history of his country. Seán's aunt did not approve of his budding patriotic sentiments. While my mother taught me to love my country and be prepared to fight for its freedom, Maryanne Allis tried to put a brake on Seán's youthful zeal. She had a hard outlook on the world. For this I do not blame her, because she had to toil and moil from morning to night for a mere existence.

Seán thought out all matters by himself. Of him we might use the term, a self-made patriot. Maryanne blamed me for leading her nephew astray. There was not a man on this earth who could lead on Seán Treacy to any course which he did not wish to follow. The truth is that in the matter of patriotic endeavour he was the leader, and I was his willing disciple.

Even though our houses were less than one mile apart, we did not meet face to face until we were in our eighteenth year. From the moment of my first meeting with him, I felt that I had known Seán Treacy all my life. He was the very soul of sincerity, and for that reason our kindred spirits clicked from the beginning. He had been delicate during his boyhood because of his fast rate of growth. He was almost a six-footer, slightly stooped in carriage. His move-ments were brisk, as if he were in a constant hurry. His hair was of very fine texture like spun-silk, almost mouse-coloured. He was short-sighted and wore glasses.

On first sight one would take Seán to be a foreigner. I remember one night when we came to a farmer's house at Deerpark, near Carrick-on-Suir, the man of the house, Paddy Arrigan, looked at the grandfather clock which showed that it was bed-time. The family were about to kneel down for the Rosary, but were slightly uneasy because of the foreigner who might not be a Catholic.

" Have you any objection, Mister, to our saying the Rosary? " Paddy asked. Seán put everyone at ease by taking from his pocket a very long beads which was a gift from a Sister of Mercy. Paddy drolly observed : " If we are to judge your holiness by the length of your beads, a walking saint of God you must be." Seán weighed about twelve stone, and in an emergency manifested the strength of a lion. This was chiefly due to his amazing will-power.

Shortly after the inauguration of the Volunteers in Dublin, a company was formed in Donohill. Some British army reservists put us through a course of drill. These fellows were called up at the outbreak of the Great War, and, as a consequence, we had no one to train us in the approved methods of warfare.

In the early days of the Volunteers a great wave of enthusiasm swept over the country and this enthusiasm was inspired chiefly by the antics of the Orangemen in the North. Then came the disastrous cleavage in the ranks; nearly all of the Volunteers of our area followed John Redmond, with the result that Seán Treacy, myself and a couple of others found ourselves odd men out.

The Redmondite or National Volunteers flourished for a time and then fizzled out completely in 1915. There were so few of our crowd left after the " split " that we had not sufficient numbers to form a local unit of the Irish Volunteers. We could be counted on the fingers of your two hands : Paddy Ryan, of Doon; Seán Treacy, myself and my young brother, Laurence; Packy Deere, Mike Ryan and Éamon O'Dwyer. I must include also Dinny Lacey and Mick Callaghan from Tipperary town.

We tried to keep in touch with the Volunteer movement by subscribing to patriotic journals, and also by attending Volunteer gatherings which were not too far distant. As the war developed, a close watch was kept on us by the police. We became known as the " pro-Germans." The majority of the people, carried away by British propaganda, hoped and prayed for victory for Britain and her allies.

The landed gentry, the well-to-do merchants and most of the "strong" farmers supported the drives that were organised to provide comforts for British soldiers. We did our best to frustrate such activities. I was still working as a railway-linesman, and the police notified my superiors about my disloyal tendencies.

The police did not confine themselves to the ordinary duties of custodians of law and order. The Royal Irish Constabulary, in familiar jargon, the R.I.C., was a semi-military force, trained in the use of arms. The main duty of the police was to spy not only on the Irish Volunteers, but also on all who were known to lend their support to the movement for Irish independence. They numbered about 12,000 in 1914, and were posted in garrisons of a strength that varied from two to about twenty, according to the population of the village or town in which they were located. They served as the eyes and ears of the British Intelligence. Being natives of the country, they had an intimate knowledge of the people, and ferreted out vital information for the British army of occupation.

From the outbreak of the Great War I continued to work on the railway and took no more active part than an ordinary member of the Irish Volunteers. We used to meet in Burke's wood, near Coolnagun, twice a week. Our company then numbered thirteen; none of us had any military knowledge. Those of our neighbourhood who would have been competent to instruct us, had either joined the British army or were not considered by us to be trustworthy for any perilous enterprise. Still we got on very well at physical drill, scouting, signalling, revolver practice, close-order drill and such work. We had to rely mainly on military manuals. By a strange irony the books which we found most helpful were the official manuals issued to the British troops. We were often seemingly innocent spectators of British manoeuvres, and I can assure you that we kept our eyes open. If the chance of picking up an odd revolver came our way, we managed somehow to find the purchase money for a further addition to our meagre armament. The best tribute to our proficiency in warfare was paid by officials of the British Government when they later described our little band as "the crack shots of the I.R.A."

We went to Limerick on Whit Sunday, 23 May 1915, to take part in a big parade of Irish Volunteers organised by the Dublin Brigade. Patrick Pearse was present. Special trains had brought about 600 men from Dublin, and there were contingents from many other places, including 250 from Cork. We marched at the rear of the Tipperary column and we were sorely tempted to open fire on the hostile crowd that pelted us with garbage as we paraded through the streets.

Treacy and I had many a chat about national matters. We were completely frank with each other. Neither of us was blessed with an abundance of money, Treacy being even poorer than myself. Whenever it was possible, I used my railway-pass to come home for the week-end. If Treacy wanted to go to Dublin, he travelled to and from that city on my pass. He had to return in good time so that I might have the pass for getting to my work.

Shortly before Easter of 1916 Treacy and I often discussed the prospect of an armed rising. I was working at that time on the line about Kilmallock. When I came home for Easter, Treacy told me that he expected a rising to take place on Easter Sunday. When the cancellation messages were received I returned to my job. The gang with which I was working consisted of about 150. Of that number I knew only one, Mick Ryan, to be a member of the Irish Republican Brotherhood. On Easter Monday night we heard about the fighting in Dublin, and I decided to go home for a word with Treacy. Limerick Junction was being held by British forces, but when I showed my railway pass I was allowed to continue on my journey. I did not make contact with Treacy until Friday. By the end of the week we learned of the surrender in Dublin. Seán had left his home on the first news of the Rebellion and cycled from one centre to another, urging the Tipperary Volunteers to take action.

On the following Sunday night, Treacy, Ned O'Dwyer and myself met at our house. We were bitterly disappointed that the fighting had not extended to the country. We swore that, should the fighting ever be resumed, we would be in the thick of it, no matter where it took place.

A short time later we were giving each other the benefit of our views of the British justice that had tried by courtmartial and sentenced to death all the members of the Irish Provisional Government, which had been established in Dublin on 24 April, 1916. They were shot at Kilmainham barracks, Dublin between 3 and 12 May, "in the most brutally stupid manner," wrote Major Sir Francis Vane, one of the British officers who had fought against them. With bitterness in our hearts, we contrasted their fate with the lot of the Ulster Provisional Government, the Government which, a couple of years previously, had been openly preaching rebellion, drilling and arming Volunteers in defiance of the British Crown and Parliament, invoking the aid of the Kaiser, and seducing British army commanders from their allegiance. These gentlemen, not one of whom had even been prosecuted, were now posing as pillars of law and order, and acting as guardians of the State. Three of them, Sir James Campbell, John Gordon, K.C., M.P., and William Moore, K.C., M.P., were afterwards made judges of the High Court, Campbell eventually became Lord Chancellor of Ireland. Carson, having entered the British Government, was made Attorney-General, and later Lord of the Admiralty and a member of the War Cabinet. James Chambers was made Solicitor-General for Ireland, and Sir John Lonsdale had to be satisfied with his peerage. Campbell was actually Attorney-General when Pearse and the other members of the Irish Provisional Government were executed. Executed also were Major John McBride for having fought on the side of the Boers in the South African War; Willie Pearse for the crime of being Pádraig's brother; and Thomas Kent of Bawnard, County Cork, for defending his home against the R.I.C. In all, fifteen were shot between 3 and 12 May. Roger Casement was hanged in Pentonville prison on 3 August. Sir F. E. Smith, Attorney-General, who led for the Crown at the trial of Casement, had been "galloper" to General Richardson, Commander of the Ulster Volunteers, during the phoney war waged by the Covenanters against Home Rule. As Earl of Birkenhead, a Unionist member of Lloyd George's coalition cabinet, he signed the Treaty on the early morning of 6 December 1921. He was the Lord Chancellor. Amongst other notorious British agitators and leaders of the Ulster "revolution," Walter Long was to be First Lord of the Admiralty, and Bonar Law became Leader of the House of Commons and Lord Privy Seal.

So much for the British concept of justice for the Irish and their concern for the freedom of small nations.

" . . . . It is believed that most of the ring-leaders are dead or captured," the *Irish Times* exulted in a leading article after the fighting had ended. "The outlaws who still 'snipe' from roofs may give a little more trouble, but their fate is certain . . . The State has struck, but its work is not finished. The surgeon's knife has been put to the corruption in the body of Ireland, and its course must not be stayed until the whole malignant growth has been removed. In the verdict of history, weakness today would be even more criminal than the indifference of the last few months. Sedition must be rooted out once and for all."

The *Irish Independent* cried out for the blood of James Connolly, leader of the Citizen Army. Thirteen executions had taken place but the holocaust was not deemed sufficient. The editor did not mince his words: " We cannot agree with those who insist that all the insurgents, no matter how sinister or abominable the part they played in the rebellion, should be treated with leniency. Certain of the leaders remain to be dealt with, and the part they played was worse than that of some of those who have paid the extreme penalty . . . We think, in a word, that no special leniency should be extended to some of the worst of the leaders whose cases have not yet been disposed of." That was the sort of advice about Ireland that appealed most to the British Government.

When I had finished with the railway-work in Kilmallock, I returned to my own gang at Limerick Junction, which was quite close to my home. We set about re-organising the Volunteers in our area. Our little company held its first public parade in August 1917. By that time, the men who had been deported after the Easter Week Insurrection had been released. Meanwhile, two by-elections, in North Roscommon, February 1917, and South Longford, May 1917, respectively, had resulted in a triumph for Republican candidates. A few months later, Éamon de Valera, on his release from Lewes jail on 17 June had been chosen as candidate for West Clare. Wearing the Volunteer uniform, which had been proclaimed to be illegal, he contested the election. He had pledged that, if his candidature proved to be successful, he would not attend the British Parliament. He won the seat by a huge majority.

Shortly after his election Mr. de Valera addressed an enormous meeting in Tipperary town on 19 August. The members of our company, wearing the dark green uniforms of the Irish Volunteers, acted as his bodyguard. The town was occupied by a garrison of over one thousand British soldiers. We did not carry rifles; instead we carried hurleys, thereby committing a threefold act of defiance. It was unlawful to march in military formation; it was a still more serious offence to wear uniforms; greatest offence of all, we were violating a recent edict against the carrying of hurleys.

Some weeks previously, on Sunday afternoon, 10 June, a meeting had been convened in Beresford Place, Dublin, to protest against the detention in British jails of Volunteers who had taken part in the 1916 Insurrection. The assembly was addressed by Cathal Brugha and Count Plunkett. Major Mills, an Inspector in the Dublin Metropolitan Police, ordered his men to disperse the crowd which included several young men who were returning from a hurling game. The police used their batons, and in the melée which ensued the Inspector was struck on the head with a hurley and received fatal injuries, the first casualty amongst the British forces of occupation since the Rising of 1916. Thereupon General Sir Bryan Mahon, Commander-in-Chief of British troops in Ireland, issued a proclamation which prohibited the carrying of hurleys in public. The result, as one would have expected from the Irish temperament, was that hurleys were brazenly carried in districts where the game of hurling had never previously been played.

Our military display in Tipperary town did not cause a bigger shock to the enemy than it did to the local Sinn Féiners, many of whom were not in favour of any stronger weapons than resolutions. They were exasperated by our audacity. We should not have acted in such a manner until the matter had been solemnly discussed in advance. A formal long-winded proposition would then be put before the meeting and a decision arrived at on a majority vote. Such timid souls often hampered our line of action, but we were not prone to worry. The political wing of Sinn Féin criticised us severely. We just listened to all the orations and prognostications and made up our own minds.

The Tipperary police informed their superiors of the open defiance of British law, and were ordered to place the culprits under arrest. Seán Treacy and I became separated in the crowd on the evening of the Volunteer meeting, and I did not learn of his arrest until nightfall. I kept well out of the way of the Peelers. Seán was taken to Cork jail where he had as fellow prisoners the well-known brothers, Austin, Paddy and Michael Brennan of Meelick, Co. Clare. He was summarily tried and sentenced to six months' imprisonment. Such trials had become a mere formality; the political prisoners refused to recognise the British courts, and turned the proceedings into a farce by reading newspapers or singing treasonable ballads while

the evidence was being produced. At the end of August or
early September, Seán and a number of other prisoners were
transferred from Cork to Mountjoy jail, Dublin. On 20
September Seán and his comrades went on hunger-strike in
protest against the treatment meted out to them by their
jailers. It was one of the first occasions on which Irish
political prisoners made use of this procedure. Five days
after the hunger-strike began, Tom Ashe died as a result
of the efforts made by the prison doctor and his attendants
to use forcible feeding. The British were made to realise
that Irishmen were prepared to die for their principles. The
tragedy infuriated the whole Irish nation, and two days
afterwards the British gave in and accorded prisoners in
Mountjoy the conditions for which they had campaigned.
Forcible feeding of political prisoners on hunger-strike was
never again attempted.

From Mountjoy the prisoners were removed to Dundalk
jail about the middle of November, and the terms of the
Mountjoy undertaking were immediately broken. They were
again treated as criminals and a new hunger-strike began.
It continued for eight days, after which the prisoners were
released under the " cat and mouse act."

Meanwhile, we had been amassing a fair supply of arms
and ammunition. Contact had been established with a
soldier in Tipperary barracks from whom revolvers and
bullets could be bought for ready cash. When Seán returned
from Dundalk, we went all out for the recruiting of earnest
and trustworthy men. Our small Volunteer unit, once
composed of those who lived in the environment of Solohead,
now blossomed into the Donohill Company. It had a strength
of approximately twenty-seven, and the members came from
within a radius of seven miles. Nowadays people would
consider a distance of seven miles of no great consequence;
but in those days such a journey over bad roads was no
easy matter. A bicycle was looked on as a rare possession,
and most of the men had to make their way on foot to the
venues fixed for drill and route marches. Towards the
close of 1917 we had extended the organisation of Volunteer
companies into the surrounding districts. During this process
we made contact with Galbally which is on the borders of
Tipperary and East Limerick. The general framework of
the organisation was fairly well defined when we formed the
South Tipperary Brigade in the spring of 1918. I was elected
Commandant in the absence of Seán Treacy who was in

Dundalk jail. An election of Brigade officers was urgent as
an attempt by the British to impose conscription in Ireland
was expected. In the autumn when Seán was free another
election brought forward a man whose name has since been
linked with the South Tipperary Brigade.

The last great German offensive of World War I
commenced in March 1918, and the British lines were
penetrated in depth. In this dire plight the cry was raised
throughout Britain, " Conscript the Irish." Within a few
weeks, on 16 April, the British parliament passed the
Conscription Act, and preparations were made to enforce
it. Sinn Féin, the Irish Parliamentary party, Irish Labour
and the All For Ireland League, which included many men
who had been in conflict for years, united in the national
danger and convened to devise ways and means of resisting
the order. They were supported by the Catholic bishops.

All eyes were turned to the Volunteers. The British
became aware that the Irish Volunteers would resist to the
death before they would allow a single Irishman to be
conscripted. The great handicap was the scarcity of arms;
of men we had a superabundance. To remedy this shortage,
we decided to make raids for arms. We knew that there
were fowling-pieces, revolvers, bayonets, swords and an
occasional rifle in the houses of loyalists. We had very
little trouble in collecting the arms. We had accurate
information regarding the houses in which the weapons were
secreted. It was our practice to call by night and demand
the arms. Some householders were unwilling to hand them
over, but dared not refuse. Many gave them willingly;
some even sent us word to call; in not a single instance was
it necessary to fire a shot but we had to proceed with all
speed. The moment that the British got wind of our
scheme, they forthwith ordered that all arms should be
handed over to the police for safe keeping. We usually got
there first. On some occasions our men had collected the
arms only á few minutes before the Peelers arrived on a
similar mission.

Seán Treacy had been arrested for the second time on
28 February 1918, and taken to Dundalk jail where he had
once more the pleasure of Michael Brennan's company, and
also that of Séamus O'Neill, a professor at Rockwell College
and later O.C. of the Cashel Battalion. At first they were
the only three prisoners in Dundalk, and they at once went
on hunger strike for the terms that had been won in

Mountjoy the previous autumn. The strike continued for ten days, and ended only after the prisoners had won their demands. By the end of March other political prisoners began to arrive in Dundalk, and generally the British jails were becoming known as "Universities for Rebels." The prisoners attended lectures by experts on military tactics, and those in Dundalk were given a special course on the making of explosives.

When word reached us that Seán had gone on another hunger-strike, we felt that some drastic action should be taken to secure his release. We decided to capture a Peeler, put him on short rations, and hold him as hostage for Seán's safety. A mountain covert was selected as a secure hiding place. We were aware that a posse of police usually went on night-patrol along the railway close to Limerick Junction. Forty of our men were mobilised to carry out the job, but all the police were confined to barracks on that night. They had scented trouble. Some time later I learned that our plan did not meet with the approval of the Irish Republican Brotherhood. From that day I severed my connection with the I.R.B.

On Seán's release from jail, Mick Collins asked him to take the post of full-time Volunteer Organiser for the County Tipperary. Brigade officers were to be elected in October, and we called a meeting of all active officers of our brigade, so that the situation might be reviewed. The six battalions which then made up the South Tipperary Brigade were represented: Clanwilliam, Kilnamanagh, Cashel, Clonmel, Cahir, and Drangan. Seán considered that it would not be compatible with his appointment as a paid organiser to hold in addition the post of Commandant which he was urged to accept.

Seán and I had previously discussed this matter of the selection of a brigadier. Seán suggested that as we were just two country lads with neither financial nor social standing, we should look about for someone whose qualifications would provide the necessary prestige. The proposition was mooted that we should ask G.H.Q. to send down from Dublin some notable officer who would take over the command of our area. Our dilemma was suddenly resolved on our hearing that a man, not a native of our county, who had taken part in the Easter Week Rising was working at Éamon O'Dwyer's. We went to interview this man whose name was Séamus Robinson. We made no mention to him of the purpose of our visit. On our return to my house at Grange we held a discussion and concluded that he would be suitable.

A few evenings later we went back to Éamon O'Dwyer's and asked Séamus if he would agree to become Commandant of our brigade. I well remember the night on which we called. We found him milking a cow, and our acquaintance with him was so slight that we addressed him as "Mr. Robinson." Treacy and I kept on talking to him while he continued with his milking. He assured us that he would do whatever we wanted him to do. When he had finished milking the cow, we expected that he might stand up to talk to us, but he took his bucket of milk and walked away, saying over his shoulder as we followed him that he would do whatever we wanted him to do, but that he could not afford to idle as he might lose his job. We went away satisfied that he would serve our purpose.

While the threat of conscription remained, young and old were lining up to join the Volunteers. It is safe to estimate that at that time nine-tenths of all able-bodied Irishmen between the ages of sixteen and fifty were Volunteers of a kind; the women had their own assocation, Cumann na mBan, and the boys were joining the Fianna or Boy Scouts. All were ready to co-operate with the Irish Volunteers. As most of our officers were in jail, having been picked up on one charge or another, those who were at liberty were busily working by day and by night. There was great enthusiasm. If the British tried to enforce conscription, a glorious opportunity would be presented of uniting the Irish people. Though poorly armed, we had made up our minds to fight; if the fight took place, the survivors would bind themselves together in bonds of steel.

Seán Treacy had had enough of prison life, and I had no desire to enjoy the hospitality of his Britannic Majesty. We went on the run and kept moving from the house of one trusted friend to another. On fine days we helped the farmers with the hay. At night-time Seán usually took a corner seat under the kitchen lamp and pored over an Irish textbook or A. M. Sullivan's history of Ireland. He liked to sing an Irish song as we went through the fields. His favourite was " Óró sé do bhatha 'bhaile "; but he had not a note of music, and his singing of " The Wearing o' the Green " did not sound differently from " The West's Awake." His monotone never varied.

In his serious mood Seán was ever harping on the fight which was bound to come. He compared the Rising of 1916 to the Rebellion of 1798, both apparent failures. Confident that all had not been lost, he set his heart on the re-organisation of the Volunteers. He felt certain that Tipperary would yet distinguish itself when the fighting began. Do not come to the conclusion that his outlook was parochial. His vision took in the entire country, but he often said that if one belongs to a certain parish, one must strive to make it the best parish in the country. If everyone was to view the matter in that light, the entire country would be renewed in spirit.

Seán Treacy considered that the good name of our county had been saved during Easter Week by Michael O'Callaghan of Tipperary town. Mick shot and mortally wounded two policemen, Sergeant O'Rourke and Constable Hurley, who tried to arrest him in the house of his father's first cousin, Peter Hennessy, at Moanour, Kilross, on a bleak mountain side about six miles from Tipperary town. O'Callaghan escaped to the United States of America, and in the following year was arrested by Federal agents and held prisoner in the notorious Tombs prison of New York. Extradition proceedings were instituted against him. Treacy and I made up our minds that if he was brought back for trial in Ireland, we would do our utmost to rescue him.

Meanwhile, though the Conscription Act had become law, Britain, fully conscious of the determination of the Irish people to resist the measure, postponed its enforcement. On 20 September an official announcement was made that the period within which Ireland must provide 50,000 recruits for the British army, as an alternative to conscription, had been extended from 15 September to 15 October. Still the recruits did not present themselves. Cathal Brugha was prepared to go to London to shoot the ministers responsible if conscription was enforced. Lloyd George, the Coalition Premier, realised that it would be " suicidal " to attempt to enforce conscription, but he was under pressure by Sir Henry Wilson and other die-hards of the Orange Order and Unionist party. Eventually he promised to enforce conscription if all hope of an armistice disappeared. The story goes that a British officer who had just arrived in Dublin went to a D.B.C. (Dublin Bread Company) café for a meal. He asked a waitress the meaning of the letters D.B.C. and was given the answer " Death Before Conscription."

Our forces made sham attacks on Tipperary town; certain roads were proclaimed as military areas; British soldiers and police and civilians were forbidden to enter those areas during the " operations." Such exercises were carried out by a few hundred Volunteers, while the town was occupied by a garrison of over a thousand British soldiers. On these occasions we made no display of arms; some of us carried revolvers in our pockets.

The armistice came on November 11, 1918, and with it the threat of being conscripted disappeared overnight. So, too, did our great army ! The small number that remained was of more use than a conglomeration of half-hearted soldiers. This select few meant to fight for independence. The others had been thinking only of saving themselves from the trenches of France; they believed, as did the old political leaders that Ireland's freedom was not worth the shedding of one drop of blood.

CHAPTER FOUR

OUR MUNITION FACTORY

SEÁN TREACY'S HEAD was full of plans for organising. I had had an overdose of it during his absence in Mountjoy and Dundalk. I urged him to begin the fight immediately. He favoured delay and we agreed to differ. In partnership with my friend, Paddy Keogh, I started a " munition factory." Many a lively dispute we had on the best method of manufacturing explosives. Seán had to pour oil on the troubled waters.

It would be a mistake to imagine that our factory was an exact replica of the Krupp works at Essen. We set up our paraphernalia in a little cottage owned by Tom O'Dwyer, of the Boghole. Three rooms were let to Denis O'Dwyer of Dervice. Denis and Tom were both well-known characters. Our equipment was of the crudest, for we had no machinery. It was a simple matter to make black gunpowder. We also turned out hand grenades by filling tin canisters with blasting-powder. These had to be ignited before being thrown; you can imagine what a risky matter it would be if those grenades had to be brought into action on a windy night. We collected every available sporting cartridge, and refilled them with buckshot.

My first encounter with the enemy took place one night as we were returning from a raid for arms. We were cycling home from Tipperary, and the front tyre of my bicycle went flat; I told the others to go on ahead and that I would overtake them. They passed the police barracks which was situated on the outskirts of the town. The police may have heard them go by, and then come out to have a look around. Perhaps they were actually on the road and were afraid to confront six Volunteers. When I had pumped the tyre and mounted the bicycle, I was immediately pulled off by a burly Peeler. In my left hand I carried a small iron bar which was useful for forcing locks. I tried its magnetic effect on the crown of his head. The bar got the better of the argument.

After that I whipped out my revolver and held it at the ready. " Surrender, or I shoot," their officer commanded. " Put up your hands, or I'll shoot the lot of you," I replied. They complied instantly.

I then stepped backwards wheeling my bicycle, with my gun still levelled at the Peelers until I reached a laneway. I dashed up the lane, mounted the bicycle, and made my escape. The alarm was raised, and the whole town was surrounded. Every street and lane was searched. By this time I had reached the safety of our factory and rejoined my comrades.

The day came when I had the sad experience of seeing our munition factory blown sky-high. I was within fifty yards of the door, but my partner, Paddy Keogh, was actually on the premises when the explosion occurred.

We never found out what caused the trouble. I had gone to the spring-well to fetch a can of water as we had to do our own cooking and cleaning. On my return journey to the cottage, I saw the roof soar upwards and at the same moment heard the explosion of grenades. In a moment the entire building was in flames. My one thought was for the safety of my comrade; indeed, I feared that he was already gone beyond human aid. I dropped the can of water and rushed to the door. I dashed up the stairs and found Paddy lying unconscious on the floor. I raised him in my arms and with a heavy heart carried him through the rain of shrapnel. I brought him to the bank of the Multeen, the stream that flowed close to the house. My heart was wrung with anguish as I laid him beside the stream. I fetched my can to throw cold water over his pallid face. Before I had time to give him a second douche, Paddy was on his feet and rushing for me—very much alive!

"You damn fool, do you want to drown me?" he shouted. He added a lot more that would not make polite reading.

The destruction of our factory was a heavy blow. Even though our funds were exhausted, the O'Dwyer's had to be compensated in some form or other. All the tradesmen of our little company set to work, and in a few days the cottage was repaired, looking none the worse for its ordeal.

In later days the Black-and-Tans wreaked a more effective havoc on it than had been caused by the explosion of the grenades.

The cottage was no longer available for my work, but in a short time we got another house from a man by the name of Jer O'Connell. This time we were more successful, because we took strict precautions.

During our stay in the new premises, our living conditions were far from happy. Of bodily comforts we had none. We had neither bed nor coverings; worse still, we had no money wherewith to buy them. We got the loan of a couple of blankets from neighbours, spread straw on the ground, and covered it with a blanket. Over this we placed a layer of newspapers, and used a second blanket as a coverlet. The sheets of paper kept us warm provided we did not shift our position. In this way we were able to get about three hours' sleep. If we moved during the night, the paper got torn and the cold penetrated to our bones.

A still greater discomfort was caused by the plague of mice! On many a night we were wakened by their nibbling at our hair. Whenever I protested, Seán would plead: "Ah, the poor little creatures! They might as well be happy when we can't. Don't be vexed with them, Dan, even if they take a lock of your black hair." I argued that it was enough to have the Peelers after us, and that if the mice had any decency they ought to leave us alone.

For some time matters went smoothly, and our work progressed pleasantly. Then our partner, Keogh, abandoned us. His place was taken by Seán Hogan—who was to be very closely linked up with Seán Treacy and myself for the next four years. The two Seáns and myself seemed to have one mind in common.

After a few months, Jer O'Connell gave us notice to quit. We had no tenant's rights. There was no Act of Parliament which we could invoke to delay execution of the writ. As we were "on the run," we dared not look for lodgings in the ordinary way, even if we had the money to pay. The Peelers knew every hole and corner, and were constantly on the prowl for Irishmen who were known to have little love for British rule.

Some cousins of Seán Hogan owned a little dairy which they placed at our disposal. Here we enjoyed the luxury of a bed and other little comforts, even though our meals were few and far between. I lived for two weeks in the dairy on rice boiled in water, without either sugar or milk. This abstemious life was not new to me. During the months which I had spent organising the Volunteers, I often fasted from breakfast to breakfast; on many a night I walked miles even for a shake-down.

One day I was alone in the dairy, which was better known as "The Tin House." I had just finished oiling a rifle, which was a recent acquisition to our armoury, when I saw a number of police approaching. I had not even a solitary .303 bullet. I slung the haversack over my shoulder and, with rifle in my hand, sprinted through the back doorway and took a five-barred gate in my stride. It was one of the few occasions on which my prudence got the upper hand of my valour. The police found the house empty and " retired in good order," as their communiques usually ran.

Lack of money was our great handicap. We did not crave for personal comforts, but we needed money for our set purpose.

Seán Treacy and I cycled to Dublin to procure some arms. We had not the price of our train fares, but it was essential that we should reach Dublin by 6 p.m. on a particular Monday. Our Brigade Council meeting had been fixed for Sunday night, and this we were bound to attend. On that account we could not leave Tipperary till 8 o'clock on Monday morning, but we covered the 110 miles and reached Dublin in good time. We were falling from hunger, but the moment that we reached the house of our good friend Phil Shanahan, a Tipperary man, all our troubles disappeared. We never wanted for anything while Phil was about.

Our business compelled us to remain in Dublin until the following Saturday. We left Shanahan's at 8.30 a.m. having in our possession six revolvers, 500 rounds of .303 ammunition, and half-a-dozen grenades, and yet we were the only ones who arrived punctually for the meeting of the Brigade Council.

The general election, which was held in December, 1918, gave the people's sanction to Sinn Féin to set up an Independent Irish Parliament in Dublin. It became the task of the Irish Volunteers to defend that Parliament and its institutions. No general election had been held for over a period of seven years. In the interval the vast majority of the people had changed their political allegiance. They had lost faith in the Irish Parliamentary party. They no longer believed in the efficacy of sending a hundred representatives to the British Parliament to figure as a helpless minority in the really important issues that concerned Ireland. Britain's treachery on the Home Rule question, her cold-blooded murder of the 1916 leaders, and her threat of conscription had brought about a strong revulsion of feeling against the Irish Parliamentary party, whose leaders had placed their hopes on British good faith. A great awakening of national spirit had stemmed from the Rising of 1916. The subsequent by-elections had given to the constituents an opportunity of manifesting the Irish people's desire for liberty, complete and untrammelled.

The general election was to be contested on the basis of manhood suffrage; it was expected that the young men of Ireland would vote overwhelmingly in favour of the Sinn Féin candidates.

The public did not clearly realise the difference between the political body, Sinn Féin, and the military organisation, the Irish Volunteers. The Insurrection of 1916 was commonly called the "Sinn Féin Rising," and our Volunteers were spoken of as the "Sinn Féin Volunteers." The tricolour adopted in 1848 as the flag of the Young Ireland party was referred to as the "Sinn Féin Flag." But misnomers did not trouble us, for the Sinn Féin party was imbued with the Republican ideals. When the Sinn Féin clubs were springing up in every parish, it was quite usual to find that the president of the club was also an officer of the local Volunteer corps. Most of the young men in the Sinn Féin clubs had been enrolled in the ranks of the Volunteers.

During the election the people went Sinn Féin mad. The enthusiasm of the speakers swept the country off its feet, but the number of active Volunteers dwindled. We threw ourselves heart and soul into the election, and worked night and day for Republican candidates. All dead walls were placarded with slogans "Rally to Sinn Féin," "Vote for the Republic," "Stand by the men of 1916." Every Sinn Féin candidate had pledged that he would not sit in the British Parliament. Instead he would work in Ireland for the establishment of the Republic. The results exceeded our wildest imaginings. Of 105 seats we had won seventy-three. The Irish Parliamentary party won six, four of which were seats conceded to them in Ulster constituencies. This plan had been adopted in order to avoid a contest that would have helped the Unionists, who won a mere twenty-six. The election had been fought and won on the objectives of Easter Week. It was the greatest manifestation of self-determination recorded in history. On the principles proclaimed by Britain and her allies, our claim to complete independence was unanswerable.

Our brigade meeting for the election of Commandant and staff had been arranged for a certain date in October, and Dick Mulcahy came down from G.H.Q. The venue was P. J. Moloney's house in Church Street, Tipperary. Séamus Robinson had been arrested some time before, and was still being held in prison. Adhering to our previous arrangement, I proposed the election of Robinson as Commandant, and my motion was seconded by Seán Treacy. The appointment was sanctioned without further discussion and ratified by Mulcahy. Treacy was elected Vice-Commandant and proceeded to act as *de facto* Commandant from that very day. I was appointed Quartermaster. Robinson was released from Belfast jail towards the end of the year, but we did not see him in Tipperary until mid-January.

CHAPTER FIVE

SOLOHEADBEG

THE VOLUNTEERS were in great danger of becoming merely a political adjunct to the Sinn Féin organisation. Treacy remarked to me that we had had enough of being pushed around and getting our men imprisoned while we remained inactive. It was high time that we did a bit of the pushing. We considered that this business of getting in and out of jail was leading us nowhere. At the moment we had nothing definite in mind, but we proposed to engage in some enterprise that would start the ball rolling in Tipperary. We had previously discussed the feasibility of attacking the

R.I.C. escort which accompanied consignments of explosives on their way to Soloheadbeg quarry. The Volunteers were in need of high explosives for grenades and demolition work. Apart from that, Treacy believed that the forcible taking of the gelignite from a police escort would have a salutary effect on the morale of the Volunteers. In this mood the Soloheadbeg ambush was planned. We expected that there would be an escort of six fully-armed police and, if they put up an armed resistance, we had resolved not merely to capture the gelignite, but also to shoot down the escort. This action of ours would proclaim to the world that there still lived Irishmen who had made up their minds not to allow free passage to an armed enemy.

The moral aspect of such action was vigorously criticised after the event. Many people, even former friends, branded us as murderers. We had thoroughly discussed the pros and cons and arrived at the conclusion that it was our duty to fight for the Irish Republic that had been established on Easter Monday, 1916. We had decided also that, when the smoke of battle had cleared away, we would not leave Ireland, as had been the usual practice. We would remain in our native land in open defiance of the British authorities. We felt that such a demonstration was bound to encourage others to do likewise. Our only regret was that the escort had consisted of only two Peelers instead of six. If there had to be dead Peelers at all, six would have created a better impression than a mere two.

At the beginning of January 1919 we received information that a quantity of explosives was to be conveyed to Soloheadbeg quarry. The consignment would be guarded by armed policemen. We made a careful survey of the locality and selected the spot for our first ambush. We knew every inch of the ground as we had been born and reared in the vicinity; Sean's own farmhouse was only a stone's throw from the quarry.

Soloheadbeg is a small townland about two and a half miles from Tipperary town, and less than a mile from Limerick Junction. The quarry stands on an eminence over a little by-road. Farmhouses and cottages are fairly numerous in the neighbourhood, but there is no village nearer than Donohill, a mile and a half distant. In this plain, dominated by the Galteemore mountain, Brian Boru and his brother Mahon fought their first great battle with the Danes in 968; their gallant army, composed of men from Tipperary and Clare, routed the invaders. They did not abandon the pursuit until they reached Limerick, twenty miles distant, and burned the town over the heads of the invaders. Their right wing swept across the hills, as the Danes fled to their stronghold.

The quarry stands to the northwest. The road by which it is approached from Tipperary town is flanked on either side by high ditches. Additional cover is afforded by a close hedge of "skough." I should explain that what Tipperarymen call a "ditch" is in reality a bank.

We had not been correctly informed about the date assigned for the arrival of the explosives. We expected the convoy to pass on 16 January; it did not come till five days later. During these five days we lay in ambush. Our men had left their homes without giving any indication of their plans. After three days we selected eight men, and sent home the remainder because we had not funds for the purchase of provisions for a larger number.

For five whole days we were watching and waiting. Seán Treacy, Séamus Robinson, Seán Hogan, Tim Crowe, Patrick O'Dwyer of Hollyford; Michael Ryan of Grange (Donohill); Patrick McCormack, Jack O'Meara (Tipperary), and I, formed the full contingent.

During these days of waiting our chief concern was to remain unobserved. We did not wish to be seen by the people of the locality, nearly all of whom were employed at the quarry. If it became known to the police that strangers were hanging around the neighbourhood, our planning would have been brought to nought. Every morning before daybreak we went noiselessly to our hiding place and remained under cover; ever on the alert, while one of our number acted as scout from the by-road to the main road along which the Peelers were bound to approach. There we waited patiently until 2 o'clock each afternoon; we then abandoned our position, feeling certain that they would not come at a later hour, as they would take good care to be back in town before darkness set in. We spent the night at my own home, and each morning about four o'clock my mother prepared breakfast. On the fifth morning she declared, "If you don't do something today, you can get your own breakfast tomorrow."

At last dawned the fateful morning of 21 January 1919. Our scout had his eyes fixed on the Tipperary road.

Suddenly the alarm was given. Dashing towards us, he gave the word of warning : " They're coming, they're coming ! " and returned to his look-out.

If any of our number felt nervous or excited, he showed little outward sign of it. In a flash every man was alerted. Our hour of trial was at hand; we were to face the enemy; in the balance was life or death. We were to begin another phase in the long fight for the freedom of our country.

Our scout returned to report the actual distance, and the number of the escort. Nearer and nearer they came. In clear air we heard the sound of the horse's hooves and the rumbling of a heavy cart. Our nerves were highly strung. We were facing men trained in the use of firearms, disciplined for such emergencies. In all probability they had completed the special course in bomb-throwing. Our little squad had scant experience in the use of firearms. We had often chaffed one another about this lack of experience, and joked about the consequences if our nerves got jumpy when the real test came. But we always brushed aside these idle fears, and took consolation from the thought, " We're Irish anyhow, and all Irishmen are fighters by nature."

The hour had come. I cast a hurried glance down the road. The driver and the County Council employee, who was to take delivery of the explosives, walked beside the horse. Two uniformed policemen armed with rifles were following at a short distance behind the cart.

One moment before, my pulse was beating rapidly from excitement; when I saw the cavalcade at close quarters, my nervousness disappeared. I felt that I could take on single-handed a squadron of those fellows. What were they but a pack of deserters, spies and hirelings ? Nearer still they came, conversing in low tones. They were almost under the shadow of our revolvers.

" Hands up ! " The cry came from our men who spoke as if with one voice. " Hands up ! " In answer to our challenge they raised their rifles, and with military precision held them at the ready. They were Irishmen, too, and would die rather than surrender. We renewed the demand for surrender. We would have preferred to avoid bloodshed; but they were inflexible. Further appeal was useless. It was a matter of our lives or theirs. We took aim. The two policemen fell, mortally wounded; James Godfrey, the driver of the cart, and Patrick Flynn, the County Council employee, looked on in stupefaction. If we had disarmed the police without firing a shot the matter would not have been so serious. The shots had alarmed the countryside. In a moment men and women would appear at every doorway. Within an hour, hundreds of police and military would be scouring the countryside for us. From that moment we were outlaws with a price on our heads.

We seized the rifles and equipment of the police, mounted the cart, and drove away. The cart contained more than a hundredweight of gelignite. We had overlooked the seizure of the electric detonators. One week later we learned that Flynn, the County Council employee, had secreted thirty of them in his pocket.

Never was a horse called upon to give such gallant service in a dash for life and liberty. Seán Hogan held the reins; Seán Treacy and I sat behind. The rest of the party had been ordered to make their escape in different directions.

On we sped, urging our poor horse to greater speed, while school-children and farmworkers watched us in amazement as we went by.

We were heading for Donaskeigh. For a great part of our journey not a word was spoken. Treacy was the first to break the silence. In the same cool tones that he might have used if we were sitting round a fire discussing a game of cards he casually remarked, " Do you remember, Dan, when we were reading about explosives ? The book says that they are dangerous if frozen, or if they get jolted ? "

The reminder did not add to our peace of mind; if ever explosives got a jolting, these did. The road was rough and uneven; heaps of loose stones were scattered along the way; the cart was of the ordinary farmyard type, and without springs.

But we had to speed on our way until we reached the spot where we had decided to hide the booty. We quickly deposited the gelignite with the exception of two sticks which I kept for a decoy. I threw them on the roadside when we had covered a good distance. We dismounted at Ryan's Cross and abandoned the horse and cart. The poor horse was so jaded from the gallop that he could proceed no further. He was found a few hours later at Aileen Bridge, four miles distant from Tipperary town. The discovery set the Crown forces in motion. In the ensuing months police and soldiers combed the countryside and actually walked several times over the dug-out in which the gelignite lay concealed. The loose sticks had led them on a false scent; they kept themselves warm by digging trenches all over the area. But their search was in vain.

And now our troubles began. We had to give a wide berth to Tipperary and its precincts. We were tired with the excitement of the day and the suspense of the previous days, but we could not think of rest for a long while yet. The weather was intensely cold; to make things worse, it started to snow. There was now the further danger that, if the snow lodged, we might easily be traced.

We turned eastwards. Previously, we had been going north; we headed south-east towards the Galtee mountains, for to them we looked for shelter. The Galtee mountains and the Glen of Aherlow have ever been the refuge of the Tipperary "felon."

We had travelled four miles by the time that we arrived at Mrs. Fitzgerald's, of Rathclogheen, near Thomastown. There we had the first square meal since early morning when my mother had given us breakfast; right heartily we enjoyed the bacon and eggs provided by our kind hostess. In that house our famous countryman, Father Theobald Matthew, had been born.

We could not afford to linger; we had yet to put many more miles between us and Soloheadbeg. We resumed our journey towards the mountains. At Keville's Cross we crossed the Cahir and Tipperary road. The wind was piercingly cold. The only other living things which we saw out in the open were two mountain-goats spancelled together near the cross-roads. Several times we lost our way. We dared not call to a strange wayside farmhouse, for at that time the people had not learned the virtue of silence. At one point Seán Treacy fell into a ravine about twenty feet deep. Seán Hogan and I feared that he had been killed. When we got him out, we found that he was little the worse for his fall; he assured us that he would fire another shot before handing in his gun. All three of us continued our journey towards the summit. When we had traversed the Glen and climbed Galteemore's rugged slopes from the Tipperary side, we lost our bearings. In the height of summer you will find it chilly enough on Galteemore. You can imagine how we felt that evening in mid-winter. It had taken us three hours to make the ascent, but after all our exertions we wandered back to the two goats, back to our starting-point. We abandoned all hope of crossing the mountain. Seán Hogan moralised: " 'Tis all very well for

poets sitting at the fireside to write about the charm of
mountains, but if they had to climb them in hunger and cold,
they would be in no mood to appreciate the beauties of
nature."

When we returned to Keville's Cross, we altered our
original plan. We crossed to the railway line and decided to
face for Cahir. A fortunate decision, indeed. We had not
gone many miles along the line when we saw the lights of
the military lorries that were scouring the roads in search
of us. Had we been down on the road, we could not have
avoided them.

Travelling on railroad-tracks is tiresome even at ordinary
times. For men in our condition it was a cruel ordeal but
we had to keep going. In the thick darkness a figure loomed
up. I was walking in front. I promptly levelled my revolver
and shouted, "Hands up!" The figure remained motionless.
I advanced with gun levelled and walked into a railway sign-
post which displayed the warning, "Trespassers will be
prosecuted." Unhappy though our plight was, the boys
laughed at my discomfiture, and I had to join in the laughter.

A little farther on Seán Hogan complained that his boot
was loose and asked us to stop for a moment. Seán Treacy
tied the lace, but Hogan did not travel much farther until he
affirmed once more that it was loose. He stooped to examine
it, and found that the whole boot had been practically worn
away by the rocks. Only a bit of a sole and the laced portion
of the upper remained.

Seán Treacy tried to keep our spirits from drooping.
Several times we asked him how far it was to Cahir and
invariably got the same reply, "The next turn of the road."
He was right, of course; as the road and the railway which
runs parrallel to it continue for thirty miles in an almost
perfect straight line, the next turn was a long way off. Now
and again we became so exhausted that we used to stand
and rest our heads against the ditch by the railway side to
doze for five minutes.

At last we reached Cahir. We were as near to absolute
collapse as men could be. We were becoming desperate. For
the first time we had to assume that outward coolness and
take the risk which later became part of our daily routine.
We walked right through the town of Cahir, a garrison-town
situated on the main road from Limerick to Clonmel and
Waterford, and only fifteen miles from Soloheadbeg. We
had to take the risk. Our blood was almost congealed with

cold; we were ravenously hungry, and there was little life left in us. We knew one good friend on whom we could rely for a night's shelter. That friend was Mrs. Tobin, of Tincurry House, near Cahir. I shall never forget her kindness to us on that night. Her house was ever open for " the boys," until it was burned to the ground as an " official reprisal " for the shooting of District Inspector Potter. For the first time in a week we went to bed. Excitement, cold and exhaustion made sleep impossible. For four hours we lay limp; we got at least rest for our weary limbs.

We rose from our bed, eager to hear news. Since we had left Soloheadbeg we had not spoken to anyone, and had not seen a newspaper. Sure enough, just as we anticipated, there were the big splash headings, "Tipperary Outrage," "Fearful Crime," "Murder of two Policemen." We read also an account of the inquest on the dead men, Constables James McDonnell and Patrick O'Connell. Most of the details furnished were absolutely false. We learned furthermore that two young men had been arrested on suspicion; neither of them had anything to do with the affair. Within a few days they were released. Two schoolboys, Seán Hogan's brother Mathew, and Timothy Connors, were also arrested by the British, as they were reported to have seen us. The father of young Connors had worked on the farm which belonged to Seán Treacy's mother. Both boys were detained for months in an effort to extract information; in the case of Connors, a protracted legal action ensued, which resulted in a verdict against the Inspector-General of the R.I.C. for illegal detention.

Meanwhile, there had been a sequel to the Solohead episode. South Tipperary had been proclaimed a "military area." Fairs, markets and meetings were prohibited; military reinforcements were rushed into the district; garrisons were established at villages which had never before sheltered a British soldier. Night and day they patrolled the roads and scoured the fields. Our little band had unmasked the British. They had to come into the open and let the world see that they held Ireland by naked force.

We also learned that a reward of £1,000 was offered for any information that would lead to our capture. A few months later this offer was increased to £10,000. Nobody ever tried to earn it with the exception of a few members of the R.I.C. They failed; many of them never made the second attempt. These are the plain, unvarnished facts concerning the first

armed encounter in which R.I.C. men were killed since the
Insurrection of 1916. They were the first of a series that
helped to bring Ireland's name once more before the world.

We spent two nights in Mrs. Tobin's house. Then we went
to Ned McGrath's of Tincurry, and from there we were taken
by Ned to Gorman's of Burncourt Castle. We had arranged
to go to Ryan's of Tubrid, and sent on word that they might
expect us. Shortly after, we changed our minds and did not
go to Tubrid; and lucky it was for us, or for somebody else.
Just at the time we had expected to arrive, the house was
surrounded by eight Peelers, and Ryan himself was arrested.

We decided to go on to Mitchelstown which is situated
at the extreme end of the Galtees. We spent a night in
O'Brien's of Ballagh, and while we were there a peculiar thing
occurred. We were sleeping in a room upstairs when strange
voices aroused us. We looked out and saw several Peelers
entering the house. At once we got ready for a fight,
expecting to see them mounting the stairs at any moment.
But they did not come up. In a few minutes they made their
departure. It was only when they had gone that we learned
that the object of their visit was to ascertain if the owner of
the house had paid the licence for his dogs !

Eventually, we reached Mitchelstown, where we met
Christy Ryan, who welcomed us and gave us the shelter of
his house. While we were there we saw eight armed policemen pass by the door. They were guarding a little packet
of blasting powder. Evidently the Soloheadbeg ambush
had taught them to take no chances; they had now quad-
rupled the escort.

We crossed into East Limerick, where Ned O'Brien of
Galbally put us up. From there we travelled on to the
Maloneys of Lackelly, the scene of a great encounter with the
British two years later. We stayed there almost one week.

We were still within a radius of ten miles from Soloheadbeg. Police and military were scouring the countryside for
us, searching houses, ditches and woods. The clergy, the
public and the press had unanimously condemned our action.
Our only consoling thought was that the men of '98, the
Fenians of '67, and the men of 1916 were condemned in their
day. As the cause of these men had been vindicated, so too
would our cause, when the scales fell from the eyes of the
people. At this time, however, scarce a word would be heard
in our defence. Our point of view was not even to be listened
to. The people had voted for a Republic; now they seemed

to have abandoned us who tried to bring that Republic
nearer, for we had taken them at their word.

Our former friends shunned us. They preferred the
drawing-room as a battleground; the political resolution
rather than the gun as their offensive weapon. We had heard
the gospel of freedom preached; we believed in it, we wanted
to be free, and we were prepared to give our lives as proof
of the faith that was in us. But those who preached the
gospel were not prepared to practise it.

Even from the Irish Volunteers, who were now known as
the Irish Republican army, we got no support. Ned O'Brien
and James Scanlon of Galbally, Paddy Ryan of Doon, and
Davy Burke of Emly, certainly stood by us; but they were
the exceptions.

When the account of the Soloheadbeg affair was published
in the press, a man who should have stood by us made preliminary arrangements for the holding of a public meeting in
the town of Tipperary. He intended to condemn our action
and proclaim that the Sinn Féin organisation had no part in
the incident. The meeting was, however, called off by another
prominent man. A local clergyman quoted from the pulpit
the old saying, "Where Tipperary leads, Ireland follows,"
but he expressed a hope that such would not be the case in
the matter of the Soloheadbeg outrage; the men responsible
would go to their graves with the brand of Cain on their
foreheads. Such were the things said about us, but we
kept on our course.

In many places we were refused shelter on nights so
inclement that one would not put out a dog. I remember one
particular occasion; we were sitting in a farmhouse by the
fireside when there was a loud knocking at the door. It was
dark, and the farmer did not wish to open until he had
learned the identity of the visitor.

" Who's there ? " he demanded.

" Police ! " came the prompt reply.

Simultaneously we drew our revolvers. The door was
opened and a young neighbouring farmer entered, laughing
heartily at his practical joke. Before we could put away our
guns the owner of the house had observed them. At once his
attitude changed. He informed us point blank that he would
not permit armed men to stay under his roof. It was bitterly
cold, but we had to go out and take shelter in one of the
outhouses. So chilled were we, that we had to drive in some
of the cows to keep ourselves warm.

We had to tramp from parish to parish without a penny in our pockets. Our clothes and boots were almost worn out, and we had no replacements. Many in whom we thought that we could trust would not let us sleep even in their cattle-byres.

When we reached the village of Doon in County Limerick, still only seven miles from Soloheadbeg, we again met with Séamus Robinson. I need hardly say that our joy at the reunion was unbounded. Although it was only a few weeks since we had parted at Soloheadbeg, we felt like brothers who were meeting after years of separation. We continued our night's march, linked arm-in-arm.

While we were in this neighbourhood, Paddy Ryan, a well-known shopkeeper and an old worker in the cause of freedom, proved a staunch friend to us. With Séamus once more in our band, we discussed the outlook and the chances of winning over the people to engage in " one good stand-up fight " against the old enemy. We drafted a proclamation ordering, under penalty of death, all British armed forces to leave South Tipperary. We sent the draft to Volunteer Headquarters for their approval; but both An Dáil and General Headquarters refused to let us go ahead. We could not understand their reluctance seeing that ours was the only logical position.

The withholding of their support was a bad blow enough; but what was our horror when we found that someone had actually worked out a plan to ship us away to America! We had not been consulted; we were simply ordered to be ready to sail in a couple of days. This was surely a sugar-coated pill; a deportation order in disguise from the very fountain-head from which we should have expected support. We refused to leave Ireland. We told them that we were not afraid to die, but would prefer to live for Ireland. To leave Ireland would be tantamount to an admission that we were either criminals or cowards. Now, more than ever, we declared that our place was in Ireland; Ireland's fight would have to be made by Irishmen on the hills and on the high-ways in Ireland, not with printer's ink in America or in any other country. This was apparently regarded as a breach of discipline. We were members of an organised body and should obey our superior officers. They persisted in their plan of sending us away; we, just as obstinately, refused to leave. At length we won, but only on condition that we should remain in hiding in some remote part of the country.

The Happy Warrior. Dan Breen had a price of £10,000 on his head when this photograph was taken on a Tipperary farm in 1921.

Sir John French, the Lord Lieutenant (left), survived the many attempts made by the I.R.A. to kill him; Martin Savage, Volunteer officer (right), fell in the ambush at Ashtown, Co. Dublin, 19 December 1919.

Section of the memorial at Solohead Cross, in commemoration of the historic action at Soloheadbeg, Co. Tipperary, 21 January 1919.

Séamus Robinson, Seán Treacy, Dan Breen, Michael Brennan (left to right) and Seán Hogan (inset).

Mick MacDonnell, Tom Kehoe, Jim Slattery (from left—seated); Vincent Byrne and Paddy Daly. All but Brennan and Slattery took part in the Ashtown ambush.

Maurice Crowe (left), Con Moloney (centre) and Seán Fitzpatrick, each of whom successively held the rank of Adjutant, Third Tipperary Brigade, between October 1918 and the Truce, 11 July 1921.

Group of Fourth and Fifth Battalion officers, Third Tipperary Brigade, at an officers' training camp, 1921.

General Lucas, Commander of the Eighteenth British Brigade, photographed in East Clare with his I.R.A. guards, July 1920. In front (from left): P. Brennan, General Lucas and Joe Keane. At back: Paddy Brennan (left) and Michael Brennan.

British infantry in full battle-dress, with armoured support, outside Mountjoy jail, Dublin.

Auxiliaries in Dublin cheer Sir Hamar Greenwood, M.P., Chief Secretary for Ireland, head of the British Administration in Ireland.

Black-and-Tans in County Limerick pose for photographer—the names and letters were entered by an I.R.A. intelligence officer to indicate notorious terrorists, after the photograph was found amongst material captured from the British.

Crowds outside Mountjoy jail, Dublin, on 24 April 1921, the eve of the execution of Thomas Trainor (inset), the father of a large family. District Inspector Gilbert Potter of the R.I.C., Cahir, who had been captured by a flying column of the Third Tipperary Brigade, was held as a hostage against the execution of Trainor. Trainor was hanged; Potter was shot in reprisal.

Jack Killeen (bottom left) and members of the Fifth Battalion column, Third Tipperary Brigade, I.R.A., during the Civil War.

Wedding photograph of Dan Breen and Brighid Malone. A church-wedding was out of the question, so the marriage ceremony was performed at Glenagat House, the home of Michael Purcell, about six miles from Clonmel and four miles from Cahir, Cashel and Fethard—all of which towns were strongly held by the enemy—on 12 June 1921. The Brigade Column mounted guard at Glenagat House on the wedding day. Dan and Mrs. Breen are third and fourth from the left, at the back. On the extreme left is Father Ferdinand O'Leary, O.F.M., and Con Moloney, Brigade Adjutant, is on the extreme right—holding a sub-machine gun.

Dan with some of the wedding guests. From left: Father Ferdinand, O.F.M.; Father Frank Davin; Jerome Davin, O.C. First Battalion; Seán Cooney, O.C. Engineers, Fifth Battalion.

We felt that we could very soon overcome that difficulty.

While these squabbles were going on between G.H.Q. and ourselves, we were suffering intensely. The cold weather and the weary, aimless travelling were very trying on us. We could not get a horse to carry us on even a few miles' journey. We had to trudge from field to field, sometimes in one direction, sometimes in another. Why should we be treated so? Was not the sky as fair in one place as in another?

From Doon we went to Upperchurch, in the north of Tipperary. There we spent a few days with Patrick Kinnane, one of a family of famous Irish athletes; our next resting-place we decided would be Meagher's of Annfield. We sent on word to expect us at half-past seven in the evening, when it would be quite dark. The four of us, accompanied by Patrick Kinnane, walked along the road, chatting and enjoying the cool spring air. We must have taken our time along the way, for Treacy looked at his watch and reminded us that we were overdue, as it was now nearly eight o'clock. Suddenly we saw something white fluttering in the darkness. We halted. It was a signal given by a girl who was trying to attract our attention.

The four of us dropped into a place of concealment behind a thick hedge. The girl approached and, when she was passing the spot in which we were hiding, she whispered: "The Peelers are inside, raiding!"

She was one of the Misses Meagher who had slipped out unnoticed by the police to give warning, for she knew by which road we would travel. From our point of vantage we saw the custodians of law and order depart to the barracks. Then we proceeded on our way, entered the house which they had been raiding, and sat down to a very pleasant meal.

From Meagher's we came south to Boherlahan and stayed with the Leahys, the famous family of Tipperary hurlers. After that we went to Donnelly's of Nodstown where we held a Brigade Council meeting. Having discussed plans for more active operations, we decided on our own responsibility to publish the proclamation concerning enemy troops. About the end of February it was posted up in several parts of the county. The newspapers printed our edict under mock-headings. It seemed a tall order at the time; subsequent events showed that we saw further ahead than either the newspaper-men or our own Headquarters staff.

After that meeting we decided to return northwards towards

Creana, having sent word ahead as we always did. We asked Patrick Kinnane to have a horse and car in readiness and we started on our long tramp for Upperchurch in the dismal night. We were met by Kinnane, Doherty and Patrick Dwyer, and headed for Murphy's house at Creana. It was three o'clock in the morning when we reached our destination. Seldom did we suffer more from cold and exposure to the elements than we did on that night; the sleet was blowing into our faces. The weather was harsh, even for February, and the district was wild and mountainous.

When we arrived at Murphy's house we were ravenously hungry. Murphy was locally known as " the Stationmaster of Creana " even though the nearest railway station, Nenagh, was fifteen miles distant from Creana. He put the pan on the fire and set about cooking bacon and eggs. So hungry was Hogan that instinctively, and half unconsciously, he began to eat the raw bacon as it was being put on the frying pan. In a few minutes he became so seriously ill that we feared he was going to die. He revived, but for some weeks afterwards he was an invalid. His illness at this juncture was very unfortunate, because we had made up our minds, in spite of Headquarters' orders, that we would try to get to Dublin; we could no longer endure the misery of our existence.

With that intent we went from Creana to the Falls of Doonass, that picturesque spot on the Shannon just across the Limerick border from North Tipperary. There we parted from Robinson and Treacy who started on their perilous journey to Dublin, while I remained behind with Hogan until he regained his strength. They arrived safely in Dublin and were welcomed by a few sympathetic friends. A full and accurate description of each one of us, with the reward offered for information that might lead to our capture, appeared every week in the *Hue and Cry*, the official police gazette. On that account it was no easy thing for them either to travel to the city, or to get about when they had arrived.

Hogan and I could not afford to stay long in the district round the Keeper mountains. Tim Ryan and Tommy McInerney brought a motor car from Limerick to take us on our way. McInerney was the driver of the ill-fated motor which had plunged over Ballykissane pier on the night of Good Friday, 1916. The passengers were Charles Monahan (Belfast), Donal Sheehan (Newcastle West) and Con Keating (Caherciveen). Their mission was to seize a wireless transmitting set then in use at a wireless training school at Caherciveen and bring the set to Ballyard, Tralee, where it was to be erected under the supervision of Austin Stack and used to broadcast news of the Rising. Unfortunately McInerney took a wrong turn after passing Killorglin and ended up in the swirling waters of the Laune. He was the sole survivor of the accident.

Tim Ryan knew of a friendly priest in West Limerick who was willing to give us shelter, and we started on our journey to meet one of the truest friends we ever made, Father Dick McCarthy of Ballyhahill. Seán Hogan sat in front with McInerney; Ryan and I shared the back seat.

Our journey was uneventful until we approached Limerick city. We were suddenly confronted by lorry loads of soldiers dashing along in the direction of Tipperary. We surmised that they were on some big round up. We did not know then, though we found out later, that they had received information that we were lying low in a certain hiding place, and scores of troops with armoured cars were being rushed to the scene.

Never since the day on which we had left Soloheadbeg did we find ourselves in such a tight corner. One flash of suspicion on the part of a single officer of the party would have ruined us. We were well aware that several British soldiers had fond hopes of earning the reward for our capture; they had made a close scrutiny of our photographs and of the posters which described our personal appearance. It was comparatively easy for them in the spring of 1919, for we were in those days the only "much wanted men," as the newspapers described us.

An endless line of lorries approached us, every soldier armed to the teeth, every lorry equipped with a machine gun. The smallest show of concern on our part meant our death warrant; the slightest sign of fear would have betrayed us. There was no turning back. To attempt such a course would have been a vain challenge by four men to several hundred soldiers. Our only hope lay in coolness and bluff.

We passed the first twenty lorries without turning a hair. We just looked at the troops with that gaze of curiosity mingled with admiration which one might have expected from any loyal citizen as he watched his gallant "protectors" go by. We had passed the greater part of the convoy and were beginning to feel more at our ease when, rounding a corner, we were suddenly confronted by a sentry with rifle at the ready who called on us to "'alt." Our driver at once put on the brakes and pulled up.

We now realised why the other braves had allowed us to pass unchallenged. We had been led into an ambush, permitted to get right into the middle of the convoy, so that we might not have a dog's chance of escaping. It was a cunning trap, but we would show them how Irishmen would face death rather than surrender. It was all up with us; but we would sell our lives dearly.

I pulled my gun. For a fraction of a second I fingered it fondly under the rug, setting my sight on the best possible target. I had my finger on the trigger, ready to take aim, when an officer dashed up.

"Sorry for delaying you, gentlemen," he apologised.

This did not look like an ambush. I waited on tenterhooks for his explanation. He was the captain in charge of the party. "Two of the 'beastly' cars, you know, have broken down," he said, "and the road is almost completely blocked." He apologised profusely for the delay, but he feared there was not enough room for our car to pass. "Awfully bad luck," but he thought we should have to get out and walk.

By this time I had quite recovered my composure. I told him that we had an important business appointment; any further delay might mean serious loss to us. "Besides," I said, "we have come from a far distance, I am crippled with rheumatism and find even a short walk difficult."

He was much impressed by my protest. In those days British officers regarded an Irishman who could travel by motor as a person of considerable importance who might get a "question" raised in the "House" if he had been rudely treated. I know what he would have said some months later to any Irishman travelling by road.

He turned to his men and ordered four of them to put aside their rifles and push our car for about two hundred yards until we had passed the broken-down lorries. We dared not manifest our appreciation of the humour of the situation by even the semblance of a smile. A section of the British Army was going out of its way to save us the trouble of walking, while thousands of that same army were searching the countryside for us. What a pretty heading it would have been for the *Morning Post*, "Wanted Gunmen aided and abetted by the British Army!"

We expressed our deep gratitude to the soldiers; assured them that they need not push our car any further and apologised for having put them to so much trouble.   A moment later we waved them good-bye, and were dashing along the road to Foynes. The speed of our car was tested for the next quarter of an hour. We feared lest those obliging soldiers might get suspicious and come in pursuit to make further enquiries. Séan and I laughed heartily when we had left them behind. From the day that we had become outlaws this was our first experience of British co-operation. It was not our last; more than once we had reason to feel grateful for their "kindness" in helping us out of difficulties.

Some hours later we reached our destination—the house of the priest to whom I have already referred. We got a right hearty welcome. No trouble was spared to make us comfortable. The housekeeper, Molly, was like a mother to us. She was a bit of a dictator, too, at times when her dictation was for our good. When she had given us a hearty meal she ordered both of us to bed, where we remained for two whole days. Can you wonder that we felt loath to leave the blankets, with memories of torn newspapers, dirty straw and damp hay still fresh in our minds?

After two days' rest I felt fully restored but Hogan was still far from well. We can never forget Molly's kindness. No trouble was too great for her. It was her kindness and good cooking that really revived us. She was always good-humoured and cheerful. It was a tonic to hear her merry laugh, her banter and her bright homely talk. It was all so different from what we had experienced during the months that had passed. Hitherto, the people who had spoken to us never raised their voices above a whisper. Sometimes we were amused when we saw the caution which they exercised before giving any sign of recognition. Whenever we met an acquaintance on the road he looked behind, to the right and to the left, before venturing to salute us. Many of them, I suppose, were afraid that if we were caught soon after having met them, suspicion might light on them; an Irishman fears nothing more than to be suspected of being an informer.

Some of our friends almost fainted when they recognised us. At this I do not wonder. Several weeks had often passed during which we had not made the acquaintance of a razor. One is not particular about personal appearance when there is an army at one's heels and a price of a thousand pounds on one's head.

Can you be surprised then that Molly's good nature and good humour were such a tonic? She was brave as well as kind. She would inspire us with hope when everything looked black. She was unshaken in her conviction that no harm would come to us; that God, as she used to say, would save us from our enemies. She kept a lamp constantly burning before the image of the Sacred Heart in intercession for our welfare, and I am sure also that she said many a decade of her beads for us.

But if Molly was a brick, the priest was a thousand bricks. Like Molly, he never counted the cost of "harbouring outlaws." We were welcome to his roof and to his table as long as we cared to stay; everything that his house held, or whatever he could command, was placed at our service. A couple of years later his friendship with the Volunteers almost proved his undoing. He was bivouacking with a Flying Column on the Limerick-Kerry border, and when the boys left before dawn to take part in an ambush, one of them by mistake took Father Dick's hat. In the skirmish that took place two of the Peelers were wounded. Later in the day the Crown forces visited the scene of the fighting and discovered a compromising article in the form of a black trilby with the lettering "Rev. Richard McCarthy" plainly visible on the inside band. A friendly policeman sent word of the find to a local Volunteer who cycled all through the night to Ballyhahill to warn the priest of his peril. He had to lie low until the Truce was declared. We certainly enjoyed our stay at Ballyhahill and would have liked to remain longer but it was not safe to stay very long in the same district. Besides, we felt it would not be fair to our host. After a stay of a few weeks we went on to Rathkeale.

Here for the first time I met Seán Finn, one of the bravest and most chivalrous Irishmen that I have ever met. He was then but a mere youth, and yet he had been elected Commandant of his Battalion. Imbued with a passionate desire to strike a blow for the old land, he was brave almost to rashness. Eighteen months later, this gallant soldier fell in his first battle with the enemy.

We did not stay long in Rathkeale. We were restless and longing for action. We were anxious, too, to know how Seán Treacy and Séamus Robinson were faring in Dublin. At this time we read the daily newspapers and concluded that they must have escaped capture. At last we got into communication with them and arranged to meet. Needless to say, our messages were never posted through ordinary government channels. We relied instead on the services of trusted friends.

In the course of time Maggie Frewin's newspaper and magazine stand at the Limerick Junction became a clearing-house for all our dispatches. Tried and true employees of the Great Southern Railway invariably called to Maggie's shop whenever the trains made a halt at the Junction. They took personal responsibility for the delivery of missives handed over by Maggie. When the war with the British ended, she married Mick Breen, Sparkie's brother.

Treacy, Robinson, Hogan and I felt that it was the decree of fate that we should be reunited so that we might stand or fall together. Seán Hogan and I worked our way from West Limerick back towards the eastern end of the county right up to the borders of South Tipperary. We had returned to the region where we had previously received shelter and hospitality, Lackelly, near Emly. Once more we found ourselves within seven miles of Soloheadbeg, a few miles distant from Knocklong where we were to have our most dramatic adventure.

At Lackelly we met Treacy and Robinson. We felt like a group of schoolboys on a holiday. Somehow, when the four of us were together all the dark clouds seemed to scatter. We forgot that we were outlaws; we talked and joked long into the night, exchanging tales of our adventures since the day on which we had parted. Treacy and Robinson had openly gone about Dublin and had quite a pleasant time. We, on our part, tried to make them jealous by telling them of the great entertainment which we had received at the priest's house; we boasted of having been helped on our way by British soldiers. Treacy and Robinson were able to retort with an equally thrilling experience. On the way from Tipperary to Dublin their car broke down right opposite Maryboro' jail; immediately several soldiers rushed to their assistance and got it restarted.

Meantime, the police and military were searching for us through the length and breadth of Tipperary. They dug gardens and bogs in their quest for the missing explosives. They watched our haunts and raided every place which we had been known to frequent. In spite of this, we were determined that we would not remain inactive. In our view, the three months that had passed since the encounter at Soloheadbeg seemed to have been wasted. The I R.A. was still an army only in name In theory there was a fairly good organisation. Every county had its brigade and its battalions; arms were not altogether lacking; but of what use, we asked ourselves, are men who are toy-soldiers? Of what use are guns that have been oiled and cleaned but never fired? The men were not wanting in courage, but they lacked initiative. In those days it was considered the height of patriotism to go to jail for one's opinions. All over the country, men were allowing themselves to be arrested for drilling or carrying arms; they never seemed to think of putting the arms to good use, rather than suffer imprisonment. At our meeting in Lackelly we made up our minds to put an end to this business of going to jail and becoming cheap heroes. We wanted a real army, not a hollow mockery. Even if such an army numbered only a few score, it would be far better than the present organisation. We expected that Soloheadbeg would have been followed by active operations throughout the country; instead, it was becoming a mere memory.

We procured four bicycles and headed straight for Donohill, back to the very scene of our first battle, right into the middle of the military net. Donohill is about two miles north of the Soloheadbeg quarry, and our route took us by the very road where we had awaited the enemy; there we had at last met them face to face. Since that fateful day, 21 January, we had not cast eyes on Soloheadbeg; you can picture our feelings as we saw once more the familiar hills and the turn of the road where the Peelers had appeared. We dismounted and lingered for a while in the neighbourhood. Doubtless, many of the inhabitants did not expect that they would ever again see us on this earth. In the old days the usual thing for men caught up in such toils was to clear away to America. But our work was in Ireland, and we were going to see it through to the bitter end.

At Donohill we appeared to the Horan family as though we had come back from beyond the grave. When they realised that we were not ghosts, they gave us a typical Irish welcome, and we joked and made merry almost till cockcrow. They didn't forget to keep somebody on the lookout in order to ensure that we would not be taken by surprise. We stayed there until the following night.

My own house was only half a mile distant; needless to remark, I took the opportunity of calling to see my mother. It was a welcome surprise for her. Ever since I had gone 'on the run,' I had not dared even to send her a card; it would have brought endless annoyance from the enemy; moreover, it might have given them useful information. Poor woman! She was very brave and in the best of spirits in spite of the fact that her little home was often raided at early dawn and midnight; her place was ransacked three times during one period of twenty-four hours. It gave me great courage to see her and to talk to her again. But I could not make a long stay. She gave me her blessing and we parted in sorrow.

The dear old soul had suffered much for the crime of having taught her sons to do their duty for their country. Her house was looted and set on fire over her head; even her hens and chickens had to pay the price of British hate, for they were bayoneted by the Black-and-Tans. Through all her trials she never lost heart and would always have her jibe at the enemy. On one occasion when the Peelers came and enquired if her son was in, she sarcastically asked them if they would venture under the same roof with him. On another occasion, in reply to the same question, she told them that I was upstairs, and invited them to enter. Their response to the invitation was a hasty retreat.

From Donohill we went to Rossmore, and then on to Rosegreen, and at last reached Clonmel, a large garrison town, which was the South Tipperary headquarters for the Royal Irish Constabulary. We spent several days in that district and were not idle. We met some of the officers of our own brigade and questioned them about plans for the future. We did our best to induce them to get things moving.

One morning I had an unusual adventure in this district; not very exciting in its own way, but one which could have had serious consequences for me. As I was cycling in pitch dark up Mockler's Hill at 2 a.m. Seán Hayes of Moyglass (later appointed a member of the Senate), coming from the opposite direction, crashed right into me. I got the full force of his handlebars over the heart and was thrown helplessly to the ground. I thought my last hour had come. The prospect of such an inglorious end did not appeal to me. To be killed in action by an enemy bullet was a fate which held no terror for me; to be killed by the handlebars of a common push-bicycle would have been an ignominious exit from this life. To make things worse, I had visions of being identified by the R.I.C. and kicked into eternity. However, I made a rapid recovery. I have made a habit of pulling myself together very quickly. After a short rest I was able to remount my bicycle and continue on my way.

On 10 May we retraced our steps to the village of

Rossmore. It was now almost four months since the ambush at Soloheadbeg. During that time we had been sleeping wherever and whenever we got the chance; sometimes in a barn, sometimes in a cattle-shed, very seldom in a bed. Our health did not deteriorate as a result of the hardship which we endured. One grows hardened from roughing it. When we got to Rossmore we were feeling fit and game for any-thing even though we had spent four nights without any rest. We could have done with a few hours' sleep. Somebody mentioned casually to us that a dance was being held at Éamon Ó Duibhir's house in Ballagh, only a short distance away. We forgot our weariness; we forgot our danger. We were young and had grown accustomed to taking risks; it was so long since we had had the pleasure of a ceilidhe.

Without a second thought we faced for Ballagh. We were soon in the thick of the night's fun. It felt glorious to be back again, even for one night, in an atmosphere of gaiety. For nearly two years I had not mingled with a crowd; here I found myself enjoying a typical Tipperary party. The music was great; the supper and refreshments still more welcome; we danced the reels and the sets with the lads and the lassies right in the middle of the Martial Law area and at a time when several British raiding parties were breaking open the doors of cottages and farmhouses in their search for us.

All the boys and girls knew us. They, like so many others before and after, could have slipped out of the house and made their way to the nearest police barracks which was not two miles distant. Any one of them could have earned a thousand pounds by informing, but such a base thought never entered a single mind. Neither did we have any suspicion of any member of the party, for we were quite certain that they would have severed their right hands from their bodies rather than touch the Saxon gold in exchange for a betrayal.

We danced all through the night; I returned to Rossmore in the early hours of the morning with a few of the boys. My three companions did not come with me, but stayed for a few more dances; we had arranged to meet at O'Keeffe's of Glenough and go to bed for a long rest Shortly after my arrival Seán Treacy and Séamus Robinson put in an appearance.

Seán Hogan did not accompany them, but none of us felt in the least uneasy. Even though his eighteenth birthday was only two days off, we knew that he was well able to look after himself.

CHAPTER SIX

CAPTURE AND RESCUE OF
SEÁN HOGAN

ALL THREE OF US were completely jaded. What with our five sleepless nights and the fatigue of a whole night's dancing, we could have slept, as Seán Treacy said, on a harrow. The sight of the cosy bed that had been made ready for us almost put us to sleep before we turned in.

Seán Treacy omitted to say his customary Rosary before going to sleep. I was too tired to breathe a prayer and I was fast asleep when I was awakened by Patrick Kinnane calling. His voice sounded very far off. He was speaking to me, I knew; but my eyes refused to open. I was suddenly brought to my senses. His words lifted me clean out of the bed. Hogan had been captured by the Peelers!

It would have been very easy for us to believe that "J.J." as we called him—his name was John Joseph—had been shot. To think that he was arrested! I would not believe it. Was Kinnane joking? I turned to Seán Treacy, for he too was on his feet by this time. I saw from the expression on his face that he realised the full horror of the situation.

I would have given a fortune for a few hours more of sleep. Never in my life did I feel so completely worn out. Robinson and Treacy were in a similar state. But the thought of "J.J." in the enemy's clutches brought us to our senses. Without a moment's hesitation we made our decision. No words were needed to convey to one another the thought that was racing through our minds. We must either rescue Hogan or die in the attempt; we knew that, had any one of us been in Hogan's position, his decision would have been exactly the same.

In a short time we got the little information that was available about the circumstances of his capture. He had left the dance shortly after ourselves and went to Meagher's of Annafield. A posse of police was seen in the distance. Seán left hurriedly by the rear of the house, but was captured by another detachment of police when he jumped to the road. It was not until a year later that the British invented the happy knack of shooting prisoners "while attempting to escape." If that fashion had then existed "J.J." would not be with us to-day, nor would our plan to rescue him have been of much avail.

Our first trouble was to locate him. Murder of innocent people had not yet come into fashion, but Martial Law had made people more careful; few ventured out late at night or early in the morning because of the certainty of being challenged by British troops who were patrolling the roads at all hours. For that reason we found from our first enquiry that no one had seen what direction Hogan's escort had taken. They might have faced for any one of half a dozen garrisons : Thurles, Tipperary, or Cashel perhaps. To be left in ignorance of their route was maddening; we knew that every hour that passed made the danger greater; we knew also that he would soon be removed to a place which might be beyond our reach. Gladly would any one of our number have taken the place of our youngest comrade. Now that he was gone from us, we suddenly discovered all his excellent qualities. We had never been in the habit of paying him compliments while he was with us.

We searched and enquired everywhere. We sent cyclists in all directions in an endeavour to pick up a trail. His captors had got too much of a start. We were almost in despair when at last we got on the scent; we traced him to Thurles barracks.

To attempt to rescue him from that place would have been worse than madness. It would have been as easy to storm the gates of hell. Thurles was a fairly large town with a big garrison of both police and military. The barracks was strongly fortified and the Peelers were always on the alert. Their position made alertness essential. They were in the midst of an area that was soon to become a theatre of active warfare. There was not the slightest hope of effecting a rescue by a frontal attack on the barracks; besides, the fact that Seán Hogan was being held as prisoner in their stronghold would make them all the more careful, for by this time they knew that he was one of the four men wanted for the ambush at Soloheadbeg. From the shreds of information which they had picked up, as well as from our disappearance, they had concluded that we were the men who had taken part in that adventure.

There was one gleam of hope. We knew that he would not be kept for any length of time in Thurles. Prisoners were detained in these local stations for not more than a couple of days during which the preliminary enquiries and remands were being effected. They were then transferred to one of the big prisons : Mountjoy, Cork, Maryboro', Dundalk or

Belfast. In the case of Tipperary men, and indeed of men from all over Munster, Cork was the usual destination. The odds were ten to one that in a day or two Seán Hogan would be taken by train from Thurles to Cork. May Maloney, in whose house we were staying, volunteered to go to Thurles and endeavour to pick up some information. She brought back word that Hogan was still in Thurles. We decided to make for Emly and hold up the train by which Seán Hogan was being conveyed. We would shoot it out with his escort and either rescue Hogan or die in the attempt. For many reasons we chose Emly. It was a small station and there were no soldiers convenient; the police we did not particularly mind. Emly was situated in a district with which we were familiar and in which we had many friends. It was close to the borders of three counties; this fact would add to our chances of evading pursuit, since the enemy would not find it easy to discover whether we retreated to the mountains, to North Cork, to South Tipperary, or to East Limerick. Above all, we had faith in the boys from the neighbouring village of Galbally.

Such operation as the holding up of a train and arranging for the removal of our companion after his rescue, to say nothing of our own escape, could not be carried out by three men. We needed help; we must get reinforcements. At once we secured the services of a special Volunteer despatch-rider; neither telegrams nor telephones were to be thought of. To trust these means of communication would be merely giving advance notice of our plans. Our first care was to send the full details of our plans to the acting commandant of the Tipperary Town Battalion, with orders to send reinforcements. Emly would be only seven miles, less than half-an-hour's cycle run, from Tipperary town. We decided on our course of action and made our preparations. Ned Reilly and the O'Keeffe brothers gave us every help. Our hearts were sad but we still had hope. Treacy, Robinson and I mounted our bicycles and faced for Emly. With the exception of one hour's sleep after the dance, we had now passed five nights without a rest. In the ordinary course Emly would have been only some thirty miles distant, but for obvious reasons we had to avoid the main roads and the neighbourhood of Tipperary town. We covered nearly fifty miles on that journey over rough and uneven roads. It was one of our toughest rides. The journeys that Sean Treacy and I had made to and from Dublin were less wearisome.

As we approached Donohill, Séamus Robinson's bicycle was put out of action. We had neither the time nor the tools for repairing it on the roadside but we had faithful friends. Patrick O'Dwyer of Donohill, whose wife was a first cousin of Seán Hogan, put a new bicycle at our disposal and we resumed our journey. Our fatigue was telling on us. We were so weary that we could have gone to sleep by the roadside, but the excitement and our sense of loyalty kept up our strength. At Oola we actually fell asleep while we were travelling, but we bestirred ourselves and went on doggedly up hill and down dale, with our teeth set and our minds fixed on rescue or death. We made a detour to the right through the Martial Law area and over the border into County Limerick through the historic village of Cullen; on to Ballyneety, past the ruins of the old castle, on the very same road by which Patrick Sarsfield rode on that moonlit night two hundred and thirty years before, when his sabre brought terror to Dutch William's troops. It was a strange coincidence that we, who now rode on a similar errand of death or glory, were Tipperary outlaws just like Galloping Hogan who on that night made Sarsfield's exploit possible. We, too, were on our way to rescue another Tipperary outlaw of the same name and clan.

While Seán Treacy was reminding us of this glorious episode, for he loved his Irish history, we were startled by a dull thud. We turned in our tracks and saw that Robinson had fallen off his bicycle and was lying prostrate, fast asleep. We shook him up, for we had to keep moving; time was precious; the three of us remounted and reached Emly at 3.30 a.m. We had stopped once or twice on the way to make further enquiry and establish a line of communication. We got another rude shock when a bomb dropped from Robinson's pocket; for a moment we thought that we were being attacked.

At Lackelly we called upon our old friends, the Maloneys, and received a hearty welcome. While we were discussing our plans over a much needed breakfast, May Maloney offered all the help that she could give and we gladly accepted her offer. She became our despatch rider for the occasion; we could not have succeeded without her help. Maloney's house was later destroyed by the Black-and-Tans, and both May and her brother Dan were imprisoned during the Civil War.

The first train on which the prisoner might come was not

due till noon. When all was in readiness a few hours before noon, we waited eagerly for the arrival of the men from Tipperary town. As the hour approached we grew anxious. The minutes grew into hours. Eagerly our eyes scanned the road from Tipperary but no cyclist appeared. What had happened ? We could not let ourselves believe that the help which we needed so badly was not at hand. Eleven o'clock; still no reinforcements. The minutes travelled all too fast. Half-past eleven came; still no sign. And the train was due at twelve noon !

We were not going to let Seán Hogan be taken away without a fight. We knew that the escort, armed with rifles, bayonets and revolvers, would consist of four to eight police-men; it was quite possible that other policemen or soldiers would be on the same train. We could only fail. At 12 o'clock the three of us rushed up to the station just as the engine steamed in.

In my hurry I dashed right into an old woman at the entrance. To save her I had to throw my arms around her. The two of us were swung round and round by the force of the collision and I finished what must have looked like an Indian war dance by falling heavily to the ground. There was no time for explanations or apologies, and I don't know yet whether the poor woman ever heard an explanation of the collision. Before she could even see my face, I was up again and racing along the platform with my finger on the trigger of the revolver.

But there was no prisoner ! We were sadly disappointed. In a sense, too, we felt a little relieved, for there would still be time to look for help before the next train was due. Waiting is always the hardest part of any fight; suspense is more nerve-racking than action.

As we returned crestfallen to our resting-place, having scanned every carriage, our pill was made more bitter by the thought that the Tipperary men had failed us. Our message may have miscarried or perhaps been misunderstood. Help must be procured from another source. We thought of the old Galtee Battalion, the boys from the mountain districts, from Galbally and Ballylanders. They were men of steadfast heart and enterprising spirit. We felt certain that they would not turn a deaf ear to a call like ours.

The next train was not due from Thurles till 7 p.m. We sent word to the boys of the Galtee Battalion; told them that their help was needed, and explained the dangerous task

on which we were bound. Within an hour the reply came.
Five of their men would join us at 5 o'clock. Never had we
got such a heartening message.

They did not fail us. In fact, Ned O'Brien, James Scanlon,
J. J. O'Brien, Seán Lynch and Edward Foley arrived a
quarter of an hour before the appointed time. Exactly two
years later, Edward was condemned to death for having
taken part in the Knocklong rescue. Paddy Maher went to
the scaffold with him for the same " crime " even though he
had not taken hand, act or part in the rescue of Seán Hogan.
Both gladly gave their lives for Ireland and their brave words
spoken from the foot of the gallows will keep their memory
green in the hearts of Irish patriots. May they rest in peace.

We were now eight strong, five of us armed with revolvers
and three unarmed. After a consultation we decided on a
change of plan. Seán Treacy, Séamus Robinson, Ned O'Brien
and myself cycled on to Knocklong, the next station on the line
about three miles south of Emly. We switched to Knocklong
because, with the exception of Emly, all the other stations
were held by strong British forces. This wayside station,
situated a couple of miles from a police barracks, was
comparatively safe. If the attempt failed we had planned
to motor to Blarney, where we could again intercept the
escort party. The other four men we sent to Emly station
with instructions to board the train without arousing
suspicion and find out in what carriage our comrade was held
captive. In that way they could give us the hint as soon as
Knocklong was reached, so that no time might be lost in
proceeding with the rescue.

May Maloney had been instructed by Treacy that if definite
information was obtained about Hogan's transfer, Michael
O'Connell, of Thurles, should telegraph such information in
code to Thomas Shanahan, manager of the coal-depot at
Knocklong. To avoid suspicion Hogan was to be alluded to as
" the greyhound." Shanahan was a coursing enthusiast and
had on the previous day despatched by rail a greyhound bitch
to be served by a stud dog at Rathcoole, Co. Dublin. This
dog was the property of Mr. Twamley, a well-known coursing
judge. Shanahan received a telegram early in the day.
" Greyhound in Thurles still, O'Connell." This greatly puzzled
him, for he had not been apprised of the arrangement
concerning the code. A second telegram arrived, but by
that time events were moving at a fast rate.

We reached Knocklong just as the train's departure from

Emly was signalled. We walked up the platform seeming cool and unconcerned but our hands had a firm grip on our loaded revolvers. In the distance we saw the plume of smoke coming from the engine. One minute later the train was pulling into the station. At the same moment the Dublin-bound train, on which travelled a company of fully armed British troops, steamed in at the opposite platform. Fortunately, it departed a fraction of a second before we began the grim struggle.

Our train had not yet come to a standstill when the signal for which we waited was given us by two different parties. In accordance with an arrangement made in Thurles on the previous day, a local Volunteer, Goorty McCarthy, had boarded the train on which the prisoner travelled. McCarthy stood at a window, prepared to give the signal. Our men were posted at another window, unaware of McCarthy's presence.

There was not a moment to be lost. The train would make only one minute's delay; we had not thought it necessary to hold up the driver. Our colleagues indicated by a slight motion of hands the carriage where we would find our man. It was a long corridor-carriage divided into about a dozen separate compartments. An outer passage-way extended along the entire train. The Galbally men were in this passage. In one of the compartments we saw Seán Hogan, handcuffed, and facing the engine. At his right hand sat Sergeant Wallace, at the left, Constable Enright. Seated opposite were two other constables, all fully armed. My job was to cover the guard's van. Seán Treacy, to whom command of the operation had been assigned, said "Come on, boys." He held his revolver at the ready and sprang to the running-board. Ned O'Brien followed close on his heels. They rushed along the corridor, burst into the prisoner's compartment, presented revolvers and gave the command "Hands up!" Only a moment before, as we heard later, Sergeant Wallace had slapped Seán Hogan's face, asking, sarcastically, "Where are Breen and Treacy now?" Constable Enright had his revolver levelled at the prisoner's ear. Orders had been given to shoot Hogan dead if any attempt were made to rescue him. It was a matter of Hogan's life or the constable's. The policeman was in the act of pulling the trigger of his revolver when he was himself shot through the heart.

Immediately pandemonium raged. Constable Ring hurled himself through the open window and took to his heels,

roaring like a maniac. Treacy sprang at Sergeant Wallace;
Constable Reilly, clutching his rifle, grappled with Eamon
O'Brien. All four were locked in a deadly struggle while
some of the Galbally contingent attempted to lend a hand.
But space was so cramped that it was difficult to distinguish
friend from foe. Jim Scanlon succeeded in wresting the
rifle from Reilly and crashed the butt-end of it on his head.
Reilly slumped to the floor.

The epic clash between Treacy and Wallace continued.
Treacy's gun had slipped from his hand in the early stages
of the scuffle. Wallace was aware of this and all his efforts
were concentrated on freeing his right hand in which he
held his revolver. But Treacy clung on for grim death by
sheer will power, for he was doing battle with a man of
great physique. Wallace's right hand was gripped as in a
vice and at last his strength began to ebb. His breath was
coming in short gasps. Treacy in a do-or-die effort wrenched
the gun from Wallace's hand, and fired at him point-blank.

Meanwhile another crisis had arisen. Reilly had recovered
from the blow on the head and in the confusion that prevailed
had managed to slip unobserved from the train with Ring's
rifle concealed under his greatcoat. From the platform he
fired random shots through the window of the carriage in
which Wallace and Treacy were struggling. O'Brien and
Scanlon were hit but their wounds seemed superficial.
I rushed from my position at the rear of the train and
though I was out of range, as I was armed only with a
revolver, I tried to draw the rifleman's fire. I succeeded only
too well. Reilly took aim. The first bullet pierced my lung,
the second found its mark in my right arm. My revolver
fell to the ground. Had Reilly kept his head, he could have
wiped out every one of us. Fortunately, I was able to pick
up the revolver with my left hand. When he saw me level
my gun he faced right about turn and fled from the platform.
Victory was ours.

We left the dead constable and the mortally-wounded
sergeant at the station. Many of the passengers had jumped
from the train and were flying, terror-stricken. The engine-
driver, who had apparently not heard the first shots, was
about to start the train while the fight was still in progress.
A girl raced to the engine and told him of the gun-fight.
He did not move out from the station until the struggle had
ended.

An inquest was held two days later at Kilmallock on the

bodies of Wallace and Enright. Ring gave a graphic account of the fight but made no allusion to the ignominious role which he had played. Reilly also gave his version. One of the jurors boldly remarked to the police : " You are simply trying to paint your own story in your own way." The police witnesses had been instructed not to answer any questions which might reveal that we would not have shot their men if they had not offered resistance.

The inquest was also noteworthy for the fact that the jury not only refused to bring in a verdict of murder but spoke out plainly. I quote the newspaper account of May 22 : " Condemning the arrest of respectable persons and the exasperating of the people, the jury demanded self-determination for Ireland and blamed the Government for exposing the police to danger." Our efforts were having their effect.

The plain people were realising that ours was a fight for Irish freedom. They realised also that we had no enmity against the police, provided that they confined themselves to their ordinary work. When they betrayed their own country by taking Saxon gold in payment for their treachery, we had to treat them according to their deserts.

This is the true story of the Knocklong rescue. After the affair, we were vehemently denounced as cold-blooded assassins. Two years later we were being hailed as heroes.

The experiences of our comrade, Seán Hogan, from the date of his arrest throw an interesting sidelight on the behaviour of the Peelers, even though their mode of action was not so barbaric in those days as at a later period.

When the dance had concluded in the early hours of that morning at Ballagh, and the rest of us had retired to sleep at O'Keeffe's, Seán Hogan went with Brigid O'Keeffe to Meagher's of Annafield. This was the same Meagher family at whose house some months previously we had had such a narrow escape when the girl waved her handkerchief to warn us of danger. Brigid, who was a near relative of the Meaghers, had decided to go to their house for breakfast.

Seán was so tired that he fell asleep at the table. When breakfast was finished he took off his belt, put aside his revolver, and lay down to rest on a sofa. Philip Meagher and his two daughters were busy about the farmyard, preparing to send the milk to the creamery.

Seán was suddenly roused from his sleep by the warning

shout: "The police are coming up the road!" He jumped to his feet and went to the door, revolver in hand.

The police had been seen from a distance by the Meaghers, but Seán could not observe them from the house. Assuming that they were coming from the north side, he took a southern course and moved quickly through a field, which is on a lower level than the road. When he had got to the end of the field, he thought that he was out of danger; he pocketed his revolver, and jumped from the fence to the road—into the arms of six policemen. As a matter of fact, they had approached from the south, and had got a full view of him as he ran along the field.

Seán was instantly handcuffed and his revolver was seized. The captors marched him back along the road to Meagher's, and roundly abused the occupants just as another section of the raiders was coming through the doorway, having made a hurried search of the house. They did not recognise Seán who refused to give his name. Just as he was about to be marched off, Brigid O'Keeffe shook hands with him and said, "Good-bye, Seán." She had given no clue to his surname. Apparently they took her to be one of the Meagher family; had they recognised her as one of the O'Keeffes, in all probability they would have come down the road to search her own house, and surprised us who were sound asleep.

Sergeant Wallace was in charge of the police party; with him were Constables Reilly, Ring and others. They marched their prisoner to Roskeen barracks and sent word to Thurles that they had captured an armed man whose Christian name was Seán. A police van was at once dispatched for the purpose of conveying the prisoner; one of the police recognised Seán as one of the much-wanted Soloheadbeg men.

After the arrest one of the Meaghers ran down the road to Patrick Kinnane's house, situated between Meagher's and O'Keeffe's, and asked Patrick to bring us word that Seán had been captured.

When Seán Hogan had fallen into their hands, the Peelers adopted every subterfuge to get him to divulge information. At first they tried to coax information from him; for they saw that he was but a mere boy. Having failed in their efforts, they changed their tactics. They beat him unmercifully but they failed in their purpose; if Seán Hogan was but a boy in years, he was a man in strength of character and loyalty to his comrades. Not a word would he breathe even though they were to torture him to death.

Having failed to intimidate him, they tried another plan. One of the policemen, making a great show of friendship, whispered to Seán Hogan that he had been betrayed by Breen and Treacy who were at that very moment journeying to London with a free pardon in their pockets and a huge sum of money, the price of their betrayal. If Hogan would reveal whatever he knew about the Irish Republican army, he, too, would be well rewarded; he would be helped to leave the country instead of finding himself on the way to the gallows. But " J.J." knew his old comrades too well to believe that they had betrayed or deserted him. All the threats and cajolery of the Peelers were in vain. He refused to answer their questions and eventually did not even pretend to hear them.

The last shot had been fired at Knocklong. We moved from the platform. The place was almost deserted. Only a few people remained as though rooted to the spot. Seán Hogan was still wearing his handcuffs; four of the rescue party were bleeding from wounds received during the encounter; even the four, who had not been wounded, were blood-stained. I was no longer able to walk, and I realised that my last shot had been fired from my revolver, even though it might at any moment be found highly desirable to have it reloaded; but my right arm was powerless and I could not reload. I looked around me. Outside the station I saw a motor car which was evidently waiting for some passenger. With my empty revolver raised in my left hand I held up the car which we decided almost instantly to abandon. A fit of dizziness had come over me as I made for the gate. I had fallen heavily against the wall and blood was gushing from my head. At last a man in khaki uniform came to my assistance. Was he an Irishman serving in Britain's army ? Or, perhaps, an American soldier who happened to be a passenger on the train ? Later reports mentioned that a soldier was courtmartialled because he had shouted " Up the Republic." Let this ' unknown soldier ' now accept my belated expression of gratitude. In the confusion I forgot to thank him. Leaning on his arm, I struggled on to the road. He half-linked and half-carried me, for I was growing weaker every moment.

While the struggle had been taking place, Seán Hogan stepped from the train, unobserved. He walked along the platform until he came to a wicket-gate which led to the street. He passed through the gateway and made his way to a butcher's shop owned by Davey O'Byrne. Davey smashed the handcuffs with a blow of the cleaver. Seán was conducted through the rear of the house and eventually made contact with the unarmed members of the rescue party.

CHAPTER SEVEN

WANTED FOR MURDER

NED O'BRIEN, TREACY, SCANLON AND I faced for Shanahan's of Glenlara. It was growing dark and we were not certain that we were on the right road. I was parched with thirst from loss of blood. I saw a woman carrying a bucket of water and asked her for a drink. She had no drinking utensil, but I took the bucket from her hand and lifted it to my mouth. When I had slaked my thirst I plunged my head into the ice-cool water and for the moment felt refreshed. It must have taken us hours to get to the house. In a field on the way we met Tadhg Crowley and some of the lads from the neighbourhood. They came to our assistance and helped us to reach our destination.

I was put to bed at once and the priest and doctor were sent for. Dr. William Hennessy, the dispensary doctor of Galbally, was very kind to me. He was reputed to be a Unionist in politics and on that account the boys were anxious to call in another doctor, but my case needed immediate attention. When he arrived at my bedside, he ordered everyone to leave the room. His words surprised me, but they brought little comfort. "I'm glad to attend an Irish man who was prepared to die for his country." He examined my wound and confessed that he had never extracted a bullet, but that his nephew, Dr. Fitzgerald of Cush, near Knocklong, who had served through the Great War with the R.A.M.C., had ample experience in the treatment of wounded soldiers. An urgent message was despatched to Dr. Fitzgerald. Both doctors regarded my case as hopeless. The priest administered the Last Sacraments. I was told that I had only about twenty-four hours to live, as the bullet had gone right through my lung and I had suffered great loss of blood. That news was cheerless enough but I was not even allowed to spend those last hours in peace.

Immediately after my arrival at Shanahan's my comrades had at once mobilised an armed guard under a chap named Clancy. They had decided that I would not be taken alive by British forces. Scouts were sent out to watch the approaches. We knew that the country would be swept with columns of troops and police. All through the night, as I learned later, reinforcements of troops were rushed to the neighbourhood; the police garrisons were strengthened at Doon, Oola, Galbally, and at all the neighbouring villages and towns. During the following days a house-to-house search was made in that part of East Limerick and South Tipperary; even the graveyards were inspected in the hope of discovering newly-made graves; the newspapers had reported that "two of the attackers were believed to have been mortally wounded."

Nor can I help recalling at this stage an incident that happened on that memorable evening. Four policemen from Elton, a few miles from Knocklong, heard the firing at the station and took to their heels post-haste back to their barracks. There they remained behind locked doors until County Inspector Egan arrived in a motor car and broke open the doors, shouting, "You cowards! Here you are hiding, while four of our men have been shot and the murderers are still at large!"

A few hours after my arrival at Shanahan's our scouts rushed in with word that the raiding parties were hot on our tracks. A hurried council-of-war was held. My comrades procured a motor car and carried me off once more without even taking time to say a prayer for the man who had only twenty-four hours to live. They drove me right through the town of Kilmallock. I did not know till the next afternoon that we had actually passed the R.I.C. barracks to which the dead Constable Enright and the dying Sergeant Wallace had been removed. There was no other means of escape; we had to get out of the net that was being drawn round Knocklong. We took our chance and luck favoured us. My comrades fully realised the seriousness of the situation and the risks that they were taking in motoring through the town of Kilmallock but I was blissfully unconscious of everything save the fact that I was soon to "cross the Jordan." When I woke up next day, I was once more in West Limerick under the care of Seán Finn.

Let me pause to tell you the sequel to the Knocklong rescue. All of us who had taken part were either already on the run, or had to go on the run henceforth with the exception of Seán Lynch and J. J. O'Brien, who returned to their daily business. Both of them afterwards joined Dinny Lacey's famous South Tipperary Column, and fought all through the Black-and-Tan war. Ned O'Brien and Scanlon fell into bad health, owing to the hardships which they had endured. They escaped to America and did not return until many years had elapsed.

In the following year a brother of Scanlon's was taken prisoner and shot dead in Limerick city. After Hogan's rescue several men were arrested on suspicion. All except three, Martin Foley, Paddy Maher and Michael Murphy, were eventually released; Martin Foley and Paddy Maher, after having been held in prison for nearly two years, were hanged in Dublin on June 6, 1921, a month before the Truce. Michael Murphy, who was an ex-British soldier, was tried in Armagh and released shortly after the Truce.

In West Limerick my comrades and I were royally treated. Seán Finn was kindness personified; indeed all the neighbours lavished hospitality on us. I must give special mention to the Sheehans, Keanes, Longs, Duffys and Kennedys; but our good times were not to last long. The enemy was once more on our track.

We moved farther west towards the Kerry border. Even here we found that the pursuit was too hot; we had to cross over into Kerry. By this time I was well on the road to recovery. Then, as at a later stage, I acquired the habit of breaking all medical precedents by keeping alive when, according to all the rules of the game, I should have died. By the time that we reached Knocknagoshel I was even able to take a short walk if someone lent me support. British troops were so busy scouring the countryside for us, day and night, that we dared not think of using motor cars or vehicles of any kind.

One bright feature always lightened our burden. It was Seán Treacy's sense of humour. No matter how dark the outlook, Seán would have his little joke. At Knocklong he had been shot through the teeth and for a long time his mouth was very painful. I was still suffering severely from my wounds. Hence the difficulties for both of us in taking food. "Dan," said Seán to me, "I wish I had your big head for half an hour. I am frightfully hungry but I can't eat. You can eat all right, but you won't." I recall still another example of his peculiar sense of humour. We were cycling at full speed from Cullen to Tipperary when suddenly Seán asked us to pull up. We were somewhat surprised; we knew how risky it was to delay in an area that was under Martial Law. We dismounted. The rain was coming down in torrents. Seán turned to each one of us separately and asked solemnly for the loan of a pin. Each one replied that he had no such commodity, the truth being that in such weather not one of us wished to open his coat.

"What need have you for a pin?" I asked, as my teeth chattered with the cold.

"Well," he replied, "I'm afraid my tie isn't hanging straight!"

I never felt so much inclined to give a punch to my old comrade and I am sure that the others felt as I did; but we had to laugh as we mounted and rode ahead, making remarks which were none too complimentary about the conceit of some people. Such little incidents helped us on our road and often dispelled our gloom.

We remained for a few days in a remote district. We were anxious for news but found it impossible to get a daily paper. One day I asked an old man if it was possible to procure such an item.

"Hardly a week goes by," the old man replied, "that someone doesn't bring along *The Kerryman*."

Eventually some recent copies of *The Cork Examiner* and *The Independent* came our way. We got great amusement from the many grotesque accounts of the Knocklong rescue. We read denunciations by leaders of Church and State of the terrible crime of having rescued our young comrade from the hangman's noose. We read also the messages of sympathy which the King and his Viceroy sent to the relatives of their hirelings. Most of the Kerry people with whom we came in contact were very kind to us; above all, we can never forget the O'Connors, the Hickeys and the Aherns of Knocknagoshel.

After our stay we returned to County Limerick, all the time keeping close to the banks of the Shannon. Our wounds were healing rapidly and we had regained our strength. Almost daily we went for a swim and we fished quite a good deal. None of us could endure a day of inactivity.

One day in June 1919, while we were still in West Limerick we had what was probably our narrowest escape

since the Knocklong affair. Sheer good luck drove us half
a mile outside a great encircling movement.

This was the sixth attempt to net us and each time thousands of troops were engaged, to catch four wanted men.
By this time they were well aware that we would offer
armed resistance and that, if luck favoured us, many of them
would bite the dust before they got us, dead or alive.
Liberal rewards were offered for any information concerning our movements. Accurate descriptions of our appearance were published in the *Police Gazette*; highly-coloured
posters were displayed outside all the police barracks; aero-
planes showered down leaflets which pledged British gold
for information received. But the police and the Intelligence
department drew blank.

The British Government was attempting to reorganise
its Secret Service. For generations a costly organisation
had been maintained but the work was not considered to
be dangerous as it related to the activities of harmless
politicians. Now, however, a considerable risk was attached.
Our Secret Service had to be reckoned with; Dublin Castle
had to bestir itself. The news leaked through that the
officials were being severely reprimanded for their failure
to catch us. The invariable excuse advanced was that the
people would not give information, that informers were very
few and very chary, and that Scotland Yard was likely to
be called upon. Rumours were afloat that certain Irishmen
who resided in Britain might be lured to undertake secret
service work in their native country. The newspapers of
the next two years can tell how several informers paid
the price of their treachery. We found all of them out
in one way or another. The final victory of the I.R.A. can
be attributed chiefly to the fact that British Intelligence had
been rendered powerless.

One word more on this subject. I know that many people
were surprised at the number of corpses that were found
with the label attached, " Spies, beware—executed by the
I.R.A." Many well-meaning persons were wondering if
there had been tragic errors of judgment on our part. I
can say that of the cases that came under my personal
supervision, there was always sufficient evidence to convince the most scrupulous. Our only mistake may have
been that we set at liberty many against whom we had
ample evidence; they received the benefit of the slightest
doubt.

The " Knocklong Gang," a title given to us in derision—constantly outwitted the spies and the battalions sent to round us up. I have certain knowledge that on many occasions they got fairly good information about our movements. After that big raid from which we had such a close shave, we deemed it wise to change our quarters once more. We crossed into East Clare, still hugging the banks of the Shannon. We kept ourselves fit by plenty of exercise, chiefly by swimming, for we were convinced that a good stroke through the water might at some time or other help us to get out of a tight corner; in fact, we lived the healthy life of primitive men. On many a day we enjoyed several hours of sun-bathing. On one occasion we were basking beside the Shannon, when a boat manned by police passed right beside us. We took no particular notice of it at the time, thinking that the occurrence was but a mere coincidence.

When we got back to the house in which we were billeted we learned that the police who passed by in the boat belonged to a search party that had got on our trail. They never suspected our identity, so that once more our recklessness had saved us, or them?

It is probable that the police were scanning the rocks or peering under bushes where they expected us to hide. It would have amazed them to know that we were often within earshot of their own barracks. It is a positive fact that only a single brick often separated us from the police garrison and that on occasions we moved back from a window as lorries went out in search of us.

I am convinced that some policemen whom we met on country roads recognised us but heeded the proverb that discretion was the better part of valour. They did not ask us to produce our visiting cards. They would not have done a service to their wives and families by attempting to arrest us. I'm not saying that they had acted unwisely.

In a short time Clare became too hot for us. The Brennan brothers were not on the best of terms with the British garrisons in that county. In fact, relations became so strained that the British proclaimed Martial Law in that area also. We crossed the Shannon once more and this time found ourselves in North Tipperary.

It was at the hospitable home of a family named Whelehan that I first came into contact with Ernie O'Malley. The famous athletes, " Widger " Meagher and Frank McGrath also paid us a visit. Frank was commandant of the I.R.A. of North Tipperary.

We spent a while in Mid and South Tipperary. We were as poor as church mice. The people amongst whom we moved were like ourselves, on the run and on the rocks.

Éamon O'Duibhir of Ballagh, in whose house the dance had taken place on the night Seán Hogan was captured, was a good friend to us and supplied us with money. On one occasion we had to sleep in Castle Blake, near Rockwell College. In later days this old ruined castle, which had a secret apartment, befriended many of the boys who were on the run.

Once again we became restive. The country showed occasional signs of following our example—an odd attack on a police barracks and the capture of a rifle or two from a British soldier. We felt that the time had come for more general action.

CHAPTER EIGHT

IN DUBLIN'S FAIR CITY

WE KNEW THAT WE COULD not remain safe within Tipperary or over the Offaly border. Time and again we discussed our position, and always came to the conclusion that we could not continue to live like hunted animals. We decided to find out for ourselves how the country stood, how we stood, and how the whole Volunteer army stood. At last Seán Treacy and I parted from Robinson and Hogan in North Tipperary. Two bicycles were put at our disposal and we set out for Dublin. We stayed for one night at Tommy Scully's in Kilasally, Offaly, and from there we went to Maynooth and called on Donal Buckley, member of Dáil Éireann.

Donal was very modest about the part he had taken in the Rebellion of 1916. Even though he was almost fifty years old and had had no experience of warfare, he did not hesitate when the chance came of striking a blow for the freedom of his country. On Easter Monday, 1916, having bade a fond farewell to his wife and children, he rallied his company of Volunteers, marched them through the Square of Maynooth College and gave the command to halt under "the President's Arch." He requested Monsignor Hogan,

President of the College, to give a blessing to his company before they set out for Dublin. The President was a pacifist and made a fine distinction. He blessed them " as men " but would give no blessing to their arms. A servant of the College was so enthralled by the sight of the riflemen in green uniform that he threw off his apron, took his place in the ranks and fought in the G.P.O. Donal told us that the most trying experience of that memorable week was not the actual fighting but the discomfort from the heat of the burning buildings in O'Connell Street. One day after a prolonged bombardment a member of the garrison became unbalanced in mind. Trigger-happy, he never ceased firing and was endangering the lives of his companions. They had to overpower him and put him in handcuffs. Donal had one very narrow escape from death. An enemy sniper had taken up position behind a nearby chimney. Donal took his rifle and endeavoured to put the sharpshooter out of action. Finding that he was aiming slightly under the target, he stooped to adjust the sight of the rifle. At that moment the sniper's bullet found its mark on the wall right at the very spot where Donal's head would have been if he had not stooped to make the adjustment. Donal proved as kind to us as we would have expected from his record. His house was put at our disposal for as long as we cared to remain as his guests, but we stayed only three or four days.

When we reached Dublin we headed once more for Phil Shanahan's. Every Tipperary man who was on the run or who wanted a good dinner faced for Phil's. We made contact with Mick Collins, at that time Adjutant-General of the Irish Volunteers, and had a long and frank discussion with him. Mick undertook to arrange that we should stay in Dublin if we so wished. With this assurance we re-mounted our bicycles and rode back to the country for Séamus Robinson and Seán Hogan.

I was dressed as a priest, not an uncommon disguise at that time. The Peelers probably suspected that a good many of the men in clerical garb whom they saw travelling through the country, knew more about guns than about theology. There would have been an outcry of indignation if a priest was placed under arrest. The old Peelers were staunch Catholics and gave the benefit of the doubt even to suspicious looking clergy. In the next year when the Black-and-Tans were drafted into the police force, not only were priests arrested and imprisoned, but three of them, Father

Michael Griffin, Father James O'Callaghan and Canon Magner were murdered.

Canon Magner, parish priest of Dunmanway in County Cork had received a letter on 10 November 1921, commanding him under severe penalties to toll the church bell on Armistice Day in memory of the British soldiers who had fallen in battle during the Great War. The letter was signed " Black-and-Tans." He ignored the order. On 15 December, he was talking on the roadway with two parishioners, Timothy Crowley and James Brady, Resident Magistrate. While they were conversing, Auxiliary Cadets from Macroom Castle approached. The lorry came to a halt and the Auxiliaries dismounted. Without warning, an Auxiliary officer shot Crowley dead. Canon Magner rebuked him. He was immediately shot dead by the same man. The Auxiliaries threw the two bodies over the fence and departed. The Resident Magistrate insisted upon an inquiry. The findings were that Cadet Harte, who had fired the shots, was guilty but proved to be of unsound mind. Mr. Brady resigned from his office.

Father Michael Griffin, a young priest of Galway city, was decoyed at midnight on Sunday, 14 November 1920, from his presbytery on a bogus sick-call. A week later his body was discovered close to the roadside at Barna Bog. He had been shot in the temple. Brig-General, F. P. Crosier, commander of the Auxiliaries, went to Galway to investigate the circumstances of the priest's death. I quote verbatim from his memoirs, *Ireland for Ever*:

" I found out that the military enquiry into the murder of Father Griffin (held in lieu of an inquest) was faced with a ' frame up ' and that a verdict of murder against ' somebody unknown ' would result. I told the military commander this and the name of the real murderer, but was informed that a senior official of Dublin Castle had been to Galway in front of me to give instructions as to ' procedure ' in this murder investigation.

" At Killaloe next day I received further evidence that the hidden hand was still at work, and was told in confidence that instructions had been received to kill the Roman Catholic Bishop of Killaloe, Dr. Fogarty, by drowning him in a sack from the bridge over the River Shannon, so as to run no further risk of detection by having his body found."

Father James O'Callaghan, an ardent Gaelic Leaguer, was

attached to the Cathedral parish in Cork. He was shot by police in a raid on Whit Sunday morning, and died some hours later in the North Infirmary.

All this frightfulness, however, was reserved for a later date. At the period of which I speak, respect for "the cloth" ensured for me a comparatively safe passage. When we reached Maynooth on the return journey, I discovered that my back tyre was punctured. I did not think it becoming my clerical dignity to mend the puncture by the way-side; moreover, I had no patience with that kind of work; I wheeled my machine to a mechanic's shop and asked him to repair it. He told me that he could not attend to the job for a few hours. I pointed out to him that I was going on urgent business, but it was all of no avail. Finally, he advised me to go to the College, Maynooth College, for the training of secular priests, where I would easily find some-one to repair it. Enraged by his refusal, I forgot for the moment that I was wearing the garb of a minister of peace and goodwill. I told off that mechanic in language more forcible than priestly, and I am sure that the poor man was shocked at the liberties which present-day clerics took with the English language. He was still staring at me when I wheeled my punctured bicycle from the door.

I had no desire to visit the College. Amongst the students I would find many friends willing to help me, but I was afraid that the President and his staff might not be too pleased to find a gunman masquerading as a clergyman; moreover, I doubted if I would be able to play the part. I need hardly say that I was no master of Latin, and I always associated priests with that language. Of course I often spoke in Lattin when I stayed at Haleys. There I ate in *Lattin* and slept in *Lattin* but I never was fluent in *Latin*.

I had to get the puncture mended. In a fit of bravado I turned towards the police barracks. At the door I met a policeman who raised his hat to me; with a show of dignity that would have done credit even to an archbishop, I acknowledged his token of respect.

I told him of my difficulties. Could he help me to repair the punctured tyre? "To be sure, Father," he replied, "in no time I can get you all that you want and, if your rever-ence won't mind, I'll give you a hand at the job."

In two minutes the whole garrison were tripping over one another in their eagerness to get solution and patches and the necessary equipment. When I entered the barracks

I could see dozens of printed notices and official documents pasted all over the walls. Amongst them was an elaborate description of Dan Breen, and a promise of a huge reward for his capture.

When the job was finished I thanked the Peelers most profusely for their kindness. They asked for my blessing and I raised my hand in a farewell gesture. I suppose it was discourteous of me not to have left my card with the sergeant.

That night I reached the borders of Tipperary and Offaly and met Treacy, Hogan and Robinson. A few days later all four of us were safely settled in Dublin, which was to be our new headquarters for months to come. Within a few weeks we were planning to shoot the Chief of the British Government in Ireland.

There were abundant signs that the war with the British was about to develop, and eventually result in an intensive guerilla struggle. Raids for arms were becoming more numerous; police patrols were being ambushed. In Dublin, British soldiers and police could still go about with comparative safety. The greatest menace to our safety came from the political branch of the "G" division of the Dublin Metropolitan Police. Their task was to track down Irish patriots, and they were always employed on political or military work. So far from devoting their attentions to the criminal classes, we knew that many of them actually made use of criminals as 'touts' or 'spotters' to shadow suspects or to act as *agents provocateurs*. The chief function of these "G" men was to guide military raiding-parties to the homes of suspect Sinn Féiners. They even made their way into Sinn Féin gatherings to take a note of the speeches, and, though many of them were known by appearance to almost every person in Dublin, they were not afraid; hitherto the only punishment which they suffered was a man-handling from the crowd. Day after day one read of raids on the houses of inoffensive people. This form of petty tyranny goaded many into action. Even boys and girls of tender age were imprisoned for the "crime" of having been caught in possession of a "treasonable" ballad.

Since July of this year 1919 several obnoxious "G" men had been shot dead, and in every case their assailants got safely away. We had to resort to such forcible measure in order to make them realise that we did not intend to tolerate spies and traitors in our midst. As a result of the

wholesale attacks made upon them they found it impossible
to stay in their homes or venture on the streets. Eventually
they took up their abode in Dublin Castle, whence they
issued forth now and again to accompany armed raiders.
Many of them resigned when things became too hot for them.
A small number of those who did not resign were never
molested, because they had themselves transferred to
ordinary criminal duties. These men had an understanding
with our side that they could go about their work provided
that they did not again indulge in political activities or assist
the military. A select few who were sympathetic to our
cause deliberately held their posts in order to provide us
with the inside information to which they had access.

When Treacy, Robinson, Hogan and I had become
acclimatised to city life, we were engaged in the tasks which
were in accordance with our hearts' desire. Now and again
a "G" man got on our track, but we soon dealt with him.
We walked about Dublin quite freely and without disguise.
Police who could identify us were sent up from Tipperary,
but their visits were invariably of short duration. They
found that it was not a particularly healthy operation to
follow too closely on our tracks. A few of them who may
have chanced to see us were wise enough to look the other
way.

We had many good friends in Dublin. Phil Shanahan's
was a great haunt of ours; one of the most amusing re-
collections I have is of a conversation which I had there one
evening with a Dublin Metropolitan policeman who had no
notion of my identity. He discussed the political situation
with me very confidentially, even the Soloheadbeg and
Knocklong affairs. He was in complete agreement with the
Sinn Féiners—he guessed I was one—but he couldn't agree
to the taking of life. I gave this simple man the impression
that my views were the same as his own.

I was known by sight to many of the D.M.P. On one
occasion I was sitting alone in Shanahan's snug when two
of their number came to the bar and ordered two pints of
draught Guinness. They wore their steel-spiked helmets
and carried revolvers in their holsters. I sat on, quiet as
a mouse, and never batted an eyelid. When they laid down
their tankards on the counter, they approached me. My
finger was on the trigger of my revolver, ready to draw
instantly if they put their hands towards their weapons.
They betrayed no such foolish intention. One of them smiled

benevolently: "Is that me bould Dan Breen? What sort of a gun are you using at present?" "I like the Colt best of all," I said, casually pulling out my revolver from my pocket. "You're in luck, then; these will suit," he said, as he presented me with a fistful of bullets which he extracted from the pocket of his tunic. We parted the best of friends. But one had always to be on the alert, so as to be first on the draw.

Shanahan's was the rendezvous of saint and sinner. A regular visitor was Peadar Kearney who composed Ireland's national anthem, "A Soldier's Song." About that time the Templemore "miracles" were capturing the public imagination. I was one of the few who concluded from the very beginning that the whole affair was a colossal fake. Phil Shanahan drove all the way to Templemore, and brought back half a barrel of water. Customers were given the full of a Baby-Power bottle of Templemore water to bring to their homes. One evening Mick Collins called and was sipping a sample, when I happened to enter the premises. I laughed at his simplicity. "Breen, you are an irreligious customer," he said to me, half in banter.

"If my religion went no deeper than to take a glass of that water," I replied, "I'd consider myself to be an outrageous impostor."

About this time Mick Collins had his office close to Boland's tailoring shop in Henry Street. I had arranged to call at a certain hour and loitered near the G.P.O. so that I might observe if I were being trailed by touts. The D.M.P. man who was on duty at Nelson Pillar on that particular morning, Constable McInerney, was elderly and extremely corpulent, tipping the scales at a good twenty stone. Members of the Dublin Metropolitan Police were compelled by Government regulations to carry revolvers, an order that most of them accepted with great reluctance. This policeman was of such a girth that it would have been virtually impossible for him to grab his gun in an emergency. I saw that he was taking me in with the corner of his eye and, as I continued to hang about, my presence must have got on his nerves. He strode over to me with ponderous steps. Even though I knew him to be an inoffensive man, I began to wonder vaguely if he was about to challenge me. My hand went instinctively to my coat-pocket. "Breen," he said with great earnestness, "don't attempt to take that gun from me. Cathal Brugha and the rest of the boys know that I would never do one of them a bad turn." Having got this solemn warning off his chest, he returned to his post on point duty.

In addition to Phil Shanahan's, Ryan's of the Monument Creamery, and Séamus Kirwan's were also open houses to us. We frequently met kindred spirits like Dick McKee and Peadar Clancy and Tom Kehoe, who belonged to the small band of gunmen who were ready to take any risk in the country's cause. Many others who later proved their mettle, did not get the chance at that time because of the dilatory attitude of our General Headquarters.

CHAPTER NINE

AMBUSH AT ASHTOWN

MY COMRADES AND I had long and serious discussions about the policy of shooting policemen and soldiers. We felt that bigger game was needed. The police and the military were but the tools of higher men. Their loss did not trouble Britain very much, for she could always get more dupes. Why, we asked ourselves, should we not strike at the very heads of the British Government in Ireland? Such action would arouse interest in Ireland's cause throughout the world; It would strike terror into the hearts of British statesmen, and it would help to render British rule impossible in Ireland. Britain could carry on all right even if a few Peelers had been liquidated; it would be more difficult to do without a Lord Lieutenant. There were thousands of Peelers but there were only a few candidates for the Lord Lieutenancy, and they would think twice of taking on the job if they had to risk their lives. We finally decided to make preparations for an attack on Lord French, the Lord Lieutenant himself! Brave and trusted men, to whom we communicated our plans, readily agreed.

For three long months we watched, planned and waited. We suffered many bitter disappointments. Lord French was very rarely seen about, and when he did make an appearance he was always accompanied by a heavy escort. Strict secrecy was observed about his movements, but our Secret Service kept us well posted. Even the public functions which were usually patronised by viceroys were rarely attended by Sir John.

Little did he realise what narrow escapes he had had

during these three months. Twice or three times we missed him by a single street—the altering of his route by a slight digression. A frequent plan of his was to make a deviation from the schedule that had been drawn up. It was a trick to upset any plot based on inside information which might be supplied by a confidante. It showed what little trust he placed in his own immediate circle. During the last three months of 1919 we planned no less than twelve different ambushes in an effort to get him. Either he failed to turn up or he arrived too late or too early to suit our designs. These plans were connected with his public functions in the city or his visits to private houses. We were hampered because we could not afford to hang too long around a particular spot; our movements would attract notice and probably lead to a sudden swoop by the military. Mick Collins was with us on the first occasion that we lay in ambush. Tom MacCurtain was also in our ranks. (Tom was Commandant of the Cork No. 1 Brigade). Dick McKee, Commandant of the Dublin Brigade, also kept us company. Dick never asked his men to take risks which he was not prepared to share.

I remember waiting with Peadar Clancy for two hours outside the door of a Merrion Square specialist, Dr. James Ashe, whom French occasionally visited. On 11 November, the anniversary of the Armistice, the Lord Lieutenant was due to attend a banquet in Trinity College. We had every hope of intercepting him on that night. Our plan was to bomb his car as he passed Grattan bridge; we knew the very hour he was expected to travel along the quays from the Viceregal Lodge to the College.

So certain were we that everything would work out according to plan that some of our men in the vicinity of the bridge, within a hundred yards of Dublin Castle, had actually drawn the pins from their bombs. On that frosty night they had their fingers pressed on the springs of the cold metal, ready to release the bombs. But he never came. For almost two hours our men endured the agony of holding the springs of the bombs; at last they had to make their escape as best they could, still gripping the cold metal.

A fortnight later French was expected at the Castle and his journey would take him across the same bridge. We knew of the arrangements and once more we took up our positions. The weather was very harsh. It was in the early afternoon and snow began to fall. But we did not mind the snow. The job we were bent upon was too serious to be interfered with by the vagaries of the weather. Some of us paced the bridge in the blinding snow, wondering were we to suffer another disappointment. While we were on the bridge a friend recognised us. Realising that we were on some job, he sarcastically remarked, "That's a most convenient spot for taking shelter from the snow!" His words brought us to our senses. Any tout in the neighbouring shops would have instantly become suspicious. When it became obvious that we were waiting in vain, we decamped. Five minutes later lorry loads of military swooped down on the bridge and searched everybody on whom they could lay hands. Detectives who had been posted near the entrance to Dublin Castle had seen us on the bridge; they telephoned immediately to the Viceregal Lodge and French cancelled his appointment; the troops came instead. We had just moved off.

Our information about Lord French's arrangements had been absolutely reliable. Doubtless, he often changed his plans at the last moment, fearing that we had been well-informed about his movements. He had surmised correctly.

It certainly was an eloquent commentary on British rule in Ireland that the head of the Government carried his life in his hands whenever he ventured through the streets of the capital. As everybody knew, he was wise enough to venture out as seldom as possible, even when accompanied by a huge escort.

At last, when our patience was almost exhausted, we got information in mid-December that gave us hope of achieving our purpose. The newspapers rarely gave any information regarding the Viceroy's movements. Even when he had crossed to Britain, the news editors were not informed until he was safely back in Phoenix Park. They were not encouraged to seek information about his movements. Sometimes, however, the newspapers were supplied with advance information which was deliberately intended to mislead the public in general, and the I.R.A. in particular. At the time of which I speak, the Irish newspapers had reported that Lord French was out of the country. It was actually reported that he was cruising somewhere in the North Sea.

Our information was more accurate. He was, as a matter of fact, enjoying himself with a select house party, at his

country residence in Frenchpark, Co. Roscommon. We knew
a good deal more about Lord French's private life than the
public ever suspected. Sufficient to say that on this
occasion we knew every member of his select escort.

Frenchpark is a remote country district. While the Lord
Lieutenant was in occupation, the house was garrisoned by
a strong force. We felt that we could easily overpower that
garrison if we had so desired. The situation of the house
would have favoured our escape when we had accomplished
our object. We would have found no difficulty in making
the journey from Dublin to Roscommon, and we believed
that we would get back almost as easily. We could readily
have gone by roads which skirted the towns, for it would
have been a much easier matter for wanted men to go from
Dublin to the west than it would have been to go south
or north.

Why, then, it may be asked, with all the circumstances
in our favour, did we not attempt to shoot Lord French in
his Roscommon residence?

The answer is simple. We knew that he would be returning to Dublin on a particular date; we decided to attack him
almost at his own door, in a city suburb. Why? Because
we had in mind the effect which such an incident would
create. Against the old soldier himself we had no personal
spite, but he was the head of an alien Government that held
our country in bondage; we knew that his death would
arouse all peoples to take notice of our fight for freedom.
His name was known throughout the civilised world. The
Phoenix Park was as famous as Hyde Park. Think of the
sensation that would be created when this man, a Field
Marshal of the British army, head of the Irish Government,
was shot dead at the gate of the Phoenix Park, in the
capital of the country which he was supposed to rule, within
a stone's throw of half a dozen of Britain's military garrisons.
Thousands of British troops, equipped with every implement
of modern warfare, could be mustered within a short space
of time. The risk to ourselves was tremendous but the
moral effect would be worth the price. The citizens of every
country would sit up and say: "The men who have done
this are no cowards. Ireland must have a grievance. What
is it?" That is the result on which we reckoned. For
this very reason we decided to ambush the Viceroy almost
at his own doorstep.

Lord French was due back in the Viceregal Lodge on

Friday, 19 December. The matter was kept a dead secret; even high officials in the Viceregal Lodge and in Dublin Castle were unaware of his plans. But we were well aware of the arrangement. This information had come from a trusted agent inside Dublin Castle.

We not only knew the day, but the hour. Further, we knew that when Lord French returned by the Midland Railway, he would not travel into Broadstone station, the city terminus, but would alight at the little wayside station of Ashtown. Accordingly we laid our plans.

Ashtown lies on the trunk road that runs from Dublin to the northwest of Ireland. In spite of the fact that it was only four miles distant from the centre of the city, the district was very thinly populated. Ashtown railway station was situated about two hundred yards from the main thoroughfare, and was served by a little by-road. The station had been laid down for the convenience of the Viceregal establishment. It was also a suitable halting-place for the unloading of horses bound for the Phoenix Park racecourse. To most people Ashtown simply meant one house, and that was Kelly's public house, commonly known as the Halfway House. It stands near the cross-roads, from which a specially constructed road led to the Phoenix Park. At the Phoenix Park gate there stood a police barracks where three or four men of the Dublin Metropolitan Police used to be stationed, but the barracks had been closed only a few days before our adventure. The Viceregal Lodge was within easy reach of the Park gate.

The Viceroy's special train was due to arrive at Ashtown at 11.40 a.m. Half-an-hour earlier our party had arrived on the scene. On that morning we had started from Fleming's of Drumcondra; I had stopped at Mrs. Martin Conlon's of Phibsboro' for a cup of tea. Eleven of us all-told were mustered for the job: Mick McDonnell, Tom Kehoe, Martin Savage, Seán Treacy, Séamus Robinson, Seán Hogan, Paddy Daly, Vincent Byrne, Tom Kilkoyne, Joe Leonard and myself.

We cycled out in pairs by the Cabra road, and went at intervals in order that we might not arouse suspicion. We left our bicycles outside Kelly's; at any hour of the day it was not unusual to see a dozen bicycles outside the tavern while the owners were having a drink. We had made ourselves familiar with every inch of the locality, every bush and turn of the road, every nook and corner. It was to our advantage that we knew the exact order in which Lord French and his escort always travelled. We realised that it would excite suspicion if we waited by the roadside. On that account our men entered the publichouse as soon as they arrived on the scene. A few of the local labourers and farmhands were taking refreshments on the premises and our appearance in pairs did not seem to give rise to any suspicion, especially as the local people were not aware that Lord French was due to pass the spot in a short time. While we were drinking our minerals, we deliberately gave the impression that our meeting was purely accidental. We talked about cattle and markets and grazing, in fact everything but politics. Even in this make-belief conversation we had to be careful; for the locals knew farming from A to Z, while some of our men knew very little about markets or livestock.

While we were talking about agricultural matters for the benefit of our audience, we were beginning to get anxious, now that the fateful hour was drawing near. I noticed Seán Treacy glancing at his watch from time to time; eager eyes kept a constant watch on the cross-roads; we had a clear view of everyone who passed by on the main road or on the road which led to the Park. The first sign of activity which we noticed was a big D.M.P. man coming from the direction of the Park gate. Evidently he knew that Lord French was expected; he took up a position near the cross-roads to control the traffic. His spiked helmet, shining buttons and spotless boots, not to speak of the care with which he pulled down his tunic under his belt, plainly indicated that he felt called upon to make an impressive display. We did not trouble very much about him, even though he had a revolver in the holster by his side.

A few minutes before the train was due four military lorries drove up from the Park gate and halted near the station. Each lorry carried its complement of soldiers who were decked out in full battle array. We knew that several armed D.M.P. men would be lined up to guard the route from the Park gate to the Viceregal Lodge. For days in advance we had made our arrangements. Nothing was left to the last moment. We had decided to concentrate our principal attack on the second car of the convoy Lord French invariably travelled in the second car. Outside Kelly's a heavy farm-cart rested on its shafts. Tom Kehoe,

Martin Savage and I had been instructed to push this cart at the last moment right across the road and block the passage of French's car; the road was too narrow to allow two cars to travel abreast, and the heavy farm-cart would compel them to slow down. At the same moment, the other members of our party were to open a deadly attack with bombs and grenades on the Lord Lieutenant's car. After the attack they were to rely on their revolvers for dealing with the military guard.

Sharp on time, the whistle of the engine sounded as the train steamed into Ashtown, but we never moved. We had two or three minutes more; a false step taken half-a-second too soon might upset our whole plan. The motor engines were throbbing; the party was about to move off from the station. We stepped out to the cross-roads. Our men quietly took up their positions. Tom Kehoe, Martin Savage and I were standing beside the farm-cart. It was time to get it in motion.

We caught hold of the cart and began to push it around the corner. It was a heavy cart, far heavier than we had expected; needless to say, we had not had a rehearsal of the act, nor had we judged the weight of the cart otherwise than with our eyes. We pushed it on to the narrow road which leads from the station. "You cannot go down there for a while," the big policeman shouted. "His Excellency is to pass along here in a few seconds."

Now I also knew that His Excellency was due. However, I could not explain to him that I had an appointment with His Excellency. Time was pressing. I tried to ignore the policeman. He evidently thought that I was too stupid for this world. He went on protesting to me, explaining how necessary it was to have the road clear for His Excellency's car.

The amazing thing, when I afterwards gave it a thought, was that he was apparently too dense to notice that I had two guns in my hands. If he had noticed, I'm sure that he would have taken out his notebook and asked me for my name and address, for it was illegal to carry arms!

I did not want to use my gun so soon. In the first place I had no wish to hurt the poor man; secondly, I knew that a shot fired at this moment would be fatal to our plans. It would at once attract the attention of the escort seated in their cars one hundred paces distant.

I did the only thing that I could in the circumstances.

I shouted at him, I threatened him, and finally told him that if he didn't clear out of our way, I would smash him up. But it was all to no avail. He kept on talking.

While we stood there, wasting moments that were precious, our comrades were wondering what was wrong. One of the men, who had been posted on the ditch that ran along the road, realised the situation. Without considering that he was threatening our whole scheme, not to speak of endangering the lives of three of us who were standing by the cart, he drew the pin from his grenade and hurled the missile straight at the policeman's head. Any of the three of us with perfect safety to ourselves could easily have settled with the obstructionist, but we had no desire to kill the unfortunate man. Furthermore, we feared that a single shot would prevent Lord French from making his approach. If an ambush had been suspected he would have sent his escort to clear the road or perhaps have continued his journey by train to Broadstone station thereby upsetting all our plans.

The policeman was struck on the head with the bomb which burst at my side without inflicting any injury; but the force of the explosion threw us violently to the ground. The policeman was not seriously injured. We quickly recovered from the shock, and had no time to bother about the policeman, for at that moment the despatch rider, who always rode forty or fifty yards ahead of the Viceroy's party, streaked past us from the station. A second later came the first motor; we dashed right in front of it and opened fire on the occupants. Our fire was at once returned, and so close were we to the enemy that my lovely new hat was shot right off my head. So fast was the car travelling that we had not time even to glance at the occupants nor indeed were we greatly concerned with them; our real object was to frighten the driver of that car into such speed that he would seek safety in flight. Meanwhile we would hurl all our force against the second car in which, as we knew, Lord French always travelled.

Our cart had not completely blocked the road, and on that account the first motor sped by, as we intended that it should. One of the passengers wore female attire. Another dash to pull the cart right across the road and the second car was upon us. From every position held by our little party a concentrated attack was maintained, and the air was rent with the crackle of firearms. The enemy brought machine-guns and rifles into action, and there we stood an easy target while we poured volley after volley into car No. 2. The three of us who had wheeled the cart into position now found ourselves doubly imperilled. Bullets whistled past and grenades burst at our feet; but so close were we to our objective, that we were also endangered by the bombs which our own men were hurling from the ditch.

With our guns still spitting fire at the occupants of the car, we sought refuge behind the cart, availing ourselves of the little cover it afforded. Another second and the cart was being riddled and the splinters from its shafts were flying round us. But our work must be accomplished and the fight must be kept up. Suddenly to our dismay another car came rushing towards us from the opposite direction. We were now in greater danger than ever for we were trapped between two lines of fire. I felt a bullet pierce my left leg, but I had not time to examine the wound, though I reckoned that the bullet had passed through. The British had by this time several rifles and a machine gun in action, but the marksmen's nerves must have failed them; otherwise we could never have put up such a sustained resistance. One marksman, however, hit his target; Martin Savage fell into my arms, fatally wounded. Poor chap! How light-heartedly he had been singing and reciting poems about Ireland and the glory of dying for one's country as we rode out to Ashtown only one hour ago. Now he was breathing his last, meeting his death as he would have wished, from a British bullet.

I laid my dying comrade down on the roadside. His lips were moving as if he had a last message to give me. I stooped and put my ear to his lips and heard the words spoken faintly but quite distinctly: " I'm done, Dan! Carry on!" To my last hour I shall remember Martin bleeding to death by the roadside on that December day while bullets whizzed as in a raging hailstorm, striking everything but myself at whom they were aimed.

But it was no time for vain weeping over the dead. Martin Savage had given his life in the cause for which he had lived, the cause for which he had shouldered his gun three years before, when, as a lad of eighteen, he had done his bit in Easter Week, 1916. For the rest of us, our duty was to carry on and fight for Ireland's sake.

By this time Tom Kehoe had got back to cover. I looked

around to see if I had any chance of escape. There seemed none. The blood was streaming from my leg; the enemy's fire was fierce and rapid, while ours had eased off; our grenades had been exploded; most of our revolvers were empty; amidst a hail of bullets I dashed round the corner for the shelter of Kelly's house and reached it in safety.

I fired one more shot; there was no counter-volley. The khaki warriors had fled for the safety of the Park; the whole Viceregal party followed. We surveyed our spoils— that hapless second car, riddled with bullets; Driver McEvoy disabled; one wounded constable, O'Loughlin, of the Dublin Metropolitan Police.

It was too risky to take any prisoners. We left the constable and the driver on the field of battle. By a strange irony of fate, our paths crossed once again. Three years later I was a prisoner in Limerick jail. McEvoy, serving in the ranks of the Free State army, was my prison officer. On my release I went to America and met ex-Constable O'Loughlin, friendless and impoverished on the streets of New York. I procured a job for him as night watchman in a large warehouse.

Our most urgent concern was to return to the city, for we knew that within half an hour Ashtown and the surrounding country would be swarming with British troops.

We held a hurried consultation at the cross-roads of Ashtown. We had routed an entire contingent of British soldiers with their rifles, their machine guns, and their armour-plated car.

We carried Martin's body into Kelly's shop. We could not afford to linger, for it was certain that the enemy would speedily return with reinforcements and take possession of that gallant soldier's dead body; it would be suicidal to attempt to remove it to the city.

With a prayer for the soul of our departed comrade, we mounted our bicycles and faced for the city. We had scarcely started when Séamus Robinson found that the frame of his bicycle had collapsed. Jumping on the back of Seán Treacy's machine he balanced himself with one foot on the step and held on to Seán's broad shoulders. A bicycle burdened with two men could not proceed at speed, and at that moment speed was our most urgent need. A man approached wheeling his bicycle, having evidently alighted when he heard the shooting. " All is fair in love and war," is a well-known adage. The temporary seizure of his machine was not against the rules. Robinson had not yet pocketed his revolver. Jumping from the step of Treacy's bicycle he held up the stranger and ordered him to hand over his bicycle. Séamus gave an assurance that if he called to the Gresham Hotel his machine would be forthcoming. I do not know whether the man ever got his bicycle; I hope he did; it was left near the door of the hotel that same evening, as Séamus had promised.

One of the boys called my attention to the blood which was oozing from my wounded leg. I alighted from the bicycle and drew a bootlace tight round the end of my trousers. It was a fortunate precaution; the bloodstains on the road would have provided a clue to my whereabouts when, a couple of hours later, the police tried to follow up the trail.

We returned safely to the city. I was feeling weak from the loss of blood and went at once to Mrs. Toomey's house on Phibsboro' road, which was on the outskirts of the city. Some hours later a search-party traced my blood-stains from Ashtown along the Cabra road but they lost the trail near the city. I was put to bed, and medical aid was summoned. I was attended by Dr. J. M. Ryan, captain of the Dublin hurling team, and by another doctor who came from the Mater Hospital, which was only a few hundred yards distant.

At nightfall Dublin rang with the newsboys' cry, " Attack on the Lord Lieutenant—Sensational fight at Ashtown—One of the attackers shot dead ! " Lord John French had escaped unhurt ! It was true. We had failed. It was the first occasion on which the Viceroy had travelled not in the second car but in the first. The car about which we had scarcely bothered actually bore safely away the man whom we wanted to dispatch. The news caused my temperature to rise. I never liked half-measures and in this instance we had not even half-done our work. Seán Treacy took the disappointment philosophically. His motto was "Always make the best of things." He tried to console me by saying, "You can't have a Knocklong every day, Dan."

We did not get any other chance of shooting Lord French. After the ambush he retired from public life. When he set out for England, armoured cars patrolled the roads that led to the mail boat, and armed detectives accompanied him all the way to London. His movements were kept a close secret from the Press until many days had elapsed.

If we could have used rifles on that day, we could easily

have shot him from Kelly's house, but at that time bicycles were our only mode of transport.   A few months previously the British had made an order that motor drivers must have a permit in writing which displayed not only the name but also the description and photograph of the driver. This order was made with a view to preventing the I.R.A. from using motor cars in their ambushes. The only men who were deemed fit to get permits would be those who could prove their "loyalty." Such men were not prone to assist us or take the risk of lending a car. The Motor Drivers' Union, resenting this degrading condition, dealt with this order by refusing to apply for permits and ended by declaring a general strike. Therefore, as we could not motor to Ashtown, we had no means of concealing rifles. We could not have strapped them on the crossbars of the bicycles. Some months later as I was walking down O'Connell Street, I met Maude Gonne MacBride and Mrs. Despard, sister of Lord John French. Mrs. Despard was a doctrinaire Republican who made no secret of her horror at the stranglehold which Britain had on Ireland's throat. But, as the saying goes, "Blood is thicker than water." She upbraided me for having taken part in the ambush against her brother.

"My only regret," I ventured to say, "is that we did not get him."

"You naughty boy! John is a good Irishman."

"Your notion and mine differ about the meaning of the word 'good.'"

"Imagine poor John killed by his compatriots!" she exclaimed with tears in her eyes.

After the Ashtown attack Church and Press denounced us in unmeasured terms; but the plain people were more guarded in expressing their opinions; the country was beginning to realise that we meant war with Britain until, to quote the words of O'Donovan Rossa, "she was stricken to her knees or we were stricken to our graves." It was the turning point. The people were beginning to appraise the situation. In private many defended our standpoint. The great majority of our countrymen were taking their bearings. Some of them were shocked at the daring force-tactics, but it was becoming obvious to all that we meant business and that it was their duty to stand by us.

On the morning after the attack the *Irish Independent* published a leading article in which we were dubbed

" assassins." The article was liberally interspersed with such terms as "criminal folly," "outrage," "murder." This was the very paper which depended on the support of the people who had voted for the establishment of the Irish Republic. It had not even the sense of decency to withhold the expression of its views until the inquest had been held and Martin Savage laid to rest. The other Dublin papers we did not mind. The *Irish Times* was openly a British organ; the *Freeman's Journal* was beneath the contempt of any decent Irishman. But we could not allow an avowedly Irish paper to insult our dead comrade.

I was confined to bed and had no direct part in subsequent events. I heard that some of the boys favoured the shooting of the editor of the *Independent*. Another course was eventually adopted. It was decided to suppress the paper. At 9 o'clock on Sunday night twenty or thirty of our men, under the leadership of Peadar Clancy, entered the building and held up the staff with revolvers. They informed the editor that his machinery was to be dismantled; they smashed the linotypes with sledges and left the place in such condition that it was hoped no edition could appear for some time. But with the assistance of the other Dublin printing workshops the *Independent* was able to appear next day. However, we had taught them a salutary lesson; somehow, we were glad that nobody was thrown out of work, because many of the staff were members of the Irish Republican army. Never afterwards did the *Independent* or any other Dublin newspaper refer to members of the I.R.A. as murderers or assassins. In later days the *Independent* was of much service in exposing British atrocities, even though it never supported our fighting policy. The proprietors got £16,000 compensation for the raid.

After the inquest on Martin Savage his body was handed over to his relatives. Before the removal to his native Ballisodare, County Sligo, the body lay all night at the Broadstone station, attended by only a faithful few. The funeral that took place the next day provided the occasion for the most signal honour that was ever paid in the west of Ireland to a dead patriot. The funeral procession was several miles long; the local Parish Priest recited the last prayers while the R.I.C. with characteristic chivalry surrounded the graveyard with their guns and bayonets. It was the best tribute that they could have manifested to a gallant soldier, even though they did not intend it as such.

It may be asked why Martin Savage's body was allowed to leave Dublin without receiving from the capital the last mark of respect which his sacrifice deserved. The answer is simple. The Government of the Republic, Dáil Éireann, did not wish to associate itself directly with our actions. Without going into details which might involve the reputation of many prominent men, some of whom are still alive, I wish to emphasise that neither then nor at any later stage did Dáil Éireann accept responsibility for the war against the British. To this very hour I do not know what were their reasons, nor do I wish to enter into any controversy on the attitude of the Dáil. I can only say what was later publicly admitted both in the second Republican Dáil and in the Free State Dáil. (See speech of General Mulcahy, December 1923: " The I.R.A. was left to carry on the war on its own initiative, on its own resources, without either approval or disapproval from the Government of the Republic.") It is as well that this fact should be known to future generations.

It was amusing to read the newspaper versions of the Ashtown attack. At the inquest held over Martin Savage's body it was stated by police witnesses that the " assailants fled and were pursued." I became almost hysterical with laughter when I read those words, remembering the British soldiers' precipitate flight for the cover of the Phoenix Park wall. It was very strange indeed that we managed to reach Dublin on our bicycles while being pursued by the men who were provided not only with rifles and machine guns but also with motor cars.

Another writer, gifted with a high imagination, stated that a tree which grew by the roadside had been specially clipped to provide a look-out for one of our scouts. Just imagine the military genius of anyone who would have posted a man on a treetop—sure target for enemy rifles— in order to view a train which was clearly visible from the roadway.

At the inquest the Crown Counsel refused to disclose the name of the lady who was in the car with Lord French.

Lord French, by the way, had travelled in mufti—this was stated at the inquest. Perhaps that is why we did not recognise him as he went by with his lady-friend in the first car.

I also learned from the inquest that Detective Sergeant Halley who had been wounded by our fire, hailed from Carrick-on-Suir, Co. Tipperary, my own native county.

CHAPTER TEN

CONVALESCENCE

HAVING RESTED a few days at Mrs. Toomey's, I was taken to the house of Mrs. Malóne, 13, Grantham Street, situated in a southern region of the city. Three months previously I had paid my first visit to her house. It happened in this way:

On 8 September 1919, Séamus Robinson and I found it difficult to get a place to sleep; we went to Phil Shanahan's and there met Sam Fahy, brother of Frank Fahy, T.D. Sam was well known to us when he lived in Tipperary. When he moved to Dublin, he had to go on the run like ourselves. We told him of our trouble and he gave us the latch-key of Mrs. Malone's of Grantham Street, assuring us that as long as the Malones lived there, "wanted" men need never want for shelter. "Mrs. Malone," he informed us, "could be trusted with any secret." She had lost a son, Michael, in the Insurrection of Easter Week.

On the day that Sam presented us with the latchkey Séamus and I made our way to Grantham Street. We had forgotten the number of the house. Fortunately it is not a long street and from the very first house at which we knocked we were directed to Mrs. Malone's. From the moment that we entered we felt quite at home. We stayed for the night and on the next morning we learned that only four days had passed since the death of one of Mrs. Malone's daughters.

We brought Treacy and Hogan to the house soon afterwards and introduced them. Both of the girls, Brighid and Áine, were active members of the Cumann na mBan. They carried our dispatches and even helped in the removal of munitions to Kingsbridge station. We were constantly in search of arms or ammunition, which we either bought or took in raids. Invariably we sent them on to our South Tipperary Brigade, for they badly needed the stuff. There were far fewer chances of getting arms or ammunition in Tipperary than there were in Dublin. Very often we consigned the contraband by train in boxes labelled 'Tea' or 'Wines' or some such commodity. At the other end we had made arrangements which would ensure that the goods would be received by a merchant who was a member of the I.R.A.

Only a few days before the Ashtown fight I had jokingly
said to Áine that she would have to nurse me if ever I were
wounded. Little did I think that what I said as a joke would
prove to be a fact. I had not expected to be installed at
Grantham Street under her care. My wound turned out to be
more serious than I had expected. I suffered also from
violent headaches. For three whole months I was invalided.
I felt in no way anxious to get away from my surroundings.
Peadar Clancy came to see me almost daily and brought me
the news. I have fond memories of the pleasant hours spent
with Peadar. Dick McKee, Seán Treacy and Seán Hogan
also came to see me regularly. The fates had decreed that
Peadar and Dick and Seán Treacy would not live to see
another Christmas.

Apart from the visits of my dear comrades, there was an
even stronger reason which made me forget the pain and
the inaction. That was the kindness of my ever attentive
nurse, Brighid Malone, now my wife. Not many a man has
the good fortune to be nursed through sickness by his
future wife whose presence counts for more than all that
medical skill could provide.

While my wound was healing I had plenty of leisure to
review the year that had passed. Soloheadbeg had borne
fruit. The best tribute was that contained in the official
statistics issued from time to time by the British Government
regarding "Crimes in Ireland." Crime was almost non-existent
in Ireland until the arrival of the Black-and-Tans. When the
British Government used the word " crime " in reference to
Ireland it generally meant active operations against the Army
of Occupation. Early in 1920 it was revealed that in the
previous year scores of attacks had been made on British
troops or police, hundreds of raids for arms had been carried
out and several police (in other words, armed spies) had been
shot dead. If the British Government thought that the
publication of these statistics would bring discredit to the
Volunteers it had miscalculated. In fact, the Irish Republican
army had set its sights on a much bigger record of such
" crimes " before the year had come to a close.

In these statistics the British took good care not to record
their own hostile actions perpetrated against the civilian
population. It was not stated that Dáil Éireann, the elected
representative Government of Ireland, had been denounced
as an illegal assembly, and that its schemes for developing
the country's industries were declared to be criminal

activities. The world was not informed that the Gaelic
League, Cumann na mBan, the Irish Volunteers and Fianna
Éireann had been listed as illegal organisations. Nor was
there any mention of the midnight raids on the homes of
peace-loving citizens. In a word, to quote an expression used
by Arthur Griffith, " England has proclaimed the whole Irish
nation as an illegal assembly."

While I was recuperating at Malones', the first Curfew
Order was issued. In an encounter with a few I.R.A. men
after midnight in February 1920 a policeman was shot dead in
Grafton Street. The British promptly issued an order making
it a criminal offence for any civilian to be out-of-doors
between midnight and 5 a.m. Within a few months that
Order was extended to most towns and cities in the south
of Ireland; not only extended but made even more
severe. At one time in Limerick no one was allowed to
leave his house after 7 p.m. In Cork the hour was 4 p.m.
It became customary for the British to clear the streets by
volley after volley of rifle fire; scores of men, women and
children were murdered in this way during 1920 and 1921.
Incidentally, these curfew regulations gave the Government's
murder gangs a free field; during the hours of Curfew no
civilian dared to be abroad and on that account no independent witness was available for bearing testimony to the
shooting or looting.

In the early spring of 1920 I left my pleasant surroundings
and traversed the fair plains of Fingal. I went for a month's
convalescence close to the Hill of Tara. It was my first stay
in royal Meath, the seat of the Árd-Rí in the days of Ireland's
glory. On that first day when I had climbed the hill I stayed
for one hour on its summit, living in memories of the past,
wondering if ever again our land would see the day when
her sons and daughters would have shaken off the shackles
of slavery and have flung their flag proudly to the breeze,
defiant and free. Little is now left on Tara to remind one of
those days of former glory. No men crowd its summit;
tradition says that the curse of a saint from my own county
brought about its ruin and decay. Still visible is the outline
of the great Banquet Hall where the High King received
homage from his vassals and entertained his subjects. A
little cross on the summit marks the " Croppies' Grave,"
where " many a Saxon foeman fell, and many an Irish soldier
true "—the last resting place of brave men who struck a
blow for Ireland in Ninety-eight and fell facing the enemy.

I knelt on the green sward of the deserted palace and prayed that the Croppies' sacrifice might not be in vain; that their dream might come true even in our generation. I hoped and prayed that I might be given strength and courage to speed the day.

There, on the sod hallowed by the footsteps of Ireland's saints and kings I realised for the first time the full meaning of that little ballad of Moore's, with its pathetic appeal that always grips the Irish heart and dims the patriot's eye:

> Let Erin remember the days of old
> Ere her faithless sons betrayed her!

And then my eyes wandered over the plains beneath my feet—richer than my own Golden Vale. Here and there I saw a stately mansion or a castle; but I knew that these were not the homes of the clansmen of our kings. They were the fortresses of those who had deprived Irishmen of their heritage. Of farm houses there were none; here and there a labourer's cottage marked the home of the Gael who had survived, to be hewer of wood and drawer of water for the conqueror. I searched the countryside for the men whom this fair land should have raised; but the roads were deserted; the bullocks had replaced the king and the peasant. I asked myself if Providence had ordained that the plains of Meath should be used only for raising cattle in order to provide food for the conquering Saxon. No! It could not be. The curse still lay on our country. The Gall still held the Gael in thrall. For many a day I wandered through that fertile countryside, dreaming of the happiness which would be ours, if only we were allowed to work out our own destiny under God's providence. Many a time I walked for three or four hours without meeting even one human being. Here and there a stately mansion; around it the gate-lodge of the serf, the winding avenue, the spreading oaks, and the green fields in which no man was visible. Landlordism, the willing instrument of British rule, had wrought this desolation. I renewed my resolve to do my share in bringing about the change that must come sooner or later.

I spent pleasant days with Joseph Dardis, Dr. Lynch and Tom Carton of Stamullen; and with Vincent Purfield of Balbriggan. From all of them I received the same genial welcome. Thank God, Britain had not been able to despoil Irishmen of the spirit of kindness and hospitality. While I was staying with Vincent Purfield, Séamus Robinson paid me a visit and was so happy in Balbriggan that he extended his stay for a few days. On Good Friday we set out for Dublin by motor with Vincent in the driver's seat, as we had decided to celebrate Easter in the city.

The British authorities in Ireland were under the impression that the Sinn Féiners would not let Easter pass by without holding some commemoration of the 1916 Insurrection. The Volunteers never obliged the army of occupation by carrying out the programme that was expected of them. On each successive Easter barricades were erected at all the approaches to the city. Fearing a surprise attack, the military placed out-posts for the searching of all pedestrians and vehicles. Having done their duty by the Empire, they removed the barricades when Easter had passed by.

As we left Balbriggan on that Good Friday morning we forgot all about this annual manoeuvre. Had we remembered, we would have remained in Balbriggan for the festive season. We had a pleasant journey until we approached the tramway terminus at Whitehall. When we rounded the corner, we observed that a troop-laden lorry was advancing towards us at a slow pace. We must have looked so harmless that the officer ordered his lorry-driver to proceed. We continued on our way congratulating ourselves on our luck. But our good fortune was short-lived. The noise of the military lorry had scarcely died away when we heard a sharp command "Halt!"

Straight ahead of us was a barricade; a score of soldiers with rifles at the ready stood to attention; an officer stepped towards us, brandishing his revolver. I thought that my last hour had come. This time there would be no escape.

Vincent kept cool as a cucumber; not one of us betrayed the slightest concern and the car drove right on to the barricade.

I stepped out of the car and I walked straight up to the officer demanding an explanation.

"I must search your car," was the curt reply. I told him calmly that we had no objection to being searched. I impressed on him that any delay would be a serious matter for us, as we had an important appointment in the city. For one moment he hesitated. Then he waved to the soldiers to clear the way.

"Very well!" he said, "you may go ahead."

"Thank you," I nodded. We entered the car and continued on our journey."

I could not have afforded to have either the car or our

persons searched. Had the officer attempted to do so, it
would have been his last display of military activity. In all
probability we would not have escaped if he had forced me
to pull my gun; there was no other way out of a nasty
situation.

During those five days our motor car was the only vehicle
that had either entered or left Dublin without having been
searched.

The bluff which had carried Seán Hogan and myself out of
a similar difficulty had now proved successful at Whitehall,
only a few hundred yards distant from the house where seven
months later I was to have my memorable fight for life.

CHAPTER ELEVEN

SMOKING OUT THE R.I.C.

I WAS feeling strong and fit again. I was anxious to be up
and doing. I could not stay idle. I felt that I had no right to
remain any longer out of the fight. Some of the events
recorded in the daily papers had made my blood boil. Tom
MacCurtain, Lord Mayor of Cork, had been murdered by
Black-and-Tans in the presence of his wife. Five months
previously, he had been in our ranks as we lay in ambush
for Lord French. Murders had also been committed in
Thurles. They were the first of several such outrages perpetrated within one year by British forces—all of which
had been either connived at or directly inspired by the
highest officials.

I resolved to be back in the fray. I returned to Dublin
where I met some of the boys and pleaded for an intensive
guerilla campaign. Dick McKee and Peadar Clancy
enthusiastically supported my views and favoured my "on
with the war" policy.

Our policy had been hitherto "unofficial." Dáil Éireann and
General Headquarters of the I.R.A. had neither sanctioned
it nor accepted the responsibility. Mick Collins promised to
push our war policy in the "proper quarters," and it must
be remembered that he was not only on the G.H.Q. staff but
was also the Finance Minister.

Our war policy was not popular. Our G.H.Q. seemed to be
lukewarm about it. The political wing certainly opposed it,
and more than one T.D. privately denounced it. We succeeded

in concealing our disagreements up to the time of the Truce. The Press continued to manifest its disapproval of our campaign, but with a difference. The salutary lesson taught to the *Independent* was having its effect. The words " shootings " and " tragedies " became very popular as substitutes for " murder " and " outrage."

At first the general public did not want the war. They seemed to forget that their vote at the general election led to the formal establishment of the Republic. Many were of the opinion that freedom could be won without any effort on their part. However, as the war progressed the vast majority of the people stood by us, and cheerfully took their share of the risks and hardships.

I had made up my mind that my stay in Dublin would be of short duration. I wanted to get back to Tipperary. Things were too quiet down there. The boys were all right and game for everything, but they needed leadership. Once more Seán Treacy and I cycled that hundred miles' journey. I had been absent from Tipperary for nearly twelve months.

We decided to intensify operations against the British in our area by attacking them in some of their strongholds— the police barracks. It was no longer safe for the Peelers to patrol the roads. They seldom ventured to move any distance from their barracks. We could not meet them in the open for that reason. But if the mountain would not come to Mohammed, then Mohammed must go to the mountain. We had to go to the police and attack them on their own grounds.

In the spring of 1920 there had begun the evacuation of the small outlying R.I.C. barracks because of the danger that the garrisons might be cut off. The British were concentrating on the larger barracks where the garrisons had been strengthened and the buildings fortified with steel shutters and barbed wire entanglements. Between 1 January and 30 June 1920, 351 of the vacated barracks were destroyed and 105 damaged. In the same period fifteen occupied R.I.C. barracks were destroyed and twenty-five damaged. The operations extended to almost every county in Ireland. In this way we prevented any possibility that about four hundred of these posts would ever again be occupied by the enemy. Hundreds of links in the British military chain had thus been severed, for the Peelers had now abandoned all pretence of being a police force. They were openly and avowedly a military force, not for the suppression of crime but for the holding of the country by brute force. When the R.I.C. disappeared from a village, our Volunteer police took over their duties. We also set up our own courts, and the enemy courts were boycotted. The robber and the house-breaker soon learned to have a wholesome respect for justice as administered by the Irish Republican courts. Our police carried out all the duties of civil police. As far as possible, they also saw that the decrees of the National Arbitration Courts were implemented. These courts were established in every county by Dáil Éireann, on 17 June 1919. But the British and their hirelings in Dublin Castle had determined that law and order would not be administered and maintained by the Republican courts and police, even though their own civil administration in the provinces had collapsed.

If any reader unacquainted with this period in Irish history thinks it incredible that a police force should have been so shameless as to allow a free hand to criminals, I shall endeavour to convince him. In cases where our police were found to have arrested persons for robbery or other forms of crime, the British practice was to release those criminals and give them protection. They committed to jail any member of the Irish Republican police on whom they happened to lay hands. In the newspaper files are reports of courts martial which bear out this statement. I learned from the Republican police of a cold-blooded murder that had been committed in County Meath by an ex-British soldier. The R.I.C. had clear evidence of his guilt. They arrested him, but did they try him? No! They released him and advised him to leave the country in case he might fall into the hands of the I.R.A. Within a short time of his release he was arrested by the Republican police, and in due course he paid the penalty for his crime.

About this time the Black-and-Tans were sent amongst us; as a matter of fact, the first of them arrived on 25 March 1920. The words "Black-and-Tan" have been adopted into many languages as a symbol for terrorism. The fact that those sadists were let loose on the Irish people speaks volumes for the mentality of those responsible for British policy towards Ireland. The frightfulness of the Tans proved to be a boomerang against those who had cast it, for the people were finally goaded into such fury that they made up their minds, "come hell or high water," never to give way before such tyranny.

Such was the Irish scene at the time when my comrades

and I returned to our native county. We decided to open a
series of attacks on police barracks. For some months previously, such attacks had been made on a small scale in
various parts of the south. A pattern had been established.

An early capture of the entire armament of a police garrison took place at Arraglin, on the borders of Cork and
Limerick, close to the southern end of the Galtees, on 20
April 1919. The coup was carried out under the leadership
of Michael Fitzgerald and, without the necessity for firing a
single shot, the barracks was stripped of rifles, revolvers,
ammunition and batons. About two months later, Michael
was arrested at Clondulane. Some ammunition was found in
the house in which he lived, and he was sentenced to two
months' imprisonment. He was released towards the end of
August, just in time to participate in a successful action at
Fermoy, under the personal leadership of Liam Lynch.

Liam Lynch was every inch a soldier. He stood six feet in
height, and from his bearing one sensed that he was a born
leader. As gentle as a child, he was a dauntless soldier; he
commanded one of the best brigades in the war against the
British, the Cork No. 2. He and Seán Moylan made an
admirable combination; their success against the British was
outstanding Tom Barry was in my opinion the best leader
of a Flying Column.

I first met Liam Lynch in the autumn of 1919. We were
introduced by Tom Hunter, Republican Deputy for Cork.
Like myself Lynch was at that period very much on the run.
On Sunday morning, 7 September, at Fermoy, he had carried
out a daring coup by which he disarmed fourteen soldiers
and the corporal-in-charge, as they were on their way to the
Wesleyan Church. Lynch's party comprised twenty-five
Volunteers from the Fermoy Company, and only six of them
were armed with revolvers; others carried clubs. In the
struggle, one of the British soldiers was killed and three were
wounded. Fifteen rifles were captured. That incident is of
particular importance because it led to one of the first of the
reprisals; on the following night the British soldiers, with the
Buffs and the Royal Flying Corps well represented, and led
by some of their officers, wrecked and looted the principal
shops of the town.

Shortly afterwards, Michael Fitzgerald, then Commandant
of the Fermoy Battalion, was arrested with others on suspicion
that they had taken part in the Fermoy job. After thirty-five
remands, three of the prisoners were returned for trial at the

Cork Assizes in July 1920. As jurors refused to attend British courts, no jury could be impanelled to try the prisoners, and so they remained in custody in Cork jail. On 11 August, Michael Fitzgerald and other untried prisoners went on hunger strike to secure release, and Michael died sixty-seven days later.

Liam Lynch had great admiration for Michael Fitzgerald, to whom he was very much attached. When Liam fell in battle on the Knockmealdowns, 10 April 1923, his last request was to be buried with Michael Fitzgerald in Kilcrumper. " Place me near my loyal and faithful comrade, Michael Fitzgerald," he asked. And there those two faithful soldiers of the Republic lie side by side.

After the capture of Arraglin barracks, the next notable victory was won by men from Midleton and Cobh under Battalion-Commandant Mick Leahy, who captured Carrigtwo-hill R.I.C. barracks on 3 January, and with it the garrison's rifles, revolvers, bombs and ammunition, following a fight that lasted a couple of hours. The police files were taken also. And on 14 February Commandant Diarmuid O'Hurley and his men of the Midleton Company took Castlemartyr R.I.C. barracks and all the arms and ammunition of the Peelers. A barracks in East Clare was surrendered to Michael Brennan and his men by Constable Patrick Buckley who afterwards joined the I.R.A. In the Civil War, Buckley fought on the Republican side. He was captured by Free State forces and slaughtered with eight comrades, at Ballyseedy, near Tralee.

Three Peelers were wounded during the attack on Bally-landers, one of the next R.I.C. barracks to be captured, on 28 April 1920. After the garrison had surrendered their arms to Commandant Thomas Malone (" Seán Forde ") the barracks was burned to the ground. The haul of arms was seven carbines, five Webley revolvers and several hundred rounds of ammunition. Cloyne R.I.C. barracks fell to Commandant Leahy and his men on 8 May, and another haul of arms and ammunition was secured.

Hollyford was one of the first R.I.C. posts to be attacked in Tipperary. The village of Hollyford lies in the valley of the Multeen, on the old road between Nenagh and Tipperary town. The way to the north stretches through mountains for about a dozen miles, but southwards the narrow valley opens. The barracks, we had been told by local battalion officers, was a strongly built, detached two-storey house, the defences of which had been greatly strengthened by the military. They had cut loopholes in the gable-ends and in some of the interior walls. Steel shutters had been fitted to the windows which had also been given steel-mesh protection against hand grenades. Steel plates had been used to reinforce the doors. The barracks, which had a garrison of twelve on the night of the attack, had been built on rising ground and was of considerable height; its ground-floor level was about six feet higher than the ground outside, and this ruled out all possibility of a break-in through the walls. A loopholed front-porch commanded a good view, and the rear gable-end was fortified by a long lean-to building. On the whole it looked a tough nut to crack.

Tadhg Dwyer was the area Battalion O.C., and Ernie O'Malley had charge of the attack, which was fixed for 11 May. O'Malley, a staff captain, was responsible only to Headquarters in Dublin. He had taken part in the capture of Ballytrain R.I.C. barracks in County Monaghan on 14 February 1920, when half-a-dozen carbines, some revolvers, assorted ammunition and police equipment were captured. He was in the South to assist with organisation, hold classes for officers and stir up as much trouble as possible for the enemy. The Brigade officers who participated in the Holly-ford attack were Séamus Robinson, Seán Treacy and myself. The task had been decided upon at short notice. On that account it was impossible to obtain help from other groups, with the exception of the Doon Battalion in East Limerick. Jim Stapleton and some of his friends from mid-Tipperary lent us their aid. Also prominent in the attack were Ned Reilly, Jack Ryan (" The Master "), and Jim Gorman of Holly-ford, who had served in the Australian army and who was at this time a lieutenant in the Hollyford Company.

Roads would be blocked or trenched, and telegraph wires cut at a specified hour. Hollyford R.I.C. barracks would thus be isolated and unable to make direct contact with other enemy posts. Before moving against the barracks, O'Malley visited the outposts and impressed on the men the importance of holding back enemy reinforcements. To Jim Gorman, who was with us on the road to Milestone, he said there did not seem to be much material available for roadblocks, except odd boulders, stones and banks of earth. " It'll be all right, don't you worry; they'll throw the road over the ditch," said Gorman dryly, pointing to a pile of pick-axes, crowbars and shovels by the roadside.

Our only means of dislodging the garrison was to burn them out by smashing the roof, pouring in petrol and paraffin, and getting the barracks ablaze. We had some hand grenades and home-made bombs manufactured by Treacy and O'Malley for use against the roof; but we had no heavy explosives. It was planned to take the incendiary material on to the roof, but there was no ladder of sufficient length to reach that height. Fortunately, there was a mason in the Hollyford Company who had been a sailor and who had also worked as a slater. There was little about ropes and ladders that he did not know. He inspected all the available ladders and from these he selected four that were in good condition. These he skilfully spliced together with ropes. The ladders would be placed against the northern gable of the building and Robinson and O'Malley would mount them for the onslaught against the roof. From the protection of a low wall, a covering party of seven riflemen and five shotgun men, commanded by Treacy, would open up on the loopholes in the front of the building, to keep the garrison fully engaged at those points once operations against the roof had commenced. I was given a roving commission.

Arrangements were made for adequate supplies of home-made bombs and inflammable material to be brought to the gable-end at which Robinson and O'Malley would climb to the barracks roof. Ammunition was to be used very sparingly when the first volleys had been fired to disconcert the garrison. Regular reports from the outposts would be received at a centre near the village.

Robinson and O'Malley looked like men from another planet as, draped and weighed by their impediments, they finally tested the ladders by swinging off the rungs. They also checked the spliced joints. Each had a two-gallon petrol tin tied to his back, and slung round his neck from cords were five or six sods of turf which had been soaked in paraffin oil. They had Mills grenades, home-made bombs, lengths of fuse and detonators. Each carried two revolvers and ammunition, and had a heavy hammer tied to his wrist. They went in ahead of the ladder party to cover the lower loopholes with their revolvers, while picked men from the Rossmore Company, in their stockinged feet, were silently hoisting the ladders into the air and moving them against the barracks. There was a deal of noise and whispering while the ladders were being manoeuvred into position, and it seemed to us that the goings-on must inevitably be heard by the police.   Robinson and O'Malley started to climb simultaneously. The Rossmore men remained at the base of the ladders, under the loopholes of the enemy, until O'Malley and Robinson had arrived on the roof.   It was then that Treacy's men opened up on the front of the building and shattered the stillness of the May night. Seconds later the explosions of bursting grenades added to the din.   Tongues of flame began to shoot along the roof. The police were replying with heavy rifle fire, and their grenades were bursting in all directions.   Verey lights, sent up at intervals for reinforcements, lighted up the hills. Police were firing at our men on the roof from the lean-to building at the rear, and also from a room further back in the main building. We endeavoured to keep them otherwise occupied by intensifying our fire against their loopholes.

A great quantity of paraffin was needed to keep the fire blazing, and Treacy temporarily relinquished his command of the sharpshooters to supervise the transfer of about fifty gallons from Hollyford creamery.   Jim Gorman climbed a ladder in order to help the men on the roof. Once the fire had taken hold only an occasional shot was necessary from the riflemen. The R.I.C. blazed away; they must have been fervently hoping for reinforcements.

By daybreak, we could see great caverns in the roof. The flames seemed to have died down, however, and the garrison continued to make a spirited defence. It looked as if all our efforts would end in failure. Suddenly, orange tinted flames shot into the air, and in a short time the entire roof was ablaze. Robinson and O'Malley had come down, having had several narrow escapes from fire and shot.

Treacy, O'Malley and myself wanted to continue the attack, although it was then broad daylight.   Séamus Robinson, however, was anxious about our outposts who held the valley positions. They were definitely endangered as there were only a few riflemen amongst them; they could be outflanked from the high ground. We were inside the ring of R.I.C. posts at Rearcross, Kilcommon and Shevry to the north; Cappamore, Doon, Cappawhite, Annacarthy, Clonoulty, Dundrum and Rosskeen to the south. The nearest R.I.C. strong-point was Dundrum, eight miles away, and it often held military.   There were military in battalion strength in Tipperary town and Templemore, and these, with strong forces in Nenagh, were no more than eighteen or nineteen miles distant.   After a long discussion, Séamus, in his capacity as brigadier, took the decision to break off the attack.

The order was given to the outposts to withdraw to their company areas. We remained in Hollyford until we were assured that the withdrawal had taken place. We had failed in our objective and had used up a lot of our war stores. But we had also gained valuable experience that was soon to be put to good account; we had suffered no casualty, though Robinson and O'Malley had been severely burnt. Besides we had left the barracks a gaping ruin.

Shortly after the operation against Hollyford—to be exact, on the night of 28 May—the famous attack on Kilmallock R.I.C. barracks took place. Although the South Tipperary Brigade was represented in the fight, I was not engaged on that occasion. The attack, led by Thomas Malone (" Seán Forde ") was carried out by the East Limerick Brigade with the aid of men from Tipperary, Cork, Clare and Kerry. The fighting lasted from midnight until seven a.m. The barracks which was regarded as impregnable, was situated in the very heart of the town, and was held by two sergeants and twenty-two constables.

The attacking force numbered approximately sixty. Of these, about thirty manned close-in barricades to deal with enemy reinforcements, and the remaining thirty took part in the actual assault. They occupied Cleary's Hotel, the Provincial Bank, and several houses on the principal street. Michael Brennan, the East Clare leader, was with the attackers who took up positions in Herlihy's premises. Under cover of rifle fire, a party smashed a hole in the roof of the building, to which they had gained access by occupying Carroll's house next door, and then moving out through the skylight. A chain of buckets conveyed paraffin to the men on the roof, and they sloshed it through the hole. A blazing torch and a grenade were thrown in, and soon the roof was in flames. After many hours of fighting the garrison managed to retreat to a fortified out-office from which they could not be dislodged; our men had eventually to break off the attack. One I.R.A. officer, Captain Liam Scully of Glencar, County Kerry, was killed when he stood openly in the middle of the street in order to fire against the post. He was answered by a single shot, believed to be the last of the morning. Of the defenders, Contables Moreton and King were killed, and six others wounded, of whom one, Constable Barry, received a severe head wound. Sergeant O'Sullivan, who commanded the garrison, was promoted to the rank of District Inspector as a reward for his gallant defence. He was transferred to Listowel where he was shot dead on 19 January 1921, less than fifty yards from the R.I.C. barracks. At one stage, Sergeant O'Sullivan was on the point of surrendering. During a lull in the fighting, he shouted an enquiry as to whether the lives of the garrison would be spared if they surrendered. Someone amongst the attackers is said to have answered back that the Kilmallock Peelers would not be afforded an opportunity of repeating the action of the Ballylanders R.I.C. Subsequent to the capture of that barracks a number of Volunteers had been arrested. Certain members of the R.I.C. testified in court to the identity of some of those who had taken part in the attack. Apparently the garrison concluded from this man's reply that their lives would not be spared.

Shortly afterwards we took Drangan barracks. The village of Drangan stands at the southern limit of the Slieveardagh Hills, in a narrow plain surrounded by rising ground. Not far distant was a number of R.I.C. barracks. There was a strong garrison at Callan towards the east, and about 150 military in the artillery barracks at Fethard, to the south-west. Military parties occasionally remained overnight in the R.I.C. posts. Drangan barracks was in the Seventh Battalion area, and Tommy Donovan, the Battalion Commandant, was anxious for a crack at it.

Attached to one gable of the barracks was a small two-storey house. A single loophole high up in the barracks gable commanded this house which we occupied on the night of the attack. Why the police were so remiss as to have left it unguarded, I cannot imagine. In fact, I cannot understand why it was not demolished when the defences of the barracks were strengthened earlier in the year, as it constituted a serious threat to the successful defence of the post. It was easy to cover off the single loophole in the gable of the barracks from the roof of the smaller building.

On the evening of the attack we were joined by Séamus Robinson and Ernie O'Malley. They had gone to assist Michael Brennan in an attack on an East Clare barracks but the attack had to be called off because the gelignite had frozen and could not be thawed out in time. In addition to these two experienced fighters, there were Treacy, Hogan and myself; Tommy Donovan, Nicholas Moroney and their men of the Seventh Battalion; Ned Reilly, Bill Dwyer, the Hanleys and Jack the Master. Men had moved in from the Callan Battalion area, from the Tipperary Town Battalion and from Rossmore. We had ample strength for the task ahead.

It was possible to command all approaches to the village of Drangan by controlling the four cross-roads which led to it. We arranged for these roads to be blockaded and patrolled, and for the telegraph wires to be cut. Drangan would be completely isolated. Our experience at Hollyford had shown us that a good pressure pump, and a length of hose to play paraffin against the roof, were essential. We had captured such a pump in a raid on Cashel railway station. Ample supplies of petrol, paraffin and explosives were assembled in the house of George Hayden. Treacy, Donovan and I had made " mud bombs " of yellow clay wrapped round gelignite to which a fuse and detonator had been attached. The clay, of putty-like substance, usually stuck to the walls or roofs against which it was hurled, and these mud-bombs were effective against the slated roofs of an R.I.C. barracks —they enabled us to strip a roof even when we could not get at it with our sledge hammers.

We moved into positions shortly before midnight. Robinson, Treacy, Tommy Donovan and Jack the Master set out to occupy the house which adjoined the gable of the barracks. The pressure pump and all the necessary incendiary material were moved up to it. It was planned to break out through the roof of the smaller building and pepper the roof of the barracks with mud-bombs. Petrol or paraffin would then be pumped in through the holes. Grenades would set the building ablaze. Treacy and Jack the Master were assigned to cover off the solitary loophole in the gable of the barracks and keep the Peelers quiet at that point.

To protect the men who would deliver the main attack from the adjoining house, O'Malley, Ned Reilly, Bill Dwyer, Hogan and myself, with some of the Rossmore men, took up positions in a haggard behind the high wall that fronted the barracks. As quietly as we could we began to break loopholes in this wall with crowbar and pick. Although we made as little noise as possible, it was inevitable that sounds of our industry reached the ears of the garrison. Besides, the dogs of the village were barking madly to indicate the presence of strangers. The Peelers sent out three men to ascertain what the row was all about, and in a matter of seconds we were exchanging fire with them. They had come up a small lane by the side of the haggard and taken us on the flank. We fired at their gunflashes, but it was difficult to hit them in the dark. Anyway, they did not tarry long. Within a couple of minutes, two beat a hasty retreat to their fortress. The third, Sergeant Robinson, was taken prisoner; Bill Dwyer of Hollyford was hit in the wrist during this exchange of fire, and he was brought to the first-aid station where Dr. Peter Conlon dressed his wound.

Verey lights turned night into day. This could mean trouble for us, for of the encircling R.I.C. posts at Killenaule, Ballingarry, Mullinahone and Fethard, none was more than seven miles distant. The attack was now on in earnest. I could clearly see Robinson on the roof of the adjoining house, and hear Donovan and Paud Egan at work with sledge hammers on a corner of the roof of the barracks just above the smaller building. Rapid fire from Treacy's Parabellum and Jack the Master's Peter the Painter made the gable loophole an unpopular post. Out front we held the Peelers' attention from the cover of our loopholed wall. Treacy left Jack the Master to keep an eye on the gable loophole and came to help with the hurling of mud-bombs against the roof of the barracks. We gave the front wall similar treatment. The Peelers replied with their rifles and grenades. An awful racket was in progress to the accompaniment of the howling of the dogs.

Robinson and Donovan, assisted by some of the boys from Poulacapple set to work with the pressure-pumps. They hosed gallons of paraffin into the cavities that had been made in the roof with sledge-hammers. The paraffin was followed up by grenades and flaming sods of turf. The roof was set ablaze and the garrison were forced to descend from the top floor. At this point we decided to break through the wall of the barracks from the adjoining house. The picks and crowbars which we had used to loophole the front wall were now brought up to make the break through. When the breach was made, grenades would be thrown in and then, covered by rifle and revolver fire, we would rush the Peelers. Overhead, black smoke belched out of holes and red flames leapt towards the sky.

Ned Reilly, Ernie O'Malley, Hogan and myself, with the help of some others, used tree trunks that had been piled near-by to make a barricade across the street as a flank protection for the men in the small house. From this cover we fired a few shots against the ground-floor loopholes. It was then that we saw a rifle-barrel with a white shirt attached pushed through one of the loopholes. " Do you want to surrender," asked O'Malley. He and I had moved close to the building in response to the signals. "Yes," the Peelers answered, "we want to surrender." We told them to throw out their rifles and revolvers at once, and to come out immediately with their ammunition. We could hear boxes of the ammunition which we badly needed exploding in the flames that roared through the building.

The Peelers were assured that their lives would be spared, and they lost no time about coming out, holding a pennant that first showed white, and then green and yellow also as it gradually unfurled and fluttered in the breeze. It was a surrender flag improvised from an Irish tri-colour they had taken from some house in the neighbourhood. Ned O'Reilly, O'Malley, myself and some of the others dashed into the building and succeeded in dragging out boxes which we hurriedly searched for papers and ammunition. The whole place was now a blazing inferno, and ammunition continued to explode. Part of the roof and the ground floor ceiling came crashing down. The fight had lasted seven hours.

Our booty comprised police carbines and Lee Enfield rifles, a few shotguns, eight revolvers, a Verey-light pistol, boxes of ammunition, bombs and bayonets. Our casualties were trifling; Bill Dwyer wounded and a couple of our men with scorched limbs. The names of the garrison were taken and the men were warned that it would be unhealthy for them to be ever again taken under arms against the Republic. They formed up in the street under King, a Black-and-Tan, who was slightly wounded in the head. He had served in the Horse Artillery in the first World War. O'Malley gave them a right turn, told them to keep five paces apart, and warned them not to look back. He then ordered them to march, and they tramped away in the direction of Mullinahone.

The entire company of those who had helped in the attack was marshalled on the village street. The Commandant delivered a brief address of congratulation and then gave the order to dismiss. Our outposts had already been withdrawn. Robinson, Treacy, Hogan, O'Malley and myself halted for a while at the cross-roads through which enemy reinforcements would have to come. Some local people brought us jugs of milk and thick buttered hunks of cake. They had remained up all night, they told us, when they heard the distant sound of gunfire and explosions.

Early the same morning, Cappawhite R.I.C. barracks,

also in Tipperary, was attacked by another party of our men, but the garrison held out and the attackers were forced to withdraw after a fight which had lasted for about three hours. One R.I.C. man was wounded, and the roof of the adjoining courthouse was set on fire.

One evening early in July 1920 word reached us that Paddy Ryan (Ryan Lacken), Captain of the Knockfune Company, would welcome our help in an attack he had planned to make on Rearcross R.I.C. barracks, in the North Tipperary Brigade area. Séamus Robinson and Seán Hogan were in Dublin, but Seán Treacy and myself, with Jack the Master, Ned Reilly, Jim Gorman, the Dwyers of Hollyford and other South Tipperary men moved towards Rearcross. There we made contact with Ryan and his men, and we were joined soon afterwards by Ernie O'Malley who had learned about the proposed attack whilst in East Limerick, and by the Yank Carty, Commandant of the Doon Battalion, with about a dozen of his men from Doon and Cappawhite. Jim Stapleton and Paddy Kinnane from the Borrisoleigh Battalion of the mid-Tipperary Brigade turned up also. Given the necessary war materials, we had enough good men available to take any R.I.C. barracks in the country, and most of them had experience in such operations. It must be remembered that the barracks still held by the R.I.C. were, for practical purposes, strongly held block-houses.

The attack was originally planned for Saturday night, 10 July. Trenches were dug, roadblocks set up and manned, signallers and scouts positioned. The telegraph wires would be cut before the attack began. At that juncture, Commandant Doherty of the Sixth Battalion, North Tipperary Brigade, arrived at the position held by Treacy, myself and the South Tipperary men. He brought an important dispatch from his Brigadier in Nenagh. In Quigley's house nearby, Treacy read the dispatch by candle-light. It was an order commanding us to return to our Brigade area. Paddy Ryan had not troubled to get Brigade sanction for his job. We were worried and with good reason. Not merely did we have no invitation from the North Tipperary Brigade to enter their area, we were now definitely commanded to withdraw from it. I discussed the situation with Paddy Ryan and Ernie O'Malley. Treacy kept out of the way. As Vice-Brigadier of South Tipperary, a breach of discipline on his part was bound to incur censure from H.Q. O'Malley

was in a different position, for he was responsible only to
General Headquarters in Dublin.

Eventually it was agreed that he would assume responsibility for the attack which was postponed until the following
night, and accordingly it was with him that the North
Tipperary Brigade would have to deal concerning our
participation. O'Malley took the line that, in the circumstances which prevailed, it was more important to proceed
and attack with our assistance rather than yield to the
authority of the North Tipperary Brigadier. I agreed with
him. Ryan should have got Brigade sanction for the job,
but now that the men and materials had been mobilised,
and with O'Malley there to take command, I could see no
good reason to abandon the project.

Trenches had to be filled in at once and road blocks
removed lest their presence should give warning of the
impending attack to the Peelers in Rearcross. The Yank
Carty and his men were sent back to their own area to
remove some road blocks and also to shoot up the Doon
R.I.C. post, so that the enemy might associate the happenings
of the night with an attempt to attack Doon. This was
important. We did not want the Rearcross R.I.C. to have
advance information of our assault.

Next morning Treacy, Ned Reilly and myself were brought
beyond the Long Stone, up a narrow lane, to Ryan's of
Bottomy. There we discovered that everybody knew what
had been planned for the previous night. On Sunday
evening we attended to our weapons. Treacy was particularly
interested in heavy cart-box bombs that had been brought
in by the Yank Carty and his men. This new type of bomb
was particularly effective against the roof of a barracks;
but men had first to get out on top to hurl it down. The
metal boxes had been filled with gelignite and tamped
tightly with old nuts and bolts and pieces of scrap iron. A
hole for a fuse had been drilled through each box which,
when fully charged, weighed about twenty pounds.

Rearcross R.I.C. barracks was a large long building, with
five windows on the top storey. It stood back some distance
off the main road, faced south, and was well protected at
the rear by a gradually sloping hill. The hill was commanded
by loopholes from which it could be raked by fire. The
defences had been strengthened by means similar to those
used at Hollyford and Drangan. All the windows were
steel-plated and loopholed, and there was wire-mesh protection

against grenades. The back wall of the garden had been lowered to about three feet to improve the angle of fire from the building, and nothing but a mass of barbed wire flourished in the garden itself. A narrow concrete path flanked by barbed wire entanglements led to the front of the barracks. A well loopholed front-porch commanded this approach. All obstacles that might give cover to attackers had been levelled, thereby ensuring that flat country to a depth of several hundred yards was dominated by the garrison. No doubt also, the Peelers had the range of every point from which they could be fired upon.

The outer defences of Rearcross were much better prepared than those at Hollyford and Drangan. About the only close-in point from which we could fire on the building was a low fence which bounded a haggard to the east.

It was important that the approaches to Rearcross should be sealed off on the night of the attack. British military were in strength at Tipperary town, Thurles, Nenagh and Newport, and a brigade had their headquarters in Limerick, seventeen miles distant. Nenagh, the R.I.C. headquarters for the North Riding, was just over twenty miles away, and we also had to reckon with the possibility of trouble from the R.I.C. in Newport, Kilcommon, Shevry, Castlefogarty, Doon and Cappawhite. Kilcommon R.I.C. barracks was only four miles from Rearcross, and Newport and Cappagh were each about eight miles distant.

Rearcross was occupied by about forty constables and two sergeants. One of the sergeants had served as a lieutenant in the World War, and it was under his supervision that the defences were prepared. Most of the garrison were Black-and-Tans, the remainder were regular R.I.C. Our force numbered about fifty all told.

The barracks building proper, as well as the adjoining general stores, belonged to a man named Flannery. We planned to get to close quarters with the garrison by entering the stores and breaking out through the roof as we did at Drangan. We had paraffin and a pressure pump, mud-bombs, and the cart-box bombs.

It was raining heavily as we prepared to take up our positions. We did not move off until O'Malley had received confirmation that the road-blocks had been renewed and that arrangements had been made to cut the telegraph wires at the appointed time. During the hours of darkness signals would be sent from certain points by flares held aloft on pikes.

Treacy, myself, and the South Tipperary contingent were posted at a grove a few hundred yards distant from the barracks. The plantation afforded a certain amount of cover. Our task was to deal with a possible break-out by the garrison or an attempted break-in by enemy reinforcements. It was hard to realise that it was summer time, with the driving rain and a high wind that chilled us to the bone.

Ernie O'Malley, Paddy Ryan, Jim Gorman, Paddy Kinnane, and Jim Stapleton entered the general stores. In addition to their weapons, they carried tins of petrol, mud-bombs, cart-box bombs and sledge-hammers. They also brought a short ladder by which they could reach Flannery's roof from the top-storey. A large barrel of paraffin and the pressure-pump were hoisted aloft.

Twenty minutes elapsed and we were wondering why the attack had not begun. As if in answer to our thoughts, great tongues of flame shot up from the roof of the barracks and simultaneously the men who had been posted behind the haggard-wall opened up with their rifles. The defenders returned the fire. Bullets whizzed through the branches of the trees. Explosions and rifle-flashes furnished abundant proof that O'Malley and his men were pushing the attack with bullet and bomb. Within half an hour the roof of the barracks seemed to be enveloped in a vast curtain of flame. The box-bombs were reverberating like muffled thunder.

One of the defenders boldly emerged from the front porch of the barracks. He raised his rifle and was about to take aim at the men on the roof who were silhouetted by the flames. Before he could pull the trigger a shot rang out from the haggard and he went into a spin and collapsed. A member of the garrison dashed out and dragged the body into the building. We learned later that the man who had been hit was the leader of the garrison, an Irishman who had served with the British army in France.

The fire was not confined to the roof of the barracks. It had also spread to the roof of the stores which were crammed with explosives and incendiaries. Treacy and I went at full speed to Flannery's and found Kinnane and Stapleton trying to extinguish the store-blaze with wet sacks; at the same time O'Malley, Ryan and Gorman were doing all in their power to intensify the blaze on the adjoining roof. Fire-fighting and fire-raising were going on side by side. While we were helping in the removal of explosives from the danger zone, heavy thuds sounded next door followed instantly by loud explosions. Gorman had tossed a two-gallon tin of petrol through a hole in the roof of the barracks and O'Malley followed this up by crashing some of the heavy bombs on top of the garrison.

When the fire on the roof of the stores had been stamped out we moved the explosives close to the foot of the ladder. O'Malley shouted down to us that Jim Gorman had been hit and that he needed our assistance. Jim was helped down the ladder by Ernie. We saw that a bullet had glanced along his wrist and ploughed its way into the arm. We gave him first-aid treatment. When the wound had been dressed, he wanted to return to the roof, but O'Malley commanded him to remain below. "You can't use two hands above, Jim, but you can be a reserve down here," said Ernie as he mounted the ladder.

Day was beginning to break and we were getting worried. There was no hope of dislodging the garrison unless we could intensify the blaze. We could not maintain the attack in broad daylight as our poorly-armed outposts would be unable to keep heavy reinforcements at bay. To make matters worse, our pressure pump gave up the ghost with a death-rattle.

We decided to slosh buckets of paraffin over the roof. Treacy and I joined O'Malley, Kinnane and Ryan. It was particularly hazardous because the roof had been so badly damaged that there remained only a small portion which could have borne our combined weight. Our eyes smarted from the smoke that billowed up through great holes. Rifle fire from the defenders sent broken slates flying through the air. Progress was so slow that we altered our plans and descended to the ground floor.

Treacy had got the sudden inspiration of filling Flannery's empties with petrol and hurling them against the roof. The bottlenecks were filed so that they might break more easily on impact. We stood back a short distance from the wall and flung them at the target. The fire took on a new lease of life and would have gone merrily if Treacy's orders had been obeyed. He had placed some men at a fixed post to protect us during our operation but they had not remained in the assigned position. Because of this, the Peelers had been given a free hand to deal with us. A grenade burst in our midst and O'Malley, Treacy and I were thrown to the ground by the explosion. A second grenade was just

wide of the mark. We got to our feet and scampered to
Flannery's back-door as fast as our legs could carry us.
O'Malley was bleeding from a deep shoulder-wound, Treacy
had superficial wounds in the hands and arms, a few
splinters got lodged in my chest. Flannery poured out a
stiff peg of brandy for O'Malley who seemed to be in a
shaky condition. I must confess that during the entire
engagement, Flannery behaved like a hero. He had had the
melancholy pleasure of seeing his house turned into a
battlefield and his supply of paraffin used in the attempt to
burn down his adjoining property and yet he made no
protest. In fact he looked almost as pleased as if the
show had been put on for his entertainment.

The attack was not broken off until 9 a.m. The military
were coming to the relief of the garrison and their approach
had been signalled. Even though the barracks had the
appearance of a burnt-out shell, no sign was given that the
Peelers had any intention of surrendering. As a matter of
fact, they had retired into a bomb-proof shelter. We had
no explosives powerful enough to demolish it. There was
no official announcement of casualties but we were informed
on reliable authority that both the sergeants had been
killed and several constables seriously wounded.

Our entire column, numbering about fifty, withdrew on
a pre-arranged route which took us through the village of
Hollyford. Seán Treacy, Ned Reilly, Ernie O'Malley, Jim
O'Gorman and myself brought up the rear. My feet had
become blistered during my stay on the red-hot barracks-roof.
I slung my boots about my neck and walked barefooted. As
the boys marched past, four abreast, all the villagers
turned out and shouted, "Up Sinn Féin!" O'Malley
exclaimed, "O holy mackerel, do you hear what they are
calling us, 'Bloody Sinn Féiners'?"

CHAPTER TWELVE

A BRUSH WITH A BRITISH
GENERAL

On 26 June 1920 a sensational event took place at Kilbarry,
four miles north-east of Fermoy. General Lucas, Commander
of the 18th British Brigade which was stationed at Fermoy,

had rented a cottage at Kilbarry for a few days' fishing on the Blackwater. As he was returning from the river, accompanied by Colonels Danford and Tyrell, the party was intercepted by Liam Lynch and his staff-officers, Seán Moylan, George Power and Paddy Clancy. The General and Colonel Danford were forced at gun-point to enter the General's car; Lynch and Clancy sat in to keep them company. Owen Curtis a member of the Fermoy Volunteers was already established in the driver's seat. Colonel Tyrell was taken by Moylan and Power to a Model T Ford which had been held in readiness.

As Lucas and Danford were being taken " to an unknown destination," they began to converse in a language which was unintelligible to Lynch and Clancy. Actually they were speaking Arabic and were conspiring to overpower their captors. Danford made a sudden spring on Clancy and throttled him. Lucas came to grips with Lynch. In the excitement, Curtis crashed into a wall and suffered slight concussion from the impact of his head against the windscreen. Clancy had been recently released after a prolonged hunger-strike and was no match for Danford. Lynch on the other hand had no trouble in dealing effectively with Lucas and was then free to go to the assistance of Clancy. He called on Danford to surrender. His request was ignored. Lynch had no option but to bring his gun into play. Danford's jaw was shattered by the first shot. The struggle had ended.

Meanwhile, Moylan and Power had gone some distance with their prisoner. They halted and waited anxiously for the arrival of the captive General. After some minutes they decided to return in order to explore the cause of the delay. When they came to the scene of the meleé, quiet had been restored. Lynch, concerned about the seriousness of Danford's injury, asked Owen Curtis who had recovered from the effects of the crash to fetch a doctor from Rathcormack. Tyrell was requested to look after the wounded man and await the arrival of the doctor. Lucas was transferred to the Model T and the party proceeded to Cork No. 2 Brigade-Headquarters.

The capture of the General happened at an opportune time. He would be held as hostage for the safety of certain prisoners, among whom was Liam Lynch's friend, Michael Fitzgerald of Fermoy, who was about to be arraigned on a capital charge.

On the next night the British military showed their appreciation of Lynch's considerate treatment of Danford by going on the rampage. " We want our f—— General; give us back our f—— General," the drunken soldiers shouted as they went through the town, smashing doors and windows right and left. It was the second time within twelve months that Fermoy had been sacked. On both occasions Lynch's exploits had been the prime cause of the disturbance.

Lucas was held in custody for four weeks. During that time he was treated with the courtesy befitting his rank and character. Every reasonable facility was given him for communicating with his relatives. He enjoyed every comfort that his captors could provide. He was paroled while he enjoyed some fishing in mountain streams. In addition, the London *Times* was made available for him each morning as he sat down to breakfast. To his credit be it said, he publicly acknowledged the kindness that had been shown to him. He is reputed to have been reprimanded by the British War Office for this open avowal. The Volunteers detained him for some time in East Clare. While he was being transferred to the mid-Limerick Brigade area on the night of 30 July, he escaped from his escort near Oola.

On the morning of 30 July Seán Treacy had planned an ambush on the road between Limerick and Tipperary. At that time our men were creating grave trouble by holding up trains and mail-cars for the censoring of letters which might provide valuable information. In this way, we often lighted on revelations concerning spies who operated in the locality. The Crown forces were obliged to take special precautions in order to prevent military mails and despatches from falling into our hands. On each day a military escort set out from Limerick by road to collect the morning mail off the train at the Junction. It was decided to ambush this party at a spot which was half a mile on the Tipperary side of the village of Oola, about six miles from Tipperary town, fifteen from Limerick city and four from Soloheadbeg. Although we had taken up a position on the main road from Limerick to Waterford, we had a great stretch of country by which we could escape southwards and motor back towards East Limerick. The terrain is comparatively flat, with thick whitethorn hedges which would provide good cover.

We expected the military car to arrive from Limerick

about 10.30 a.m. At 10.15 the road was effectively blocked by the felling of a large overhanging tree. We then took up our position, keeping well out of view; for it must be remembered that in the village of Oola, almost in sight of the spot selected for the ambush, there was a strong garrison of Peelers. On the other side, two miles away at the Limerick Junction, was another R.I.C. garrison.

Sharp on time the military car came tearing along from Limerick. Just when they turned a corner and were almost about to drive into the barrack-compound we opened fire. Every soldier jumped instantly from the car and took cover to reply to our fire. The encounter lasted for half an hour. After our first volley two of the soldiers dropped their rifles and rolled over mortally wounded; the others continued to pour volley after volley in the direction from which our fire came. We were faced with an awkward situation. We numbered only seven and we had only ten rounds of ammunition per man. To add to our troubles we saw another military car approach from the Limerick direction. These reinforcements may have arrived by accident; as our ammunition was running low, there seemed no possibility of continuing the fight and so we decided to break off the engagement. While we retreated, we held the enemy at bay by an occasional discharge of shot. At this stage, a group of uniformed members of the R.I.C. armed with rifles, advanced from the village. If our supply of ammunition had been ample, a couple of our number could have been detailed to feign an attack on the barracks and keep the police indoors. In the circumstances we had to continue our withdrawal. The sum total of enemy casualties was three killed and three wounded. We escaped unscathed.

Next morning we learned something of which we were in ignorance while the engagement had lasted. Brigadier-General Lucas was actually present with the enemy forces. He had, as I have told, escaped on the previous night. During the hours of darkness he had wandered through the fields, not knowing his exact position. He had endeavoured to avoid any of our men who might have been sent in pursuit of him, and had hoped to get in touch with some of his own forces. On the morning of the ambush he arrived at the village of Pallas, three miles on the Limerick side of Oola, and must have been picked up by the passing car. On the next day the British newspapers splashed the headline, "Attempt to recapture General Lucas."

A few days after this engagement at Oola, I returned to Dublin and while I was there I underwent an operation for the removal of grenade-splinters which had become embedded in my body during the attack on Rearcross police barracks. I had been on the run for eighteen months with a price on my head. I was becoming more reckless. The war was going on to our satisfaction. The struggle of the Irish people was taking the shape for which I had always hoped. The Black-and-Tans and the Auxiliaries—the latter were ex-British officers endowed with a special flair for savagery—were out by day and by night, looting shops, setting fire to private houses and murdering prisoners. The more savage were their methods of repression, the more determined the Irish people had become to fight to the bitter end. Practically the whole country—apart from the hard core of Unionists who never changed their allegiance—was now on our side, providing us with food and procuring valuable information for us whenever they could not give us more active assistance. Many, whose political views differed from ours, were being driven into our ranks for the simple reason that if they stayed at home they would be murdered at dead of night. In fact, their only hope of safety was to go " on the run."

The Irish Republican army was daily increasing in number and becoming more and more skilled in military tactics. I had prophesied to Seán Treacy that if the fight for freedom were once started, the whole country would rally to our support.

Meanwhile, I must refer to my trusty Dublin friends at whose houses my companions and I were ever welcome, even though torture and imprisonment would have been the fate of any householder convicted of having harboured us. I cannot recall all of them at the moment, but some I shall never forget : Séamus Ryan of The Monument Creamery; the Bolands of Clontarf; Séamus Kirwan of Parnell Street; the Delaneys of Drumcondra; the Duncans of Irishtown; the Dohertys of Connaught Street, who proved good friends to me during my American visit; Martin Conlon, and last but not least, Phil Shanahan.

Hitherto we had been relying chiefly on men who would take part in a barracks attack at night and resume their ordinary daily work next morning. For many reasons that became difficult in practice. They could help only at night; the urgent need of attention to their own business might

often prevent them from taking part in a military engagement. The disappointment which we had suffered at Knocklong showed what serious risks were incurred in having to
rely on "doubtful starters." Part-time Volunteers could
not undergo the necessary training; they could not go very
far from home; most compelling reason of all, they lived
in an atmosphere of peace and not of war.

We wanted full-time soldiers who were prepared to fight
by night or by day, ready for any adventure. They would
constitute a mobile force capable of striking at a given
moment in one district and on the next day springing a
surprise thirty miles away. Could we get such a mobile
unit? Of course we could. In addition to those men who
were permanently on the run—their number was daily increasing—there were scores throughout the country who
would volunteer for full active service. Furthermore, the
British practice of assassinating men whom they suspected
of being Volunteers was making it impossible for any
known member of the I.R.A. to remain at home or to go
about his daily work. We were being encumbered with
hundreds of men who would only be in the way unless
they were organised in proper military units, acting under
disciplined and daring officers.

At long last we convinced the Headquarters-staff of the
desirability of such a scheme. The flying columns were
organised and they bore the brunt of the war during the
next twelve months. Perhaps the most successful aspect
of this system was that it enabled active counties like
Tipperary and Cork to send columns into counties such as
Kilkenny and Waterford where Crown forces were having
too quiet a time.

During the autumn Dinny Lacey was constantly with me
in Dublin; many an exciting adventure we shared, dodging
or defying the "G" men or the spies who got on our trail.
The unending nervous tension in the city made it imperative
for him to return to his native parish for a brief rest.

Dinny was born in Goldengarden, in the heart of Tipperary.
He was educated in Donaskeigh School in the parish of
Father Matt Ryan, well-known patriot and "General of the
Land War." Dinny had been a great sprinter and foot-
baller; in fact he was "an all-round man." His home was
only about a mile distant from mine; we had known each
other from boyhood. When he was a mere boy, he went
to Tipperary town and soon became his employer's most

trusted man. In due time he was appointed manager of
a large coal and provision emporium. He was a non-smoker
and total abstainer, was deeply religious and attended daily
Mass. He had been always a keen student of the Irish
language and from the very start of the movement became
an enthusiastic Volunteer. In Easter Week of 1916 he was
one of the small band who answered the call to mobilise
for action at Galbally, six miles from Tipperary; but Mac-
Neill's countermand sent him home; like the rest of the
men of Tipperary, he did not get a chance of striking a
blow during that week.

In the summer of 1916 he was one of the most enthusiastic
in favouring the reorganisation of the Irish Volunteers as a
fighting force. Modest and unassuming, he was ever on the
look-out for a rifle or a revolver, and spent his own money
freely in making such purchases. He gave everything, even
his life, in the cause of freedom.

During 1917 and 1918 I came into frequent contact with
him once more. He took part in the attack on Kilmallock
barracks and shortly afterwards had to go on the run.
Henceforth he became one of the most daring fighters.
So much was he hated by the Black-and-Tans that they
burned down the house in which he had lodged during his
stay in Tipperary. Poor Dinny! He escaped British bullets
only to be killed early in 1923 by the Free Staters in the
Glen of Aherlow. During my stay in Dublin Seán Treacy
and myself had many adventures in the company of Mick
Collins' most trusted men, Liam Tobin and Tom Cullen.
Special jobs were often assigned to the four of us by Collins.
Liam and Tom were dare-devils and brave to a fault. Liam
was ice-cool in a crisis, Tom was of an impetuous nature,
a very fine character but a very bad shot.

One night I was taken by Tobin and Cullen on a very
urgent mission. They hoped to have the pleasure of an
encounter with a particularly obnoxious " G " man. The
plan was to decoy him along to Exchange Street. Cullen
and I were instructed by Tobin to stand in the archway
leading to the *Evening Mail* office. While we were there
a big powerful man stopped under the arch to take shelter
from a heavy shower and got into conversation with us
chiefly about the weather. After a few minutes he looked
furtively up and down the street. " I don't think it will
clear at all. I'll be off," he said and made a hasty departure. Up came Tobin. " What delayed you ? " we asked

with impatience. "You promised to send along that 'G'
man."

"Weren't you talking with him for ten minutes!" he
said in exasperation. But we had no clue as to the man's
identity. However, the "G" man got such a fright when
he realised how close he had been to his doom that he
resigned next morning and took the first boat to England.
He never again set foot in Ireland.

One of my most amusing experiences occurred one day
on the road from Dublin to Bray. Pat McCrea had
"borrowed" a British colonel's private car without seeking
the colonel's permission. He made some minor alterations,
chiefly in the matter of number-plates and the colour of
the body. McCrea asked me to accompany him on a run
to Bray Head, for he thought that I needed a change of air.
While we were cruising along the road without a care in
the world, Pat noticed in the driver's mirror that we were
being pursued by a Lancia car which had a full complement
of Auxiliaries. He opened the throttle until the speed-
ometer registered seventy, but the Lancia passed us with
ease and a slow-down was signalled. There seemed no
other course open but to obey, and either bluff or attempt
to shoot our way through. An officer dismounted from the
Lancia and approached us, his face wreathed in smiles.
"You may not know it, sir," he said to Pat almost apologet-
ically, "but your rear right wheel is out of alignment."

Pat expressed his deep gratitude. The officer and his
Auxiliaries continued on to Bray. We made a detour at
Shankhill and sniffed the ozone at Killiney.

CHAPTER THIRTEEN

"FERNSIDE" AND AFTER

I WAS BECOMING OBSESSED with the idea that if I remained
in Dublin my days were numbered. The British had touts
and spotters everywhere. They had promised liberal rewards for information; at this time they were making
desperate efforts to restore their Secret Service and match
it with ours. Everywhere one saw the khaki uniform and
the guns and the lorries. It was quite a common thing for
an ordinary pedestrian to be held up and searched six or
seven times during one day. The Crown forces jumped off

lorries and searched and questioned passers-by. They boarded tramcars and "frisked" every passenger. They surrounded whole blocks of buildings and, for days on end, kept a cordon drawn tight while every house was being searched from cellar to attic. All these things were of daily occurrence.

During the same period people were being brought to the Castle and tortured for information. Letters were opened in the post; hotel servants were bribed; an elaborate system of telephonic code was arranged for the touts and spotters. Is it surprising that in such circumstances I was often hard-pressed to make my escape? I was being shadowed at every step and I knew it, but I always carried my gun strapped to my wrist, concealed in the sleeve of my coat, ready to meet every challenge.

At last came an adventure which I thought would prove to be my last. On a certain Friday night I was standing alone at the Henry Street corner opposite Nelson Pillar. I had arranged to spend the night at Professor Carolan's house, which was situated between Drumcondra and White-hall. The Whitehall car came along; I jumped on board and went on top deck. Five men sprang on to the tramcar and came up the stairs close on my heels. I immediately recognised two of them. They were members of the Murder Gang. This group was composed of about fifteen R.I.C. men from various parts of the country where the I.R.A. were most active. Each had been attached to the Political Branch of the Force in his own district for a number of years, and it was his business to know all the Volunteers in the neighbourhood. They were now on the look-out for country Volunteers in the streets of Dublin, and it was their business to murder them. In a letter captured by our Intelligence Department on 1 June 1920 a British general, one of five newly appointed divisional commissioners of the R.I.C., referred to "the new policy of stamping out terrorism by secret murder."

The leader of the Murder Gang was a former Head Constable from Galway, who had originally come to Dublin to identify a prisoner. For a few years previously he had served as an ordinary constable in my own part of Tipperary. He evidently liked the atmosphere of Dublin Castle and the R.I.C. Depot in the Park, for he remained in the city and conducted his own private campaign against the I.R.A. from the Depot. The group of "R.I.C. Political Branch" men whom he enlisted in the notorious Murder Gang might be described as having a natural talent for murder. Kindred spirits, they were mainly renegade Irish like himself, but included also some English, Scottish and Welsh. All of them lived in the Depot. Members of the gang were not only highly paid; in addition, they had received an assurance that, no matter what evidence was brought against them, they would never be obliged to stand trial. They did, as a matter of fact, succeed in murdering a number of our men— and some innocent civilians also—under particularly revolting circumstances. Seemingly, it did not matter how many civilians died if there was any chance of one of our men being amongst them. Some of those people may have been the unfortunate victims of false information, private vengeance, or just the gangsters' lust for blood.

The organisation of the Murder Gang was kept a close secret, even from military and police officials. Its members used assumed names which they changed frequently, and even when giving evidence in secret, they were known only by their ciphers. We knew a good deal about them through our own Intelligence Service. We knew the names of most of the Gang and the murders in which they had taken part. Our Headquarters had provided us with photographs of some of them. They were always armed, dressed in civilian clothes, and usually moved about the city streets in a body, well strung out as a protection against attack. It was very difficult to attack them in the crowded streets of the city without endangering the lives of peaceful civilians.

The full tale of the infamies committed under cover of curfew by the Murder Gang will probably never be told. The Broadstone station was the scene of their first crime in the city. There they met a Volunteer named Howlett on his arrival off an incoming train, and they assassinated him on the platform. On 22 September 1920 they shot John A. Lynch of Kilmallock in his bed at the Royal Exchange Hotel, Dublin. He was not a Volunteer and had never carried arms. In all probability he was murdered in mistake for Liam Lynch. The murder was done by the leader and two other members of the Gang. With these were Captain G. T. Bagally, General Staff, Shipp Street barracks, and a British Intelligence officer named Lieutenant Angliss who posed as an Irishman and used the name "MacMahon." The murder party was accompanied by a small detail of military from Dublin district headquarters. Captain Bagally and Lieutenant Angliss were soon to pay for their part in this atrocious crime, for both were amongst the Secret Service officers who were shot on the morning of Bloody Sunday. The Murder Gang also raided during the hours of curfew the house of a Dublin Volunteer officer named Carroll. He was not at home, but they murdered his aged father instead.

Dublin Castle was the fountain-head of all the British murder gangs operating in various parts of town and country, and the presiding genius who directed murder from there was the notorious Brigadier-General Ormonde Winter, the " Holy Terror," as he was known, who performed his task so well that he was knighted soon after the Treaty was signed. He was chosen to be head of British Intelligence in Dublin Castle, on the recommendation of General Sir Neville Macready, Commander-in-Chief of the military, and General H. H. Tudor, Inspector-General of the police forces. We tried to get Winter at Westland Row station on the night of his arrival to take up office. In an exchange of shots with the police, a bullet ripped the sole off Seán Treacy's boot. Winter's braves murdered my staunch comrades, Dick McKee and Peadar Clancy, Commandant and Vice-Commandant respectively of the Dublin Brigade. Both had been observed by a military-police sergeant named James Ryan, as they entered Fitzpatrick's house off Gloucester Street, in the early hours of Bloody Sunday. Ryan, who lodged off Gloucester Street, and who had been on Intelligence work for some time, telephoned the information to Dublin Castle, and McKee and Clancy were captured in the raid which followed, about 2 a.m. Ryan, who was known in the area as " Shankers " Ryan, was a brother of Becky Cooper, a brothel keeper. His brother-in-law was with him in Hynes' pub in old Gloucester Place, about 10 a.m. on Saturday, 5 February 1921, when he was executed for his treachery. For some time prior to Bloody Sunday we had suspected him of spying, but our request for permission to shoot him was turned down. There was not sufficient evidence against him, we were told.

Conor Clune, a young Irish language student from Clare, was arrested earlier in the night at Vaughan's Hotel, Parnell Square. He had no connection whatsoever with the I.R.A. and had merely availed himself of a " lift " in a motor car, to come from Clare for the week-end. He was a football enthusiast and, as he had to attend to some business in the city, he timed his arrival for the challenge match between Tipperary and Dublin at Croke Park. He went to Vaughan's to discuss Gaelic League business with Piaras Beaslai. All three prisoners were taken to the Castle and foully murdered. They were tortured, battered, bayoneted and then shot through the head. The murderers were led by Captain Hardy, an Orangeman, and Captain King, an Englishman, both notorious members of the Castle Murder Gang.

"Poor Dick was beyond recognition," James MacNamara, one of Collins' agents in the Castle, told Charlie Dalton of the Dublin Brigade. "I saw the battered corpses being taken away to King George V hospital. They flung them into a van. I was nearly mad, but I had to act my part. I had to look on while Captain X (the notorious Captain Hardy) pulled back a canvas screen to satisfy his hate with a last look. He flashed his torch on poor Dick's ghastly face, screaming at him as if the dead ears could still catch an echo of his words, and at the same time hitting the body with his revolver."

Accordingly, when on that night I recognised two of the Gang on the tramcar I did not need to be a Sherlock Holmes to make up my mind that their three companions were also of the same ilk. But it was not the history of the Murder Gang that I was recalling when I realised my predicament. I was in a tight corner. To attempt a retreat from the car would be a plain invitation to them to open fire. Besides, there was the bare possibility that their presence on the car was a mere coincidence. Perhaps they did not recognise me at all. Perhaps they were on some other job.

All these thoughts flashed through my mind in a mere fraction of the time that they take to relate. I had to keep cool so as to avoid betraying by the slightest sign that I was excited or panicky. There was nothing for it but the old game of coolness and bluff that had served me so well on the road to Foynes and at Whitehall a few months before.

I sat down on the three-seater bench at the rear of the car, just at the top of the steps. Then I pulled out a packet of cigarettes and lit one. Immediately two of the Gang sat down on the same bench, one on each side of me. A third remained standing right opposite me, gripping the railings. The other two went along the centre passage to the front of the car. In all my life I never felt less comfortable than at that moment. I realised my danger but saw no way out of it.

Neither they nor I made any move. The car started on its journey, crowded with passengers who little realised the real-life drama that was being enacted. It was after eleven o'clock and everybody was hurrying homeward before the midnight hour when curfew began. If a man were to be seen on the streets after that hour he could well prove to be a target for a hail of bullets.

As the car passed up Parnell Square I began to feel reassured. Previously I had travelled in the company of detectives and policemen who never recognised me. Perhaps my luck was still in. All of a sudden both the man on my right and the man on my left made a simultaneous move. Their right hands went to their hip-pockets. They were about to draw their revolvers. I beat them to the draw. In an instant my three would-be assassins were rushing headlong down the stairs. I was at their heels with my revolver levelled. They sprang from the car on to the street and I followed closely. Now came another moment of suspense. Would they face about and open fire?

It was not a favourable spot for a fight. The streets were crowded with pedestrians. Armed police might appear at any moment. If the three gangsters attempted to fire, the only course for me was to get in the first shot. If they remained inactive, so also could I. But I could not afford to lose time. There was only one more Whitehall tram and I had to get that or run the risk of being picked up by a patrol.

We were in the centre of Dorset Street, almost opposite Gardiner Street Church. I tried a little ruse. I stepped on to the footpath and ran a few strides towards St. Joseph's Terrace. I halted and stamped my feet on the pavement as if I were on the double. At my first move the three men who were a few yards ahead of me quickened their pace and turned into the little avenue which runs parallel to St. Joseph's Terrace. They had been deceived by my manoeuvres and ran to intercept me at the other end.

While their footsteps were still resounding, the last tram from the city came along but did not slow down. I jumped to the platform and left the Murder Gang behind. I often wondered why their confederates who had boarded the tram did not try to apprehend me when I set off in pursuit. Loyalty to comrades did not seem to be their motto, least of all in moments of danger.

I slept that night at Fleming's of Drumcondra. Next

morning I told Seán Treacy of my adventure. "You cannot escape much longer," he laughed uneasily. A few moments later he put his arms around me. There were tears in his eyes while he implored me never again to go out alone. In fact, from that very day we kept almost as close to each other as a pair of goats that have been chained together to prevent them from straying too far afield.

Next morning we went to Mrs. Fitzgerald's of Hollybank Road, almost beside Flemings. Mrs. Fitzgerald was a Tipperary woman, and we had often enjoyed her hospitality. On that day we were tired and sleepy and we spent most of the time in bed.

On the following day we went to Croke Park, the headquarters of the Gaelic Athletic Association. It had been our custom on Sundays to visit Croke Park, provided that there was no urgent matter for our attention. We usually had a game of "Forty-Five" with officials who might be at hand. Andy Harty, D. P. Walsh (both fellow-countymen of mine), Luke O'Toole and Alderman Nowlan were all good friends with whom we often spent a pleasant evening when the football and hurling contests had ended.

I well remember this particular Sunday because it indirectly led up to the fight at Drumcondra. The stakes at our card-games were never high, but at that time a few shillings seemed like riches. On that evening the game proved unusually exciting; the "kitty" gradually blossomed into a nice sum, and I don't mind admitting that I cast jealous eyes on it. Luck favoured me, even in gambling; I won the pool; never since has money been more welcome.

At this particular period our plans were not very definite. They were not altogether of our own making. About a fortnight previously Dinny Lacey had returned to Tipperary and we had promised to join him within a week. Contrary to our usual habit, we had failed to keep our appointment; the fault was not ours. It was due to the action of Headquarters.

The war was going on even better than could have been expected. In the south our men were gaining the upper hand. In spite of torture, burnings and lootings the people were standing by the Volunteers. It was death for the man who dared to harbour a rebel, and yet in every parish shelter was provided for our Flying Columns. In spite of an Anglicised Press, the people had realised that we had adopted the right attitude and that their cause was ours.

Ireland could never have peace or prosperity until we had driven the British out of the country. Delighted by the change in public opinion, Seán and I were becoming reckless. The hotter the fighting, the more proficient became the Irish Republican army. Headquarters, having realised that the rank and file were getting too far ahead of them, began to take a kind of semi-official responsibility for the actions of the Volunteers.

In pursuance of this new policy, Headquarters had now actually planned a certain operation to take place in Dublin for which our help was needed; for that reason we were unable to return to Tipperary as soon as we had arranged. But these plans never matured, and we were kept dallying round the city. A certain event brought us good cheer. I got a tip for a race, a "dead cert" that was to come up at the Phoenix Park races. Luckier still, I was in possession of the money which I had won at Croke Park. All our worldly wealth went on the horse. And it won!

Now for a little of the pleasures of life. In our poverty the few pounds which I had acquired seemed like untold riches. Of course I did not regard it as my personal property; it belonged to our little company. Whatever we had, we shared. We must spend this money before our return to Tipperary. Any day might be our last in this world. A fusillade of bullets might speed our departure from this earth before we had drawn up our wills; the thought which worried us was the possibility that our money might provide the Black-and-Tans with the wherewithal to toast our health when we had gone to glory.

We knew that we had to be ever on the alert. The net was drawing round us. On the night of 10 October 1920 an incident occurred which revealed our constant peril. Seán Treacy and I had decided to stay at the house of Séamus Kirwan, 49 Parnell Street, where we had often stayed. Séamus invariably gave the full run of his house to his fellow countrymen. All his assistants and employees belonged to the I.R.A., and whenever we lodged there they took the precaution of being well-armed.

On this particular night we had just entered when a man rushed in at our heels and told Séamus that "the two men who had just come into the shop had been shadowed." Seán and I rushed out to the street; the tout, who was standing near the door, ran for his life. He was a good judge. We changed our plans and went elsewhere. Hence-

forth we knew that Kirwan's would be a marked house.
I did not stay there again until the period of the Truce.
The warning which we had received on that night illustrates
how loyal the people were to us. Frequently we got
friendly warnings from newsboys and fruit-vendors who had
seen touts hanging about.

Only a few days previously I had met a group of the
Dublin Castle gangsters face to face in Talbot Street. We
recognised each other simultaneously and drew our guns.
They did not bring them to bear on me or attempt to fire.
I don't know why. As I had no desire to engage a whole
group unless forced to do so, I didn't fire. I walked quietly
away, unmolested.

To return to the spending of our winnings. Our first
little dissipation was to go on the following afternoon to
the pictures at La Scala Theatre which had just been opened
in O'Connell Street. In the theatre we met Kay and Dot
Fleming of Drumcondra; with them was Mrs. O'Brien, wife
of Eamon O'Brien of Galbally, who had taken part in the
Knocklong rescue. It must have been a surprise to Mrs.
O'Brien to meet in a cinema the two men whom all the
troops and police in Ireland had been instructed to shoot
at sight. We had grown used to taking these risks. Indeed,
it was quite possible that not one of the audience would
get home without being held up and searched, either at the
theatre door or in the street or in the trams.

We left the theatre together. Just as we stepped into the
street the first man I set eyes upon was one of the men
who had boarded the tram with me a few nights before.
I could make no mistake about him, for he was one of the
two who sat beside me on the tram. Standing on the path
and closely scrutinising the audience as they emerged, he
was pretending to be looking for a friend. I felt certain
that he was looking for me.

For a moment I felt tempted to draw my gun and shoot
him there and then. But I was between the two girls and
I did not want to alarm them. Besides, if he had a con-
federate, the return of fire was sure to endanger the girls.
The five of us were facing for Nelson Pillar, waiting for a
tram to Fleming's house in Drumcondra. As the Pillar is
less than a hundred yards from the theatre, I considered
it safe enough to walk on. I said nothing to the others,
nor did I cast a second glance at the Castle man. I knew

that he must have seen me, and I had a fair idea that he was following us.

Just as we approached the tram, I stepped back to let the others get a few yards in advance. Kay Fleming whispered, "There is a friend following." She must have seen him also. The girls of those days were well trained to use their eyes.

Seán and his three companions stepped on to the tram. I followed immediately behind. As I mounted the footboard I wheeled round sharply and faced my enemy. He read the message in my eye. Had he attempted to board the tram, I would have riddled him. But he was quick to see my move; he slunk back and lost himself in the crowd as our car started for Drumcondra.

At Fleming's we discussed the incident over a cup of coffee. Often since that night I have regretted that I had allowed him to escape scot-free. Had I known as much when I stood on the footboard as I did some hours later, the Crown forces would have been one man the less; that very man or one of his confederates must have boarded the next tram to Drumcondra and picked up our trail.

We left Fleming's about 11 o'clock. In case we had been seen when we entered the house and were still being shadowed, we left by the rear. It was a bright moonlit night. We went as far as Botanic Avenue. Seán and I debated for a few minutes whether we should go round to our friend Mrs. Fitzgerald of Hollybank Road, or go on to Professor Carolan's. We turned to the right and walked to the bridge which spans the Tolka. The streets were already deserted. As we stood for a moment on the bridge to look round and listen, we heard the distant rumbling of military lorries moving out on curfew patrol.

From the bridge to Carolan's is about a seven minutes' walk. It is on the main road to Belfast, and is situated in a middle-class residential quarter. On the left as one goes from the city is situated the Training College for National Teachers; on the right, some distance back from the road, is another well-known institution—All Hallows Ecclesiastical College.

We had a latchkey to Professor Carolan's house, "Fernside." It was one of the many latchkeys in our possession, all of which had been given to us by friends to whose houses we were welcome at whatever hour we might wish to call.

I had already stayed a few nights at "Fernside," having been introduced to the family by Peter Fleming. I well remember how heartily I was received by the family on that first occasion, and how thoughtfully Mr. Carolan himself showed me over the whole house, calling my special attention to the back garden. He pointed out a low wall which offered the best means of escape in the event of a raid. "I don't expect you'll need it," he said, "but it is no harm to know your way about." He was a kindly lovable man whose clear earnest eyes would inspire one with confidence. A native of Sligo town, for some years past he had been on the teaching staff of St. Patrick's Training College.

The house is one of a type common enough in suburban districts; a two-storeyed brick building of eight or nine apartments. A grass plot, fenced with iron railings separates "Fernside" from the roadway; on the left a door served as tradesmen's side-entrance. In an emergency an active man would have no difficulty in springing over such an obstacle. At the rear of the house is a long garden which, is separated from the adjoining garden by a seven-foot wall. Close to the house and directly under the bedroom window was a conservatory.

On all previous occasions we had reached the house before 11 p.m.; on this night we did not arrive until 11.30. As there was no light to be seen, we concluded that the family had already retired. We let ourselves in as noiselessly as possible and made our way to the room which was reserved for us on the first floor at the back. This room overlooked the conservatory, the end portion of which adjoined the wall of the house directly under the window-sill of our bedroom. I am convinced that no member of the family was aware of our presence in the house.

We undressed and shared the solitary bed, Seán occupying the inside position beside the wall. I placed a loaded revolver on a chair which I had set down close to the bed. Seán had a loaded Parabellum under his pillow. We did not feel sleepy. For a while we chatted about our future plans and the prospect of our return to Tipperary. Our conversation lagged. My mind became obsessed by a strange presentiment. Perhaps it was the after-effects of my recent perilous adventures. I tried to sleep but for once sleep would not come. Seán, too, was still awake, but not disposed to chat. I felt half-inclined to tell him of the foreboding that was disturbing me, but he was himself the first to speak:

"Dan, do you find any strange feeling coming over you? I can't sleep, can you?"

He had, in fact, put the very questions that were agitating my mind. I told him so, and we both laughed.

"We may have a raid to-night, Seán," I said, half joking. "I wonder if there is any danger that we were shadowed on our way to the house? If we were surrounded in this place, we'd have a very poor chance of escaping."

A full minute passed before Seán replied: "Somehow, Dan, I wouldn't mind at this stage if we were killed. The war will continue whatever happens; if we're to be killed, I hope that we will die together." Another brief silence, and we both dozed off.

Suddenly we sat up in the bed. We could distinctly hear the heavy tramp of marching men. There was a low murmur of voices at the rear of the house. Through our window shone the beam of a dazzling searchlight. A single peal from a nearby church-tower signalled one o'clock.

There was a crash of glass at the front of the house, and the hall-door was burst open. From the stairs came the sound of rushing footsteps.

We sprang out of bed. Simultaneously we gripped our revolvers. Fingers were groping on our door. I held my breath. Seán pressed my arm and whispered, "Good-bye, Dan, until we meet above." Crack! Crack! Two bullets came whizzing through the door. Crack! Crack! My German Mauser pistol was replying.

There was no light save the flash of the shots. Outside on the landing a heavily-accented "English" voice was shouting, "Where is Ryan? Where is Ryan?"

Bullets were flying from every direction, and our door had been pushed partly open. I blazed away on to the landing. Blood was streaming from my right thumb, but I felt no pain. I heard a thud on the landing as if somebody had fallen.

Seán could not find his glasses. This was a severe handicap to him as he was very short-sighted. Worse still, his gun had jammed. I shouted to him to get back to the window. He stepped back, just as another bullet buried itself in the wardrobe. I felt a sharp pain in the region of my spine. Feeling certain that my days were numbered, I told him to make his escape, and that I would join him when I had fought my way through. I raked the landing with my Mauser and heard the sound of footsteps retreating down the stairs. Towards the back of the house I could hear the sharp ping of rifle shots.

I dashed out of the room on to the landing, and saw a group of soldiers coming up the stairs, their electric torches pin-pointing me as a target. One bullet grazed my fore-head, another passed through the fleshy portion of my thigh; two hit me in the calves of my legs and one lodged in my right lung. But I still kept my stand and fired at the raiders until the gun was empty. As a matter of fact, when I pulled the trigger for one more shot, I thought that the mechanism had either jammed or had become overheated from the constant firing. For a moment my case seemed hopeless; but I discovered that the last bullet had been fired. I reloaded. I knew by this time that the house was surrounded and that there was little hope of escape. But the rage of battle had taken possession of me. I was going to be killed; but I would sell my life dearly.

As I blazed into the group of soldiers there was a hurried rush for safety. They were now in retreat and I was pursuing them down the stairs. When I got to the first floor they were charging headlong into the street. I gave them a parting shot. There was no further target for my Mauser. Now and again I heard the sharp report of rifles being fired at the rear of the house, mingled with occasional groans and cries. My heart was grieved to hear the wailing of Carolan's young son.

I rushed back to my room. At the door I tripped over two dead bodies; a third was writhing on the floor, groaning in anguish. I had to pull them out of the way before I could close the door. I don't know how I had missed tripping over them when I charged out of the room. In the heat of battle one does not notice everything that is taking place.

Once back in my room, I banged the door and turned the key in the lock. I knew that I had not a moment to spare; for, with the large contingent of troops which they had apparently brought on the raid, they were bound to make another attack. I sprang to the window. A search-light played for a moment on the back of the house and a fusillade shattered the panes of glass.

The lower half of the window was open. Seán had made his escape by that exit. I stepped on to the window-sill and dropped to the roof of the conservatory. In the clear moon-light I could discern the glitter of several steel helmets. The soldiers were blazing at me. Before I could drop from the conservatory I realised that I would have to fight my way through them.

With the revolver which I held in my left hand I smashed a hole in the glass roof. Then I gripped a beam and swung from it, my German pistol intent on its target and making sweet music in my ears. Right well did it accomplish its task, for within a minute there was not a soldier to be seen.

I was still dangling from the roof of the glasshouse. I swung back on the roof and jumped to the ground.

I looked around for my comrade. There was no sign of him. I called out his name, but got no reply. I lay flat on the ground to avoid offering an easy mark for any venturesome Tommy who might put his head over the garden wall. I continued to call out for Seán. But there was no reply. I thought that he might have been hit as he was leaving through the open window; perhaps he lay wounded in the conservatory. I began to fear that he had fallen into their hands. I consoled myself with the thought that after all he might have got away, though the chance was a poor one.

I had been fighting on the landing and on the stairs for several minutes; when I had not returned to the room, Seán may have concluded that I was killed while he was trying to get his revolver to function.

I had neither hat, boots nor overcoat. I had had only barely time to slip on my trousers and jacket. I was bleed-ing from head to foot, but I had to move quickly. I was even beginning to feel that I might escape.

While I was figuring out what course to take, the enemy returned to the attack. Several grenades burst around me quite close to the conservatory. I steeled my will for further conflict and rose from the ground. A short distance away I saw that low dividing wall which my host had been so careful to point out on my first visit. I appreciated his foresight as I made for the garden-wall; a little distance from the glass-house I found the dead bodies of two soldiers. Then I knew Seán had passed that way.

He might have escaped, I began to hope; but there was still the danger that he had been shot when he had reached further down the garden.

Just as I came to the wall a soldier's head appeared outside. He saw me and levelled his rifle, at the same time calling on me to halt. He fired and missed. I fired, too. When I dropped over the wall, clear of Carolan's garden, I stumbled over his body. I don't know whether he was dead or badly wounded.

Another group of soldiers close at hand opened fire on me; this must have been the party who had been ordered to cover the rear of the house. They may have mistaken the exact position or perhaps their timing was bad. Be that as it may, I pumped shots at them in return as I rushed for the nearest wall. I got over but did not recognise my surroundings. I continued to make my way through plots fenced by low strands of wire. I cleared the last fence and found myself on a thoroughfare and was almost instantly confronted by an armoured car. I fired at the man in the open turret and I must have got him. For a few moments the occupants held their fire. When I had covered about twenty paces they opened up with a machine-gun. The bullets sprayed the walls and sent up showers of splinters from the roadway and from the sidewalk but never once was I hit. By this time I knew that I was on the main road, between Carolan's house and Drumcondra bridge. It would be madness to continue along the road; if the armoured car did not pursue me, I was almost certain to run into some of their outposts near the bridge.

On my right, as I ran towards the city, was the limestone wall which surrounds St. Patrick's Training College. Could I once scale that wall and get into the College grounds, my chances of escape were good. But it was about ten feet high. I had neither boots nor socks; the big toe of my right foot was broken and causing me more pain than all the other wounds. I was nearly blinded with the blood that flowed down my forehead. I had received several gashes from the broken glass. But, when a man is fighting for his life, he gets strength that he has not at ordinary times. Mustering all my energy, I sprang from the ground and caught hold of a coping-stone. In later years, whenever I passed along that road, it was a source of wonder to me that I could have accomplished such a feat. When I got to the top of the wall I felt almost happy. My hope grew stronger. I dropped down and faced southwards through the College grounds. I was beginning to lose consciousness. I have no recollection of having scaled the high wall at the other end of the College grounds nor of my journey through Millburn Avenue or Milimount Terrace. And yet, some interior voice must have warned me that I was still within a few hundred yards of "Fernside"; at any moment I might once more run into a group of soldiers. I crawled along as noiselessly as I could. I was guided solely by instinct. I was dazed; and yet able to drag myself along. I had lost all sense of time and distance.

At last I reached the bank of a river. I knew that it must be the Tolka. There was no friend's house convenient in which I could seek shelter. My one aim was to put some distance between me and my pursuers. I dared not venture on to the road and look for a bridge. I had to cross the river, and there was only one way of doing it. Fortunately, it was not deep. Up to that moment I had become oblivious of my wounds but, when I saw the water turn crimson as I waded through, I began to fear that I would not have the strength to cross. I braced myself for a final effort and scrambled to the opposite bank. I saw that I was close to the rear of houses. I could struggle no further. I was bleeding freely. My only hope, if I were not to die of exhaustion, was to seek the shelter of one of these roofs.

I do not know what instinct guided me when I selected one particular back door. It was as if an angel had whispered that this door and this only, held out hope to me.

I knocked. I realised well enough what a spectacle I must have presented at such an unearthly hour, half-clad, dishevelled and blood-stained.

For the second time I knocked. A man opened the door. My appearance was sufficient explanation; I mumbled that I needed shelter, and instantly swooned. As though from far away I heard his words: "I do not approve of gunmen, I shall call the military." A woman's voice reprimanded him: "If you do, I'll report you to Michael Collins."

For a short time I relapsed into unconsciousness. When I came to, I experienced their kindness of heart. They did not ask me who I was, or how I had received my wounds. They simply said, "Come in. Whatever we can do for you we'll do it."

The woman speedily summoned Nurse Long who lived nearby. They dressed my wounds and gave me some stimulant, procured by the nurse from my friends, the Flemings. She risked her life as she had to pass twice through the excited cordon of soldiers.

I learned later that my good Samaritans were Fred Holmes

and his wife. They tended me with the care and attention that they would have bestowed upon their own son. There was no need to tell them how I had come to be in such a plight; I was a stranger and yet they took me in and saved my life. Gratitude is but a poor word by which to express my feelings towards that family. Later in the morning I told them who I was. They assured me that everything that lay in their power would be done to enable me to reach a place of safety. I well knew that I could not prolong my stay in a house which was less than half-a-mile from the scene of the fight.

In the early hours of the morning Mrs. Holmes took a note to Phil Shanahan's for delivery to Dick McKee. I wanted to be removed as soon as possible. I also wanted to report to Headquarters that Seán Treacy had been killed.

While I was awaiting the reply, I learned from the people of the house that in each of the houses on either side a Black-and-Tan was lodging. You can imagine how lucky I was to have selected that particular back gate.

In a short time Joe Lawless, Maurice Brennan and Tom Kelly arrived by car. They had been sent by Dick McKee to take me to the Mater Hospital, where he had already made arrangements for my reception. I was provided with an outfit—my jacket and trousers were in ribbons—and carried to the car. My keenest regret was not for my suit of clothes but for the six pound notes and the watch which I had left behind in the bedroom. Probably some enterprising officer enjoyed one good night out of his windfall. I need hardly say that my losses did not form the subject of compensation-awards when the Truce came.

I was driven along Botanic Road and through Phibsboro' towards the Mater Hospital. At Phibsboro' corner a D.M.P. man motioned to us to halt. For a moment we feared that something was amiss, but relief came in a few moments. We were merely being asked to slow down while a convoy of Auxiliaries passed on their way to raid some houses in the locality in their quest for Seán and myself.

We continued on our journey and approached the entrance to the hospital in Eccles Street. I saw Dick McKee, himself a very much wanted man, moving slowly along the sidewalk. With a slight wave of his hand he motioned to the driver to pass the hospital. A little further down he crossed to tell us that we could not go into the hospital for some time as two Inspectors of the Dublin Metropolitan

Police with some military and Auxiliaries were actually raiding the hospital in their search for wounded men.

"Dan," he said, as he gripped my hand for a moment, "ye got the very men whom we had marked down for special attention even if it took us years to meet them."

Our car crossed from Dorset Street into Mountjoy Square, and finally drove into an old stable in Great Charles Street. This was one of the favourite dumping-grounds for the arms of the Dublin Brigade; it was discovered shortly afterwards by the enemy.

It is easy to imagine how sick and tired of life I was as I was being driven into this old stable; picture my delight at seeing Seán Treacy waiting to welcome me! He had escaped without as much as a scratch. Briefly—for he had not many minutes to spare—he told me of his adventures. He had got safely through the rear of the house, fully convinced that I had been killed. For hours he had wandered almost naked through an unfamiliar countryside until at last, as dawn broke, he knocked at a door in a desperate effort to gain shelter. The door was opened by his own cousin, Phil Ryan of Finglas! Truly, the fates were propitious on that morning.

In our joy at the re-union we almost forgot our peril; the streets of Dublin were being searched that day as never before by hundreds of troops. Our scouts finally reported that the way to the Mater was clear, for the police and military had left the hospital. The boys were anxious that no time should be lost until I was placed in skilled hands; we moved on at once towards the Mater. They took me by stretcher into the hospital and, as I lay on that stretcher, I shook hands with Seán Treacy for the last time.

Little did I think on that evening that never again on this earth would I set eyes on my faithful friend, one who was dearer to me than a brother. Had I known then that it was to be our last meeting in this world, I would have had little heart to bear up with my plight. Poor Seán! the comrade of my adventures, the sharer of my hopes. His face is always before me, and until my last hour on this earth his memory will remain forever green in my heart. I have often knelt at his grave in Kilfeacle to have a word with him, telling him, in the words of Charles Kickham, about "the fate of poor old Ireland and of sorrows of my own."

When I arrived at the Mater Hospital I was taken to

DEATH IN THE AFTERNOON

It was late in the afternoon of 14 October 1920. Fifteen years old John J. Horgan was in the vicinity of Nelson's Pillar. He was apprenticed to Maunder Brothers, pictorial representatives in Dublin of *The Daily Sketch* and *The Daily Graphic*. Horgan carried a press camera and was in search of his first scoop. In search of a scoop also was Gordon Lewis, Pathe Gazette movie newsman, and from a window in Talbot Street he had his camera trained expectantly on the Republican Outfitters, the much-raided stores across the street. Each was to get his scoop with spectacular success—for both were on the spot to "shoot" the Talbot Street gun-battle which resulted in the death of Seán Treacy, two enemy agents and a number of civilians. John J. Horgan's pictures were given world-wide circulation by an international press agency; audiences in most parts of the world saw the Pathe news film made by Gordon Lewis, and many others saw it in recent years as part of the Gael Linn film, *Saoirse?* Some frames from the news film, and the Horgan pictures are reproduced by courtesy respectively of Maurice Baum, Dublin; and of Seán Horgan, Dublin, son of the late John J. Horgan.

Seán Treacy lying dead beneath the window of Spiedel's pork shop in Talbot Street, Dublin. Propped up near the halldoor on the left and partly hidden by some soldiers is Christian, one of the British intelligence agents who was fatally wounded by Treacy—from the Gordon Lewis sequence.

John J. Horgan's dramatic pictures. Last seconds in the life of Lieutenant Price, British intelligence officer, as he opened fire on Seán Treacy to prevent his retreat in the direction of Nelson's Pillar. Auxiliaries who arrived on the scene after the shooting had ended found Price beyond human aid. Treacy had killed Price instantly and fatally wounded Christian, another British intelligence officer, before he was himself shot dead, from behind, by a third enemy agent.

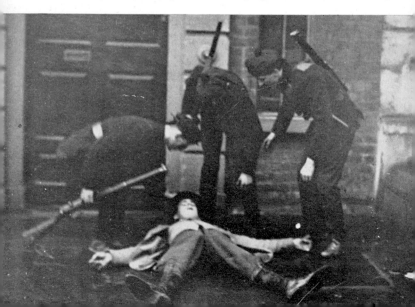

Christian, already dying, was borne to one of the military lorries by a number of plain-clothes men who included Castle touts and members of the Murder Gang. Civilians who had sought refuge in private houses and shops nearby, rushed to the scene when the shooting had ceased —from the Gordon Lewis sequence.

The dead were removed to the lorries and taken away by the military whilst hundreds of curious civilians looked on. Seán Treacy's body was taken to the King George V Hospital where the remains were identified—from the Gordon Lewis sequence.

The armoured car which was used in the Talbot Street shooting and the British officer who commanded it. To make certain of killing Treacy, a machine-gunner opened fire without regard for the safety of the British agents who were at grips with him—from the Gordon Lewis sequence.

Members of the Murder Gang—a photograph secured by I.R.A. intelligence and numbered to identify the men in it. Those numbered 1, 2 and 3 were Irishmen.

This is the room in Dublin Castle in which Dick McKee, Peadar Clancy and Conor Clune were murdered on Bloody Sunday. The photographs were "staged" by the British propaganda department in the Castle, some hours after the murders had been committed. It was part of a clumsy attempt to prove that the men had been killed whilst attempting to escape.

Michael Sadlier, Dinny Lacey and Dinny Sadlier (brother of Michael), all three of whom fell on the Republican side in the Civil War.

Scene near the entrance to Dublin Castle, at Dame Street, shortly after the Truce had come into effect at 11 a.m. on 11 July 1921. The Castle was then the headquarters of British civil and military administration in Ireland and the focal point of the opposition to the aspirations of the Irish people.

Paddy Dalton (left), known as "The Armoured Car," and his great pal, Martin ("Sparkie") Breen, both of whom were killed fighting on the Republican side in the Civil War. They lie side by side in the Republican Plot in St. Michael's Cemetery, Tipperary.

Lying-in-state of General Liam Lynch, Chief of Staff of the Republican forces in the Civil War. He fell in action on the Knockmealdowns, 10 April 1923.

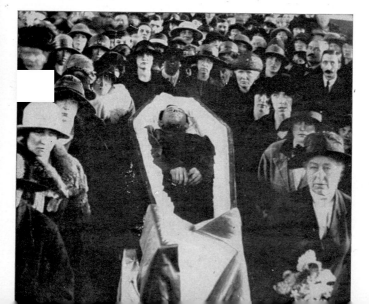

the private nursing home and Surgeon Barnaville took me under his special care. I am convinced that I owe my life to his unceasing attention.

Next day D. P. Walshe called and told me the full story of the Drumcondra fight or at least that portion of it which I did not already know. He had learned some of the details from the newspapers, the rest from our Intelligence Department.

It seems that in spite of our precautions we had been shadowed to Fleming's and later to Carolan's by the very man whom we had seen outside the theatre. Their Secret Service was able to report that "Breen and Lacey" had gone to "Fernside."

I have never discovered whether Seán Treacy was actually mistaken for Dinny Lacey, or whether the similarity of the surnames had confused the spy.

At once every "G" man in the Castle was mobilised for the raid, but they refused point-blank to go on the job. Their superior officers were incensed at this display of cowardice and mutiny; but they could not afford to betray the weakness of their position by letting the news leak out that the entire political branch had refused to go on a raid. The "G" men were not punished for their indiscipline; but with a view to covering up the mutiny, they were ordered on that same morning to raid the shop owned by J. J. Walsh (Postmaster-General in the early days of the Free State régime).

Meanwhile the military chiefs had been informed of the position. They had asked what kind of a job it would be, and were told that they might expect plenty of gun-play.

I learned later that one of the officers was a Major G. O. S. Smyth, member of a blood-thirsty, ill-starred family. His brother, Colonel G. B. F. Smyth, R.I.C. Divisional Commissioner for Munster, made the notorious address to the Royal Irish Constabulary in Listowel barracks: "If persons approaching carry their hands in their pockets, or seem to be suspect characters, shoot them down. You may make mistakes occasionally, and innocent persons may be shot, but that cannot be helped. No policeman will get into trouble for shooting any man." He was shot in Cork for those words. I had tried to get him near Clonmel but I missed him. I got the credit, wrongfully, for the shooting of this man. At that time Major Smyth had been on service in Egypt. He applied for Intelligence work in Ireland, was accepted, and brought over eleven picked men with him to avenge the death of his brother. They became known as the " Cairo Gang."

When he heard that I had been traced to a house in Drumcondra, he called his braves to help him " capture Breen alive and skin him." He had been warned that I was quick on the draw. " Not quick enough for me, the rat! " he affirmed. I'm still in my skin. He was the first to be killed on that night. With him fell another officer, Captain A. L. White. A corporal named Worth, who accompanied them on the way to our bedroom, was severely wounded. These casualties the British officially admitted but we knew that their losses were heavier. As a matter of fact, many years later I was having a chat with Joe Connolly, Captain of the Dublin Fire Brigade. One of his men said to me, " How are you, Dan ? " I asked him who he was. " I am one of the men," he replied, " who went with the ambulances to clean up after yourself and Seán Treacy. We took away thirteen dead men from ' Fernside ' and its precincts."

Some hours after the fight at " Fernside " tracker-dogs were brought on the scene. They followed my trail from the house and on through the College grounds as far as the river-bank but they lost the scent when they came to the Tolka. Fifty bloodhounds had been specially imported by Brigadier-General Ormonde Winter for the tracking down of members of the Irish Republican army.

What saddened me most of all was the news that our faithful friend, Professor Carolan, had been very seriously wounded. The official report stated that the Professor had been shot in the first exchange of firing. This was the report of a secret military inquiry concerning the shooting of the officers.

Long before this event the British had forbidden the holding of coroner's inquests. Ordinary jurors, being honest men, would insist upon finding out the truth and would thus expose the whole murder-campaign.

John Carolan survived for several days. He was actually in the Mater Hospital at the same time as myself, but in a different part of the institution. For a time there were high hopes of his recovery. During that period he made in the presence of witnesses a statement which will be found in the Dublin newspapers of 21 and 22 October of 1920. It was the death-bed protestation of an honourable man. A further proof of its accuracy is that the newspapers which published it were not suppressed, as they would have been within half an hour were the report inaccurate.

In that statement Professor Carolan made it quite clear that at the time when he was shot we had already made our escape. We had been a quarter of an hour out of the house, he declared, before he was put standing with his face to the wall and deliberately shot by a British officer. When he opened the door for the raiders they enquired who was in the house; the faithful man said he thought that Ryan was the name, a name quite common in our part of the country. Our accents would not prove his answer to be false had we replied to questions about our identity. That accounted for the shouts we heard, "Where is Ryan? Where is Ryan?"

A revolver was kept pressed to the poor man's temple all the time and, when the gangsters saw that their leaders had been killed, they murdered him as a reprisal. Generous, noble and patriotic, he dared to shelter us when few of our friends would have done so. I shall always think of him and his family's kindness to us, and regret from the bottom of my heart that he met such a sad death. May he rest in peace.

On the evening of 12 October, while I was being taken into the Mater, the village of Finglas, only one mile distant from the house where I had been befriended, was invested by hundreds of British troops in full war kit. They had either traced Seán to that district or had suspected that I had travelled farther than I actually did. Every house in the village and the surrounding countryside was searched, but in vain.

One other sequel to the Drumcondra fight I must relate before I proceed with my own story. James and Michael Fleming, and Éamonn O'Brien's father, who was staying with the Flemings, were arrested that morning. That is the best proof that our footsteps were dogged on that night. Michael Fleming was sentenced to three years' penal servitude for refusing to give information about Treacy, Hogan, Robinson, Lacey or myself. He had been offered a bribe of £10,000 by Lt. Colonel D. L. McLean, Chief Intelligence Officer. His sentence was later reduced to nine months. James Fleming was released after a few hours, and Éamonn O'Brien's father was released almost immediately. McLean was one of the Intelligence officers shot on Bloody Sunday. Some months later in the House of Commons attention was called to my speeding of Smyth and his companion on their passage to eternity. I quote from House of Commons Debates:,

IRELAND

Murders

Lieut-Commander KENWORTHY asked the Chief State Solicitor for Ireland whether a reward has been offered for the death or capture of the honourable Member for South Cork; if so, whether he will state the sum of money offered; whether rewards have been offered for the death or capture of other leading Irishmen; what are the amounts; whether any rewards have been claimed; whether any rewards have been paid out; and on what vote or votes will these sums be found?

MR. BROWNE: The answer to the first and third parts of the question are in the negative. The second and fourth therefore do not arise. The only case in any way similar to that indicated in the question is an award which was offered for the capture of Daniel Breen who, there were strong grounds for believing, was the murderer of Major Smyth, D.S.O., M.C., and Captain White, D.S.O., at the house of Professor Carolan, "Fernside," Drumcondra, on the 11th October last. The award was offered in the case of this man solely on the ground that he was wanted for the specific crime of murder.

Lieut-Colonel J. WARD: Was the award offered successful in bringing the murderer to justice?

MR. BROWNE: No, Sir. I am sorry to say it was not.

Lieut-Colonel WARD: Would a larger reward have any possible result? This murderer ought really to be brought to justice.

MR. BROWNE: That will be considered.

Thursday, 14 October 1920 is a date I shall never forget. It was my third day in the hospital.

In the afternoon one of the Sisters came quickly into my room. Before she spoke I could read from the expression on her face that she had serious news. A few hours previously I had heard some firing in the neighbourhood, but that, I had been told, had been an encounter at Phibsboro' corner where an attempt was made to capture an armoured car; one of our men lost his life in the effort. The ambush had taken place only three hundred yards from the bed on which I was lying. But the Sister had more serious news. The hospital was surrounded by troops and armoured cars, and a search for me was in progress. My bed was beside the window. I raised myself on my elbow particularly from Surgeon Barnaville and the nuns. It must not be forgotten that at this time the British had issued orders that any doctor or nurse who attended a patient suffering from gunshot wounds was obliged to report the case to the Castle. The purpose of the order was to enable the police to track down wounded men. To their credit, be it said, the members of the medical profession, irrespective of their political views, refused point-blank to obey such an edict.

My wounds began to heal so rapidly that I was able to get out of bed for a short time each day. About one week after my arrival an exciting incident took place. Our whole block was surrounded and I began to fear that the sleuths had picked up my trail. From my window I could see the troops taking up their positions. I moved towards the skylight—skylights had often proved useful to us. From my position I saw an Auxiliary on the roof with a rifle in his hand. This time, I concluded, there was no chance for me. I was caught like a rat in a trap.

I returned to the front window and could see a solid line of khaki and steel lined up on the street. A throng of curious sightseers had gathered. Some, I suppose, were full of anxiety lest any soldier of Ireland should be entrapped. Others, doubtless, were proud of the Empire's army, and fondly hoping that it would gain further laurels in the reconquest of Ireland.

As I surveyed the mass of spectators, I recognised the figure of Mick Collins. Sometime later I learned the reason of his presence. He had seen the troops moving in the direction of the district in which I was a patient, and had actually collected a few of the boys who would be ready to attempt a rescue. Their services were not needed. The soldiers raided almost every house in the locality, including the house next door, but they never entered Dr. Barry's. I felt grateful for Mick's solicitude.

It was considered advisable to remove me once again. Early in November I was taken to Dun Laoghaire to the house of Mrs. Barry, where Miss O'Connor and Miss Mason tended me with care. I made a rapid recovery. I had been there only three or four days when once more almost all the houses in the avenue were raided. The British spies were hot on the trail but losing the scent.

Late on Sunday evening, 21 November, I received a detailed account of the dramatic events that had happened since the early hours of that day of terror, appropriately named Bloody

and looked out. On the street I could plainly see the Glengarry caps of the Auxiliaries who were on guard.

"It is all up this time, Dan," I reflected, "and you can't even pull a gun!"

Somehow I felt resigned. For the sweet music of the shots which I had heard that morning told me that the fight would continue. I cannot say that I was not excited. Now and again I heard the throbbing of engines. Perhaps they would go without finding me. But they were only driving up and down in order to keep back the crowds. I looked out once more and saw that the Auxiliaries were still there. The minutes grew into hours. Would the raid ever end? When would the door open to admit the raiders to my room? After a two-hours' search they departed without even coming near that section of the hospital in which I had been placed.

It was only when they had moved away that I learned the purpose of their swoop. On that very morning a young Volunteer named Matt Furlong had been wounded in an accident which occurred near Dunboyne, a village which is sixteen miles distant from the city. He had been experimenting with high explosives to be used in a Stokes trench mortar. His comrades rushed him in a dying condition to the Mater, and the police learned of his presence in the hospital. He bore a close resemblance to me. The poor fellow died while the raid was in progress. The Black-and-Tans may have concluded that they had seen the last of Dan Breen.

EXECUTIONS AND REPRISALS

While I lay prostrate on my bed in the Mater Hospital my faithful comrade, Seán Treacy, was not idle. All his concern was for my safety. When he learned on Thursday evening that the hospital was surrounded, he went immediately to Headquarters to organise a rescue party of which he himself would be a member. In less than one hour he and other trusty comrades were mobilising their men. In his zeal for my safety he forget about himself and went openly through the principal streets of the city. He was shadowed, and I am firmly convinced that the man who shadowed him was the very man who three days previously had traced us to Drumcondra.

Seán had almost completed the arrangements for the

rescue when he went to the "Republican Outfitters" of Talbot Street to have the final details settled. This was a shop owned in partnership by Tom Hunter and Peadar Clancy. It was perhaps the best known meeting-centre in the city for members of the Irish Republican army, but it was so closely watched that it was never advisable to remain there for any length of time.

When Seán arrived at the shop, he found Dick McKee and the sons of Count Plunkett, George and Jack, who were attached to the Headquarters staff; also present were Joe Vyze and Leo Henderson, officers of the Dublin Brigade.

Peadar Clancy and a lady-friend had just left the shop and had only got as far as Nelson Pillar when they saw an armoured car and two lorries filled with soldiers dash from O'Connell Street into Talbot Street. Even though Peadar surmised that the shop was about to be raided, he saw no possibility of giving word to the boys. In the space of one minute the raiders had arrived at the drapery establishment. Seán Treacy was standing near the door when the lorries pulled up. One of the Volunteers, warned of danger by a sixth sense, ran from the door to the street and immediately a soldier sprang from the lorry to intercept him. At the same time an Auxiliary Intelligence officer called Christian who was dressed in civilian clothes, jumped from the first lorry and shouted: "That is not he. Here is the man we want." He rushed towards Seán Treacy who was about to throw his leg across the bicycle which was resting on the kerb. Actually Treacy might have made good his escape had he not taken the wrong bike, probably McKee's, which was too big for him, thereby losing valuable seconds. Seán saw that he was cornered and pulled his gun, but from the first it was a hopeless fight. In spite of the odds against him, Treacy did not waver. He grappled with an Intelligence officer, Lieutenant Price, who was in civilian clothes, and shot him dead. In addition, he inflicted serious wounds on Christian. Meanwhile, another enemy agent had crept up from behind, and from a distance of about five yards shot Treacy, who slumped to the ground.

The whole contingent of British troops and Auxiliaries, regardless even of their own comrades who had been in grips with Seán, turned their rifles and machine gun on the man whom they feared. In this burst of firing, two civilians who came in the line of fire were also killed and a constable of the D.M.P. was severely wounded.

During the days that followed, no one breathed a word to me about the fight that had taken place in Talbot Street. I am not given either to superstition or to flights of imagination, and yet I knew beyond any shadow of doubt that Seán Treacy was dead. I saw him standing at the foot of my bed with a radiant smile on his countenance. Towards nightfall Mick Collins came to see me. "Where is Seán?" I asked. Mick averted his eyes and replied, "He's out in the country." Ten days passed before I learned the full story.

Seán Treacy's body was taken to King George V hospital. The remains were identified by Norah O'Keeffe and Mollie Gleeson before removal to the Pro-Cathedral, Marlborough Street. Next day the coffin was conveyed by train to Limerick Junction and thence to Solohead church. When the funeral took place next day to Kilfeacle graveyard a solid phalanx of mourners extended from Solohead to Kilfeacle, a distance of five miles. The day was observed as a day of mourning in Tipperary, and all the neighbouring towns and villages. Banks and business premises were closed and blinds remained drawn. An order was issued by the O.C. British forces, Tipperary, that there must be no military parade. This order had to be complied with; otherwise, the procession would not be allowed to proceed. The Volunteers evaded the regulation by walking in single file on either side of the road. At Barronstown, two hundred cycles were seized and brought to Tipperary military barracks. In spite of the official repressive measures British soldiers openly paid tribute to a gallant opponent by saluting as the hearse passed by. At the graveside, Con Maloney, Brigade-Adjutant, delivered a brief and poignant oration. When the green sod was rolled over the grave three volleys were fired by Volunteers who melted away in the crowd. Seán Treacy's last resting place at Kilfeacle has become a place of pilgrimage for all who revere his memory. His name has been inscribed in letters of gold on the roll of Ireland's patriots.

As it was considered likely that the Mater Hospital would be raided again in an attempt to discover me, Gearóid O'Sullivan and Rory O'Connor brought me by motor to Dr. Alice Barry's house on the south side of the city. I shall always remember with gratitude the devoted care which I received from every member of the hospital staff,

Sunday. Fifteen enemy agents had been marked down for execution on that morning. Four escaped. Two Auxiliaries who became involved were shot dead near Mount Street bridge. Incidentally, what has always been referred to as the "tragic error" of the shooting of Captain McCormick of the Royal Veterinary Corps, in the Gresham Hotel, is a myth perpetuated from some early writers. I have no doubt that he was not shot by mistake. One of the Gresham Hotel execution squad confirmed that he was on their list as a spy, and that his mission to buy mules was his cover. These British officers, seeming to live like ordinary citizens, were in reality spies. When a country is at war, spies who have been unmasked must face the penalty. Even British Ministers justified the employment of spies by professing that Britain was "at war with Ireland." It could not be allowed that one set of rules should apply for their minions and another for Irishmen, and the fact that even the British ministers acknowledged the existence of a state of war was proved by the agreement for the Truce, the parties to which were the commanders of the British military forces in Ireland and the representatives of the Irish Republican army.

That morning's operation was one of the most successful ever effected in Dublin. Our side suffered some casualties. Frank Teeling was captured and sentenced to death, but he escaped from Kilmainham jail before the execution could take place. Paddy Moran was tried for having taken part in the shooting of one of the officers, even though at the time of the shooting he was four miles from the scene. He was hanged in Mountjoy jail on 14 March 1921. I knew Paddy well. I met him for the first time at Mrs. O'Doherty's in Connaught Street, Dublin. He was an upright man and a faithful soldier of Ireland.

Diabolical reprisals were taken later on that day for the execution of the British spies. Large detachments of Auxiliaries and Black-and-Tans drove to Croke Park where ten thousand people, many of whom had not even heard of the early morning shooting, were spectators at the football match between Tipperary and Dublin. The British forces surrounded the grounds and instantly discharged volley after volley into the crowd, killing fourteen people and wounding fifty-seven.

The second reprisal touched me more closely. It was the murder, already described, of Peadar Clancy and Dick McKee. Sir Hamar Greenwood, instructed by his agents of Dublin Castle, invented the usual villainous lying explanation. It was stated that Clancy and McKee had attacked the guard and attempted to escape. Imagine two highly intelligent officers attacking an armed guard in the heart of a fortress from which escape was well-nigh impossible. An independent medical examination showed that Peadar and Dick and also Conor Clune had been subjected to the most incredible tortures before they were done to death.

Mick Collins and Tom Cullen made the arrangements for the obsequies at the Pro-Cathedral. I mention this to their everlasting credit.

Dick and Peadar! Two of our bravest officers; the staunchest supporters of our war policy. They met their death only five weeks after Seán Treacy and did not even get the chance of putting up some show of resistance.

From Dun Laoghaire, Éamon Fleming motored me across the Dublin mountains and brought me to a farmhouse in East Wicklow. Éamon introduced me under an assumed name, but the man of the house laughed heartily and assured him that he knew me well as Dan Breen, for he had been a patient in the same section of the Mater Hospital when I was there some weeks before.

At this time I had to keep moving rapidly from place to place. Fresh troops were now being poured into the country. Hundreds of Black-and-Tan recruits were being mustered. Every assurance was given to them that they need not fear that they would incur any penalty for letting themselves loose in a campaign of murder, loot and arson. And they took the hint.

CHAPTER FOURTEEN

WITH THE THIRD TIPPERARY BRIGADE

I SPENT A FEW DAYS in Annamoe at Bob Barton's. From there I went farther south. A few days before Christmas I found myself back in my own brigade area of South Tipperary. Once again I met all my old comrades: Séamus Robinson, Dinny Lacey, Seán Hogan, Seán O'Meara and many others. My health had improved but the doctor would not allow me to walk any considerable distance.

The war was at its height. Our columns were moving about in broad daylight with rifles on their shoulders, welcomed everywhere by the people, even though the "crime" of harbouring rebels was punishable by death. The enemy ventured from their strongholds only when they could move in mass formation, accompanied by armoured cars. The British machinery of Government had completely broken down. Litigants flocked to the Republican courts, heedless of the warning that British magistrates would commit to prison all who were convicted of pleading in the Republican Courts. The orders of the so-called Government were ignored by all our public bodies. In a word, Britain's only claim to rule Ireland at this time was by virtue of her occupation force of approximately 60,000 regular troops, and about 15,000 police who included Black-and-Tans and Auxiliaries.

I spent a while in the neighbourhood of Solohead and then went on towards Cahir and Rosegreen. I passed most of the remaining period of the struggle in the neighbourhood of Fethard, Cahir and Rosegreen. Our columns were daily engaged in active warfare. Dugouts had been constructed for sleeping accommodation and for the concealing of arms. These underground lairs had very narrow entrances, barely large enough to admit a man's body.

In April 1921 we were in Cahir district when our Brigade Intelligence Officer reported that a convoy of British troops was in the habit of passing between Clogheen and Cahir on every Wednesday morning. We decided to ambush this convoy on 22 April. Word was sent to the columns to mobilise at the spot chosen for the attack. Con Moloney and I had arrived in the neighbourhood on the previous night and fell in with our column. At this stage of the conflict we travelled about in a motor-car; the reader will appreciate the change that had taken place since the early days of our resistance. In 1919 when the war had not yet started, I dared not stay in my own county otherwise than "on the run," and now in 1921, when the war was at its height, I could, with comparative safety, use a motor car.

At 5 a.m. all our men rose to get ready for the ambush. When all preparations had been made, Moloney, Lacey, Hogan and I visited the positions.

The convoy usually passed about 10 a.m. Long before that hour the Volunteers were on the alert with guns in their hands. The hours passed by, but no convoy made its appearance; nevertheless, we remained in readiness until 1 p.m. As there seemed to be no prospect of a fight, Con and I decided to return to Brigade Headquarters—" somewhere in South Tipperary."

We had left the position only half an hour when the military lorries came along. Our men called upon the enemy to surrender but they replied by opening fire. A sharp encounter followed in the course of which one soldier was killed and two wounded. The remainder of the patrol then surrendered to our men, who disarmed them, took over their equipment and set them at liberty.

No time was lost in retiring from the position, for the firing had probably been heard in Clogheen and Cahir, both of which towns were occupied by strong British garrisons who would rush reinforcements to the districts. The Volunteers were marching off in column formation with their booty when a motor car rounded the corner at a place called Curraghclooney and almost ran into the rear guard. The car was halted. The driver was asked to reveal his identity. He stated that he was District Inspector Gilbert Potter, of the R.I.C., Cahir.

He was immediately taken prisoner. Our column had not proceeded much farther on their way when they were ambushed by a strong detachment. A brisk engagement developed; although heavily out-numbered, our boys not only fought their way through without casualty, but even succeeded in carrying their prisoner along with them. Their success can be attributed chiefly to the able leadership of Dinny Lacey and Seán Hogan.

At this time a Volunteer, Thomas Trainor, was under sentence of death in a Dublin jail. The British had already hanged several of our soldiers, but our side had set its face against reprisals. On many a day on which members of the Irish Republican army were hanged as criminals, British soldiers and police fell into our hands but were always released on handing up their arms.

Trainor's was a particularly sad case. He was the father of a large young family. His execution was fixed for 25 April. With Potter in our hands, we decided upon a course of action which might save Trainor's life. We sent a special courier to Dublin to propose an exchange of prisoners. If our proposition proved fruitless, Potter would be executed.

The message was delivered in Dublin Castle two days before the time fixed for Trainor's execution. The British refused the offer, but notified that in exchange for Potter's release they were prepared to allow four named prisoners to escape as if by accident from internment camps. We decided to have no further parley on the matter.

On the 26 April we received word that Trainor had been executed. We felt that it would show weakness on our part if we did not carry out our threat. We thought, too, that it would have a salutary effect if similar offers were to be made at a future date. Potter was in our reckoning not a British soldier but an Irish traitor. We informed him that he was to be executed. We gave him every facility for communicating with his wife and children. He was reputed to be a wealthy man and tried to bribe his guards by offering a substantial sum for his release. They promptly reported the matter to me.

I was very distressed at having to carry out such an unpleasant duty. We had considered the matter most carefully and concluded that we had no alternative. Potter was a kind and cultured gentleman, and a brave officer. Before he was executed on 27 April he handed over a diary, a signet ring and a gold watch with the request that we should convey them to his wife. We fulfilled his request.

As an official reprisal for his death, the British military authorities blew up ten farmhouses in South Tipperary. Amongst them was Mrs. Tobin's of Tincurry where Seán Treacy, Hogan and I had sheltered on the night after the Soloheadbeg ambush.

The execution of another British officer took place under similar circumstances. Major Compton-Smith, D.S.O., of the Royal Welsh Fusiliers had been captured by men of the Sixth Battalion, Cork No. 1 Brigade. He was held as hostage in the hope of saving the lives of four of our men, then under sentence of death in Cork jail. They were Thomas Mulcahy and Patrick Roynane, taken at Mourne Abbey, on 15 February; and Maurice Moore and Patrick O'Sullivan, captured at Clonmult on 20 February. Word was sent to Major-General E. P. Strickland, Commander of the British Sixth Division, that Compton-Smith would be shot if our men were executed. All four I.R.A. men were executed on 28 April in Cork military barracks. Compton-Smith was shot the same day.

On 12 June 1921, just one month before the Truce, I was married at the front line of battle. I have already told how I met my bride, Brighid Malone, and how she and her sister

had befriended us when friends were few. I fell in love
with Brighid at first sight and laid siege to her heart. To
Brighid's constant care I owed a speedy recovery from my
wounds. During the months that I spent in her mother's
house, our mutual affection blossomed, and in due time
we became formally engaged.

After the fight at Drumcondra, Brighid came to see me
whenever it was considered to be safe for her to do so.
We decided to " get spliced " as soon as I was completely
recovered. I well knew the risks which I was asking her
to accept, but she never hesitated in making her decision.
To be known as a friend of mine involved being exposed
to all the tyranny of which the British were capable. What
then would it mean for the girl who could be charged with
the terrible crime of becoming my wife ? Spies would
constantly follow her steps; her home would be raided night
and day; she herself would suffer insults and perhaps have
to undergo torture from the police in their effort to extract
information about me. But she never flinched. Early in
1921 we decided that the marriage would take place in
June. Brighid would have her holidays at that time, and
for that reason her journey to the country would not arouse
undue suspicion.

By the end of May we had completed all the preliminaries.
A church-wedding was out of the question. Churches were
frequently raided; the Black-and-Tans and Auxiliaries did
not hesitate to add sacrilege to their list of outrages.
Moreover, it was essential to avoid the publicity which was
bound to follow if our marriage took place in any of the
local churches. And so, we decided to have the marriage
ceremony performed at Michael Purcell's of Glenagat House,
about six miles from Clonmel, and four miles from Cahir,
Cashel and Fethard. All of these towns were held by
enemy forces; armed patrols scoured the district by day
and by night. The spot which we selected was in the very
midst of hostile territory.

The Purcells had a long record of service in the country's
cause; both Michael and his wife had seen the inside of a
prison cell during the Land War and had been ruthlessly
evicted from their homestead; by this time however they
had won back their farm.

During those days the rival forces were locked in deadly
combat. On either side heavy casualties were being
inflicted. The reader can appreciate the risk which Brighid

had taken when she arrived in the district on the Sunday before the wedding. It was seven months since we had parted; you can imagine our joy at meeting once again.

Meantime, I had sent word to the various sections of our column telling them of the coming event. During the early morning of 12 June all members of our column converged on Glenagat. Trees were felled to provide road-blocks; armed guards were posted at the approaches. Glenagat was as impregnable as the South Tipperary Brigade could make it; if the British forces had attempted to visit the area, they would have got a warm reception. On the night before the wedding I shared a sleeping tent with Seán Hogan, Dinny Lacey, Mick Sheehan, Con Moloney, Seán Fitzpatrick, and several other officers. I should have said " spent the night " for I got no chance of sleeping. The boys would insist on talking all through the night, and giving me the advice that bachelors usually give to one who is destined soon to become a benedict. If ever I found myself a target for sustained fire, it was on that night, though fortunately it was all blank shot.

Shortly after sunrise we reached Glenagat House. Father Murphy, Curate of New Inn, had already arrived and Brighid was there too. Father Murphy said Mass and both Brighid and myself received Holy Communion. Seán Hogan acted as my best man and Áine Malone was bridesmaid. When the ceremony had ended we sat down to breakfast, and a right merry party we were. Father Ferdinand O'Leary, O.F.M., Seán Cooney and his sister arrived on the scene just as the breakfast was about to begin.

We adjourned to Jack Luby's of Milltown House for a real country wedding. All through the evening the boys and girls of the neighbourhood took part in the dancing and singing as though no war was being fought. Our out-posts remained on the alert, with reliefs taking over so that all might share in the merriment. Even while the boys danced, their guns were close at hand. We had grown used to the war. British terrorism could not kill the spirit of the people.

From Glenagat district we went across to Donohill, my native parish. Larry Power of Coolnagun, Captain of my old company, made certain that we had nothing to fear from the enemy, and I knew that my comrades could be trusted to the death.

Here we spent our honeymoon, moving from the house

of one friend to another, for all of my friends were anxious
to entertain us. As I did not carry my marriage certificate
in my pocket, our position, on at least one occasion, was
embarrassing. A certain straight-laced lady, who shall be
nameless, could not be convinced that myself and Brighid
had been lawfully married. On that account she would
not allow us to share a bedroom in her house. John Quirke,
Paddy O'Dwyer, James Ryan and Jack O'Brien, of Ballin-
vassa, took their turns to act as our host, and spared no
pains to make us happy.

Truly, it was a strange wedding and a strange honeymoon.
No wedding marches, crossed swords, confetti or continental
tour; nothing but the affection and welcome of trusted
friends. Neither my wife nor I would have preferred a
different setting.

CHAPTER FIFTEEN

THE TRUCE

EARLY IN JUNE 1921 a rumour was afloat that negotiations
were taking place about a cease-fire. It did not surprise us
when we learned that a Truce had been arranged to take
effect from 11 July 1921.

In many respects we welcomed the respite. For some
time our area had been running short of munitions. Some
weeks before the Truce was signed, some of our men had
gone to France with the object of purchasing munitions
and running them through the blockade. In an effort to
co-ordinate military tactics, the various brigades of the
Irish Republican army were being grouped into divisions.
It was a delight to relax from the hard life of campaigning
and enjoy the blessings of peace. Everywhere we were
acclaimed as heroes, even by the people who, two years
before, had been denouncing us as assassins. While the
Truce lasted I attended several race meetings, and made
scores of friends among the racing people. Now and then
Hogan and myself got a good tip and benefited very con-
siderably. It was our only chance of making a few pounds,
for the Irish Republican army was still on a volunteer
basis and the men received no gratuity. I visited all my
old friends in Tipperary and Dublin and got a cordial
welcome. The I.R.A. was devoting special attention to the

northern areas in an effort to equip local units in order that, if the fight were to be renewed, they would play a more active part and thereby lessen the burden of the southern counties. I gladly offered my services and went to Ulster where I met Charlie Daly (a Kerryman and a true patriot). I spent five weeks in his company, instructing the northern boys in the use of the gun and the bomb. It was hard work, but I enjoyed it. We saw a great portion of Ulster in our long walks and occasional pleasure-drives. To make it more exciting, we paid an occasional visit to Belfast.

I returned to Dublin about the end of September and received a presentation of a gold watch and chain from the Dublin Guards. At the function some very nice things were said about me by Paddy Daly and others who later became high-ranking officers of the Free State army.

I remained in Dublin until a few days before the signing of the Treaty. When I discovered that a compromise was being made, I journeyed to the south. I was convinced that, if we could show that the army was standing solid for what it had fought to achieve, the Dáil would not betray the army. The soldiers, I felt, would keep the politicians on the straight track. I could not bring myself to believe that the Dáil would take upon itself the responsibility of making a compromise. In this I was sadly mistaken. Our bitterest opponents of former days were the strongest supporters of the Treaty.

I came to Dublin on 7 December, the very day on which the terms of the Treaty were made public. I met Liam Lynch, Seán Hogan and several officers of the Irish Republican army. I urged Liam Lynch, who was then in command of the First Southern Division, to end the Truce right away and resume the war against the British. In this way we might have kept our army united. Nobody favoured my suggestion. Some held out the vain hope that, even if the Treaty were accepted by the Dáil, it would be rejected at the polls. It is a self-evident truth that when a country has become war-weary, the majority of the people will always accept a compromise.

Disheartened at the failure of my efforts to persuade the boys to make common cause against the enemy, I went to London and was introduced to Mahatma Ghandi, the most intelligent man and the most implacable foe of Britain whom I have ever met. While Ghandi got the credit of not sanctioning any resistance other than passive to British rule in India, he confided to me that he could see no other way of accomplishing the liberation of his country. He considered that armed resistance would have resulted in the slaughter of millions of his countrymen, the vast majority of whom had no experience whatever in the use of arms.

But I met other Indians in London who favoured armed revolt. I offered them my services in the hope of getting in one more blow for the cause of freedom. I got a rude shock when my advances were repelled, the reason proferred being that no Irishman could be trusted, seeing that his countrymen had abandoned the fight for the freedom of their own country. An emissary of Abdul el Krim, Leader of the Riffs, offered me a large sum of money if I would proceed to Morocco and help in the Rebellion of the Riffs against the Spanish Government. This agent went by the name of Patton. When he told me that some of my former enemies, the Auxiliaries, had already enlisted in the rebel army, I declined the invitation.

Saddened at heart, I made up my mind to leave Ireland and set my face for America. But before taking this step I came back to Dublin to act as best man at Séamus Robinson's wedding. That same evening I crossed to Holyhead feeling completely broken in spirit. I reflected with sorrow that all our efforts had come to naught. Men, in whom we had trusted, were telling the world that the fight for freedom had been won even though the Free State Government would be obliged under oath to pledge its allegiance to a foreign king. By the time that the Treaty was ratified our country was " rent in twain " and yet they called it freedom. Was it for this chimera that brave Irishmen had fought and died?

Had our army taken the field I would never have left Ireland. I prophesied that within twelve months Ireland would be in the throes of a civil war.

Before I left Ireland I addressed an open letter to Commandant Seán McKeon, T.D., in which I made perfectly clear my attitude towards the Treaty. To quote my exact words:

You are reported to have stated to-day in An Dáil that this Treaty brings the freedom that is necessary and for which we are all ready to die. You are also reported to have previously stated that this Treaty gives what you and your comrades fought for. As one of your comrades, I state emphatically that I would have never handled a gun or fired a shot, nor would I have asked any of my comrades, many of whom fell on the battlefield, to raise a hand to obtain this Treaty.

Let me remind you that this day is the second anniversary of Martin Savage's death. Do you suppose that he sacrificed his life in attempting to kill one British Governor-General in order to make room for another British Governor-General?

I take no party's side, but I still stand by our old principle of Complete Separation and entire Independence.

When I reached London I made contact with Seán Hogan. The novelty of the big city helped to keep our minds from the tragedy of Ireland. During our stay we met P. L. Smyth, the well-known Dublin Commission Agent, who proved a kind friend to us.

CHAPTER SIXTEEN

AN AMERICAN JOURNEY

IT WAS NO EASY PROBLEM to find a way of travelling to America. We had no passports and very little money. Both difficulties were eventually resolved. A British naval captain (who hailed from the County Cork) secured passports for us under assumed names. A London butter-merchant named Chris Cullen generously paid our fares on a liner that sailed from Southampton to Montreal.

After a brief stay in Montreal we slipped over the Canadian border and made our way to Chicago. Here we were met by my brothers, John and Pat, and my sister, Mary, who had been in the United States for some years. We met so many kind friends that we were made to feel almost as if we were at home. You can imagine our delight on meeting once again Ned O'Brien, of Galbally, who had recovered from the wounds which he received on that memorable day of the Knocklong rescue. We were introduced to Mrs. McWhorter, a staunch supporter of Ireland; Michael Mulryan, Jim Delaney and Colonel O'Reilly. All of them proved most hospitable to us. We were taken on a tour of the sights of Chicago, not least of which were the huge meat-packing factories, many of them owned by Irishmen or by men of Irish descent.

We went from Chicago to Philadelphia and were greeted by a host of friends, including Joe McGarrity, that veteran worker for Ireland. We spent some days under his roof where so many great Irish patriots, Seán McDermott,

Pádraig Pearse, Roger Casement and Éamon de Valera, had been entertained. Luke Dillon, too, extended a welcome; and our old Dublin friends Séamus and Mrs. O'Doherty. The kindness of the O'Doherty family to me knew no bounds.

From Philadelphia we travelled to California. There I met many Irish friends, including Father Peter Scanlon, Father Dan Kelly (senior) and Father Dan Kelly (junior) who hailed from my part of the country. I was delighted to meet once more Mick McDonnell, our old comrade of the Ashtown fight. Although it was mid-winter when we arrived it seemed like an Irish summer.

Meanwhile, I had kept in touch with affairs in Ireland. The American papers were giving prominence to the development of events at home. It was plain that our old comrades were irrevocably divided and heading for civil war. Every day brought fresh stories of new differences and minor conflicts which could end only in one way. In America, our countrymen were likewise divided.

Early in March came the news that Limerick was on the verge of an outbreak. Different posts in the city were being held by the rival sections of the Volunteers, some of whom supported, while others opposed the Treaty. Ultimatums had actually passed between the rival commanders, and it looked as if at any moment a single shot might set in motion a conflict that would soon spread throughout the land. I was staying at Menlo Park with Father Dan Kelly when I received a cablegram from Liam Lynch requesting me to return at once to Ireland. An agreement had been made in Limerick between the rival sections, and this pact momentarily averted an armed conflict.

Within two days of the receipt of the cablegram I took the train to Chicago where I spent a few days with my relatives and friends. I went on to Philadelphia and received the same warm greeting from Joe McGarrity, Luke Dillon and the O'Dohertys.

Hogan and I figured out that New York would be the best port from which to attempt a passage to Ireland. Here we were once more confronted with the difficulties regarding money and passports which we had experienced in our outward journey. We could easily have got passports from the British Consulate if we had made the application as British subjects, but we would have preferred to rot in America rather than demean ourselves in such a base fashion. We paid a visit to the Carmelite Fathers in 39th

Street, and to the Irish Offices in 5th Avenue, where I met Liam Pedlar.

At last, through the help of some Irish friends, we were taken on as stokers on a vessel that was sailing for Cobh. Seán and I set manfully to our work and had spent four hours at a task which was novel to us. The vessel was due to sail within an hour when somebody got suspicious of Hogan. He was questioned as to his nationality and his experience on other vessels. When his answers were deemed to be unsatisfactory, he was promptly ordered off the ship.

This was a nice dilemma for me. Our four hours' hard work and our efforts to secure the jobs had come to naught. I could not leave Hogan penniless and alone in New York. I made up my mind that I would not travel without him. It was no easy matter for me to escape from the ship. The crew were already marshalled for the voyage; to attempt to return to shore was a serious offence for which I might find myself in irons. The risk had to be taken. I walked straight to the gangway, but was held up by an officer. I explained to him that I had important business to transact on shore, but that I would not be detained longer than a few minutes. He must have taken me for a harmless member of the crew; he accepted my explanation and allowed me to leave the ship. I never again set eyes on himself or his ship. The loss was not all on his side. All our money had been invested in guns, and these were aboard. It would be madness to try and retrieve them. My comrade meant more to me than Krupp's factory.

We met with a few bitter disappointments before we got on another liner. At last we found ourselves on the high seas, bound for Cobh. We landed in Ireland early in April. A friend, to whom my wife had telegraphed, met me at Cobh and brought the happy news that not only my wife, but also a son, were awaiting my arrival in Dublin.

CHAPTER SEVENTEEN

THE CIVIL WAR

WHEN I REACHED DUBLIN, I found that the situation was even more critical than I had anticipated. The old Republican army had definitely split into two sections—the new Free State army and the I.R.A. The British troops had evacuated

Beggar's Bush and Wellington barracks, and had handed them over to the Free State troops. The Republicans had seized and fortified the Four Courts and made it their head-quarters. Similar cleavages of opinion existed all over the country, although the South remained overwhelmingly Republican so far as the army was concerned. It was clear that at any moment civil war might break out. War was in the air. All through the night the noise of gunfire could be heard; armoured cars were patrolling the streets.

I was sick at heart when I reflected that we who had been such loyal comrades were now about to turn arms on one another. I decided that, should fighting commence, I would not be the one to incur blame. I visited the strong-holds of each party in an effort to explore the possibilities of averting a conflict. I urged the old fighting crowd to come together, but there seemed no hope of an agreement.

I met Seán O'Hegarty (Commandant of the First Cork Brigade), Florrie O'Donoghue (Adjutant of the First Southern Division), Humphrey Murphy of Kerry, Tom Hales of Cork, and Seán Moylan, T.D., all of whom were opposed to the Treaty. After some discussion we decided to seek out some officers on the other side in a last attempt to find a way out. We made contact with Mick Collins, Dick Mulcahy, Owen O'Duffy, Gearóid O'Sullivan and Seán Boylan.

After a long exchange of views, agreement was reached upon a certain basis of settlement. This agreement was put down in writing and all the members attached their signa-tures (Seán Moylan was the only one who refused to sign). This document was published in the Press on 1 May. I give it here in full :

> We, the undersigned officers of the I.R.A., realise the gravity of the position in Ireland, and appreciate the fact that, if the present drift is maintained, a conflict of comrades is inevitable; we hereby declare that this would be the greatest calamity in Irish history and would leave Ireland broken for generations.
> To avert this catastrophe, we believe that a closing of the ranks is necessary.
> We suggest to all leaders, army and political, and to all citizens and soldiers of Ireland, the advisability of a union of forces on the basis of the acceptance and utilisation of our present national position in the best interests of Ireland; we require that nothing shall be done that would prejudice our position or dissipate our forces.
> We feel on this basis alone can the situation best be faced, viz.:

(1) The acceptance of the fact, admitted by all sides, that the majority of the people of Ireland are willing to accept the Treaty.
(2) An agreed election with a view to
(3) Forming a Government which will have the confidence of the whole country.
(4) Army unification on the above basis.

The agreement was signed by Tom Hales, Humphrey Murphy, Seán O'Hegarty, Florrie O'Donoghue, Seán Boylan, Dick Mulcahy, Owen O'Duffy, Gearóid O'Sullivan, Mick Collins and myself. Five of the signatories opposed the Treaty and five favoured it. (Florrie O'Donoghue and Seán O'Hegarty remained neutral during the Civil War).

These proposals came in for severe criticism. Republican Headquarters forthwith issued a statement repudiating the terms, and suggested that it was an attempt to split their ranks. I received a full share of adverse criticism. A Republican journal, *The Plain People,* described me as a "Judas with perhaps this difference : I had not got the thirty pieces of silver." To this day I do not know who was the editor of this paper. Perhaps he considered his accusation just. I paid no heed to these observations because I believed that it was my duty to strain every nerve in an effort to avoid civil war.

On 3 May the signatories of this document were received by the Dáil, and Seán O'Hegarty addressed the House. A Committee representing both sides of the Dáil was appointed to discuss the proposals.

The next step was to see what could be done to bring about a reunion of the army. A conference was arranged and several meetings were held but neither the military nor the political leaders could come to any definite agreement. However, a temporary pact was entered into between Éamon de Valera and Michael Collins; in the forthcoming election, Free Staters and Republicans would stand as a United Sinn Féin party. In accordance with that agreement all the outgoing members of the Dáil were once more nominated, and it was agreed that after the election a coalition ministry should be formed.

When the election came, some difficulty arose about a vacancy which had been created in East Tipperary by the resignation of Alderman Frank Drohan. He had resigned before the division on the Treaty, and a dispute originated as to whether Republicans or Free Staters should nominate his successor. I was eventually selected, because I was considered to be more or less neutral. I had not been consulted on the matter and I knew nothing about the arrangement until I saw it announced in the daily papers. I protested against the proposal, but for the sake of harmony I agreed to allow my name to go forward even though I had no political ambition. I was a soldier first and foremost and made it quite plain that I would take no part in the election campaign. However, both sides nominated me, but I was defeated at the polls.

I had hoped that, as a result of the pact between Collins and de Valera, we would have an uncontested election, thereby preserving a united front. The Labour party and the Farmers had prepared to send forward candidates of their own in opposition to Republicans and Free Staters. Before the polling Mick Collins delivered a speech in Cork urging Labour and other parties to carry on with their campaign. This was a flagrant violation of the agreement.

In North, Mid and South Tipperary we succeeded in inducing the Farmers' candidates to withdraw from the contest. If all parties had been as patriotic as the farmers of Tipperary, civil war might have been avoided. They had suffered from the Black-and-Tan terror more than any other section of the community. Martial Law had for three years prevented the holding of fairs and markets. Many of their farmhouses and creameries had been wrecked and yet they had stood loyally by us all through the war. Their self-sacrifice deserves to be remembered.

The Labour candidate would listen to no argument. He cared nothing about this idea of presenting a united front to the enemy. He was ambitious for power and insisted upon going forward. He boasted afterwards that he was "not afraid of Dan Breen or of his gun levelled at my temple." Even in election campaigns it is not playing the game to circulate such slanders. My countrymen know well that I would never aim a gun at an unarmed opponent.

Mick Collins's violation of the pact had made me suspicious. I felt too that Britain would never permit a coalition ministry of Free Staters and Republicans, but my hope was that, if a crisis came, the Free Staters would throw the Treaty back in Britain's teeth rather than have brother fight against brother.

I do not wish to add fuel to the flame of bitterness that was occasioned by the Civil War; but I must insist on emphasising that I worked might and main in an effort to prevent it. When I learned with horror that the Free Staters had at dead of night placed British guns in position to shell the Four Courts, I felt there was only one course open to me—to throw in my lot with old comrades and carry on the fight for the Republic.

In the course of that fight I lost nearly all my old brothers-in-arms. Even in the war against the Black-and-Tans, Tipperary suffered less heavily. My heart is sorely grieved when I remember those faithful friends who fell during this disastrous conflict: Dinny Lacey, Jerry Kiely, Martin Breen, Big Paddy Dalton, Paddy MacDonough, Donal Ryan, Liam Lynch, and several others with whom I campaigned.

Paddy Dalton, bravest of the brave, was known as "the armoured car," a huge man who did not know his own strength. Martin (better known as "Sparkle") Breen was his great pal. During the years of combat they were constant companions; in death they were not separated. They lie side by side in the Republican Plot of St. Michael's graveyard, Tipperary.

When the Volunteers paraded through the towns during the Truce-period the people were much impressed by Paddy's giant stature and someone invariably remarked for the benefit of all within earshot, "My God, isn't he a fine man!" On such occasions Paddy would be very embarrassed, for he was a very "quiet-going" man, altogether different from "Sparkie" who was gay as a lark. "Sparkie" was only five feet six in height and reached no higher than Paddy's elbow. One day both of them were marching down the street of Mullinahone when the usual compliment about Dalton's majestic bearing was overheard. "Sparkie" nudged Paddy, "Which of us do they mean, Dalton?"

"Sparkie" Breen was leader of No. 1 Column of the Third Tipperary Brigade from August 1922 to 10 January of the following year. Whenever his Column happened to fall in with No. 2 Column, "Sparkie" would come down the line asking, "Where is Cooney of the Main Guard?" Having found Seán Cooney he would march with him for the rest of the day or night, telling stories and making everyone laugh, provided that it was safe to relax; otherwise, the columns marched in silence. Conversation was not allowed and smoking was prohibited in areas where detachments of the Free State army were bivouacking.

These two Columns were constantly on the move. Number

One kept mostly to the northern side of the brigade-area and Number Two to the southern side. But they often travelled outside their own particular beats. Number Two moved on a perimeter that extended from the Nire into Newcastle, down to Clogheen, on to Ballyporeen and almost into Kilbehenny, County Limerick; across the Galtees, over the Suir at Knockgraffon, up as far as Ballingarry and back by Slievenamon. A crossing of the Suir was usually made near Carrick, and when they reached the far bank they proceeded to the shelter of the Comeragh mountains.

Number One's assigned route was through the Glen of Aherlow and along the Suir valley as far as Knockgraffon. From there they swung over into the Rosegreen district and made their way by Drangan, skirting Slievenamon on the return journey to their base. The men felt most at home in the Glen, especially in the area north of Slieve-namuck and in the countryside close to Kilfeacle.

In the early days of the Civil War a false rumour was set afoot that the Glen people were in favour of the Free State, and would give a hostile reception to Republican forces. The rumour nearly proved disastrous to No. 2 Column, whose Commandant was Tom Sadlier. On a foggy morning an advance guard of this column donned Free State army uniforms which had been captured from the soldiers at Carrickconeen and came down the mountainside expecting to be received with open arms. Some of the inhabitants, seeing the green uniforms, gave the alarm to Martin Breen's No. 1 Column which was billeted in Glen-cushnabinna. Several of Martin's men rushed out half-dressed and disappeared in the fog. Sadlier accosted a young man who was driving a horse and cart laden with milk-churns and asked him to lead the way to some billets. The youth refused and looked down the barrel of Sadlier's gun without blinking an eyelid, saying, "Shoot and be damned." When the men were at last settled in billets, the misunderstanding was cleared up. "Sparkie's" Column had reformed and were about to attack the "Free-Staters," but found to their surprise that they were dealing with their own comrades of the Fifth and Sixth Battalions, the men who hailed from the territory south of the Galtees. The latter then learned from their comrades of the Fourth Battalion that, were it not for the dense fog, fire would have been opened on them as they descended from the mountain into the level plain of the Glen of Aherlow.

Martin Breen and Tom Sadlier used to lead their Columns through rich grasslands and poor moorlands, over hill and bog, deep into mountain defiles and pleasant valleys. In due time the men learned to distinguish the different parts of the county not only by the various kinds of land through which they passed but even by the particular brand of "crane" (an instrument for hanging pots over the fires), which was in use at farmers' houses. The design of the crane varied with the particular fuel that was being burned, turf, timber, coal, or culm-balls.

A member of a flying-column could always be recognised, not only by the rifle and revolver which he usually carried, and by the trench-coat, bandolier and leggings which were part of his regular outfit, but also by the razor and tooth-brush which he sported after the manner of a fountain-pen clasped to his breast-pocket. Discipline in the matter of personal cleanliness was very strict. A column-man with a dirty or unshaven face was unheard of. The large open razor was in vogue, because safety-razor blades were not easily procurable. Some of the "cut-throat" razors had a strange history. One officer, attached to the Fifth Battalion, used a razor which had once belonged to a major of the Auxiliaries.

It was no uncommon sight in the summer and early autumn to see the men of a flying-column bathing in a river or in the pool of a mountain-stream. The usual procedure was to get up a good soap-lather and swim about for a while. If no towel were available, the men would roll in the grass when they emerged from the water. Shirts were washed by being immersed and rubbed in the water. When they had been wrung out they were hung on bushes to dry. The men dressed minus the shirts and by the time that the column was ready to parade the shirts had become dry and well-aired. The Suir, Tar, Anner, Aherlow and Arra washed many a good man and his shirt in those days.

An order, issued from Field-headquarters on 24 July 1922, prescribed that columns on active service should as far as possible be billeted in mansions which were owned by persons hostile to the Republic. In practice, however, columns were generally billeted in farmhouses. As time went on, mansion after mansion was given to the flames by the Republicans, so that it would have been difficult to adhere to the instructions given in the said order. Some mansions which escaped the ravages of fire continued to be used by the columns until the end of the war. One of these was the Earl of Donoughmore's at Knocklofty. The Earl, to use the words of an I.R.A. officer, "was not a bad skin," and whenever the columns called at his mansion there were always six or seven beds available, as well as plenty of good food. Another "Big House" where the columns occasionally billeted was Coole House, Knocklofty, owned by a Mr. Fitzgerald. On one occasion when a number of men from No. 2 Column were staying in this house a remarkable incident took place. After breakfast Mr. Fitzgerald brought the party of men (who belonged to the machine-gun section) into the orchard and came to a halt before a large statue of the Blessed Virgin. "My dear boys," he said, "this is the fifteenth day of August, Lady Day; kneel down and we'll say the Rosary." The men knelt down and, having taken the rosary-beads from their pockets, answered very devoutly the decades which were given out by the man-of-the-house. When they had finished they made the Sign of the Cross and rose up from their knees. "None of you boys here present will be killed in this war," Mr. Fitzgerald prophesied. "All glory to Mary Immaculate," affirmed the officer who related the story, "that prophecy was fulfilled."

When billeted on the people of a district the men were frequently obliged to sleep three in a bed. Sometimes four men had to try and do as best they could with one bed; a bed for two men was a luxury, and a bed to oneself was as rare as a white blackbird. On several occasions the men had to sleep in dirty beds, but even a dirty bed was better in the eyes of some than a haybarn. In spite of such conditions no man on active service with the columns was known to suffer from insomnia though many developed what came to be known as "the Republican itch." On night-marches the column would fall out at intervals for the space of about ten minutes, many of the men availing of this short halt to rest on their backs in the centre of the road (the grass on the roadside being wet with dew); others preferred to remain in a standing position. On fine days the men lay down to rest on the grassy sward, for their legs had grown weary from the interminable walking. The frolicsome young ones sometimes indulged in "sod battles" during those intervals, much to the irritation of the more staid members. The periods of rest were much appreciated by the men, one of whom said that the luxury of lying on one's back was, even on a dusty road, "the nearest thing to heaven."

Most of the columns had a machine-gun section. The guns were usually of the Lewis and the Thompson pattern. There were also some Hotchkiss guns in their possession. The gun-crews took turns in carrying the heavy weapons. The Lewis gun weighs about thirty-three pounds and, as it was generally carried on the shoulder, it often happened that a man's coat became frayed at that particular spot from the friction. On more than one occasion this helped the opposing army to identify prisoners who belonged to the machine-gun section. A story is told of a Volunteer from the Eighth Battalion who was known to his comrades as "German" Hennebry. On his capture by Free State troops he was asked to what section he belonged. "To the Red Cross," he replied. "I suppose," remarked an old ex-British soldier who was questioning him, "it was carrying the bandages that wore the hole in your coat."

About the beginning of October suggestions were made by many people of various political views that there should be a truce of some kind. The Free State Government repudiated any suggestion that agreement could be come to with the "Irregulars," short of a total surrender of arms. They issued a proclamation, nevertheless, promising an amnesty and free pardon to all who should deliver up their arms and ammunition before 15 October; furthermore, that an undertaking must be given to cease all armed activity against the Free State, and neither to aid nor abet such armed opposition for the future. These pourparlers came to nothing but they called forth an interesting letter from the father of two well-known officers of the Third Tipperary Brigade, one of whom was to die at the hands of the Free State soldiery in less than a month from the date of the letter. The writer was Patrick Sadlier of Rathkenny, Fethard, and the letter, which appeared in the *Clonmel Chronicle* of 7 October 1922, was as follows:

> Dear Sir,—Having read the letters of Father Carolan and Madame Maude Gonne MacBride, I am in entire agreement with their views. I know perfectly well that the soldiers on either side do not want to take the lives of their opponents, but of course the Republicans cannot honourably surrender their arms. That would spell defeat.
> Why, then, not have the arms stored in armouries under guard of men elected by themselves?

One of my sons, Denis, gave up his life for his country, and the others are quite as ready to sacrifice theirs if need be. But God knows it is high time that we be once more united to work for the welfare of our poor, distracted country.

Yours faithfully,

PAT SADLIER.

The suggestion of storing the arms was substantially the same as that made in March 1923 by the Archbishop of Cashel, namely, that arms be stored away by the Republicans until a general election had been held; they should then be delivered up to whatever government might be returned to power. This proposal was endorsed by Mr. de Valera as one of the conditions for a truce. To such proposals, as to all the others subsequently put forward, the Free State Government turned a deaf ear. It would have been better for the country and, perhaps, for the future stability of the Free State, if those terms had been accepted.

On 26 October Paddy Dalton was killed in action at Donohill. He was staying with some of his men in the district and happened to be in Dwyer's publichouse when a ration party of Free State soldiers arrived by motor-lorries. The officer commanding the troops ordered his men to dismount and advance in extended order for the purpose of surrounding Dwyer's. Immediately Paddy and his companions rushed through the front doorway, firing as they advanced. In the confusion that occurred most of his men got away to open country. Paddy took shelter in a cowshed at the rear of the premises and kept the opposing forces at bay by maintaining a steady fire. He dashed through the haggard but was shot dead as he attempted to clear the fence.

His funeral took place on the following Sunday afternoon. From far and near his friends came to pay their last respects to one of Tipperary's noblest sons. The Last Post was sounded and three volleys were discharged over his grave by a firing-party of six Volunteers.

Following close on the death of Commandant Dalton came the sad news of the death of another fighting officer of the Third Tipperary Brigade, Commandant Michael Sadlier. At early morning of 3 November he was trapped at William Heffernan's, Marlhill, by a party of Free State soldiers who were making a house-to-house search in the district. Mick and his fellow-officer, Paddy Loughlin, took refuge in a hiding-place under the stairs. Such hiding-places were no longer of any avail, for they were well known to the men from the locality who had joined the Free State army. One of the soldiers was holding a lighted candle when Mick and Paddy were ordered by the Free State officer to come out with hands raised. The candle was suddenly extinguished and Mick fell mortally wounded from a discharge of shots. He was removed to Cashel hospital and died on the following night. His last words, spoken to his grief-stricken father, were, "I forgive them."

Commandant Mick Sadlier's remains were laid to rest beside those of his brother, Denis, in Drangan churchyard. All business was suspended in Fethard and blinds were drawn as the funeral procession passed through the streets of the town. A unique tribute was manifested by the flying of the Tricolour at half-mast over the Garda barrack, thereby giving testimony to the respect in which the deceased Republican officer was held by all the people irrespective of their political views. At the graveside Pat Sadlier gave utterance to a remark which many people, Republicans and Free Staters, heartily endorsed: "My son is gone. My only regret is that I have lived to see the day when Irishmen are turning their guns on one another. I hope this state of affairs will end soon."

"Sparkie" Breen met his death on 10 January 1923. He had paid a hurried visit to his home in Tipperary town, and was making his way through the fields with Denis Ryan and Jim McCluskey to rejoin their Column when they were observed by a detachment of Free State soldiers who were approaching from the direction of Limerick Junction. The commanding officer called upon the three men to halt and upon their refusal to obey he instructed the soldiers to open fire. Martin and his companions took cover behind a fence and returned the fire. Meanwhile some of the Free State party had outflanked them. The three men were surrounded but, even though there was no possibility of escape, they refused to surrender. They considered that it was better to die fighting than to be put up against a barrack-wall and shot, a fate which might well be theirs if captured under arms. The fight, such as it was, lasted hardly two minutes. "Sparkie" was shot through the head and died instantly. Denis Ryan was severely wounded and died six months later. Jim McCluskey surrendered.

From the inception of the Volunteers Martin Breen had

taken a prominent part in the fight for freedom, and had proved himself a soldier of resolute courage. It was a tragic irony that he should have been shot down by his own countrymen, almost at the threshold of his own home.

Early in January of 1923 rumours of peace-talks began to circulate, and my name was mentioned as one who was prepared to parley. The Dublin correspondent of the London *Observer* was passed along to me for an interview. "The fact is," so ran his despatch, "and I learn it from Breen himself, that while he is as much in favour of peace as anyone could be, his business is to fight. He leaves peace-making to others.

"Indeed, when I saw him, Breen was panoplied for war rather than for peace. He carried, slung from his shoulder, a formidable machine-gun, and his companion was similarly accoutred. How I came to meet Breen need not be explained here. Sufficient to say that for three hours we talked peace, and at the end of that time we had got no further than the pious expression from Breen that he and his associates wanted peace as much as anyone else and they would not prolong the struggle one moment longer than necessary."

The Neutral I.R.A. Men's Association attempted to bring about an agreement between the rival forces, and with this object in view, appealed to both sides, as a preliminary, to agree to a truce of one month. This appeal fell on deaf ears, neither the Free State nor the Republican authorities being willing to consider the proposal. But it had a tragic aftermath.

Sickened at heart by the suicidal conflict, members of the above-named association requested Dinny Lacey to come to Rossadrehid in the Glen of Aherlow to discuss their proposal. Dinny knew the great personal risk that he was incurring, but he threw caution to the winds and left Mount Bruis on Saturday, 17 February, with seventeen men. They reached Ballydavid that evening, footsore and weary. Having made arrangements with the men to meet at Rossadrehid next day at 3 p.m., he divided them up into small parties and sent them to their respective billets in the neighbourhood. He himself, with Vice-Commandant Paddy MacDonough and Captain Bill Allen, stayed for the night at the house of a farmer, Rody Ryan, of Ballydavid.

On that very night not less than a thousand Free State troops, drawn from Cahir, Cashel, Clonmel, Tipperary and

Limerick, were preparing to invest the Glen of Aherlow in one of the most extensive round-up operations yet undertaken in Tipperary. At dawn on Sunday morning they had taken up their positions; the Glen was encircled and columns of troops poured in from every side.

The sound of rifle-fire from the direction of Ashgrove House was the first intimation Lacey received that an attack was in progress. Some of his men were billeted at Ashgrove House and he decided instantly to go with his two comrades to their relief. As they were about to set out from Rody Ryan's house they saw a contingent of Free State soldiers enter the farmyard. An exchange of shots took place and at once several Free State soldiers who were in the vicinity appeared on the scene. Dinny raked the opposing forces from an improvised shelter near the doorway, MacDonough and Allen kept up a constant fire from the kitchen and parlour windows, but from the beginning their resistance seemed hopeless. MacDonough was severely wounded in the hip and slumped to the floor. Dinny did not realise the seriousness of MacDonough's plight and called to him and Allen to make a dash for liberty. MacDonough, badly wounded as he was, rose up from the floor and all three emerged from the doorway with guns blazing. The very audacity of the move momentarily threw the invaders into disorder; three of them fell mortally wounded. But the soldiers regrouped and resumed the attack. MacDonough was hit once more and could go no further. (He was removed in a Free State ambulance and died in Tipperary hospital next day). Lacey scaled a high fence at the end of the haggard and helped up Bill Allen. When they jumped down to the opposite side they heard the cry of " Hands up " from a group of Free State soldiers who lay concealed in the ditch. Lacey raised his gun to fire and at once came an outburst of rifle-fire. He was shot dead.

Even from his opponents came a paean of praise, " gallant," " fearless," " resourceful and tireless," " iron disciplinarian." There was a manifestation of universal grief at the untimely passing of the great Republican soldier, Dinny Lacey. May he rest in peace.

By the late spring of 1923 it was becoming obvious that the Republican army had disintegrated to such an extent that a further continuation of the struggle seemed useless. The jails and internment camps were full to overflowing with Republican prisoners. Most of the leaders realised the hopelessness of the position and urged that the war should be ended. The Chief of Staff, General Liam Lynch, maintained that the army was sufficiently strong to continue resistance for an indefinite period. A meeting of the army executive was held in Pierry Wall's cottage, Knocknarue, Ballymacarberry, at which Commandant-General Tom Barry proposed the following resolution: " Further armed resistance against the Free State Government will not advance the cause of the independence of our country." Tom Barry's proposition was defeated by one vote.

The presence of the army executive and the Republican leaders in the Nire Valley became known to the Free State Intelligence Service. Ten thousand troops were mustered for the purpose of encircling the mountains of South Tipperary, North and West Waterford. I was billeted with Captain Jerry Kiely at Stephen MacDonough's of Lisvarnane in the Glen of Aherlow. In the early morning Free State troops surrounded the house. We decided to fight our way through. I opened the back-door and hurled grenades at my opponents. Such confusion was caused that I succeeded in escaping to a nearby wood. I expected Jerry to follow me, but he disregarded our previous arrangement. Instead of accompanying me, he left by the front door, armed with a Thompson machine-gun. The gun jammed after the first round and he was shot down.

Two other Republican officers, Ned Somers and Theo English, were trapped in the secret room at the old ruins of Castleblake which had proved a safe refuge for many a " wanted " man when closely pursued by Black-and-Tans. It had escaped detection all those years, but it was well known to Lieut. Patrick Kennedy of the Rosegreen district. Having placed his men at strategic points within the ruins, he advanced to the hide-out and called on the occupants to surrender. There was no reply. He and Lieut. Moran proceeded to remove the boards. A bomb was flung through the opening. Kennedy was mortally wounded and Moran's left arm was shattered by the splinters. Somers and English emerged with guns blazing, but both were shot dead in an attempt to fight their way through.

The facts concerning Liam Lynch's death are well known. The spot on which he fell is marked by a noble memorial in the form of a Round Tower set on Croghan West, a desolate, windswept mountain under which nestles the village of Newcastle. The memorial dominates the landscape, and can be seen even from the plains over which the columns marched in bygone days.

After Liam's death Austin Stack, Frank Barret, Daithi Kent, Seán Gaynor, Maurice Walshe, George Power, Andy Kennedy and I came up from Araglen and decided to make for the Nire Valley. We reached Mount Melleray after midnight. Before daybreak we resumed our journey through the foothills of Knockmealdown in the direction of Cappoquin. After an hour's march we crossed the main road and were advancing uphill when heavy fire was opened on us. We took cover and divided into separate parties, some of whom succeeded in slipping through the cordon. Austin Stack was captured, and in his possession was found the draft of a memorandum prepared at the house of the brothers, James and John Wall of Knockanaffran, for the signature of the several members of the army executive. The memorandum authorised President de Valera to issue an order for the immediate cessation of hostilities. De Valera was present at Wall's but took no part in the discussion. While the session was taking place in "the room," he had paced restlessly on the kitchen floor. The document also furnished certain proof to the Free State army chiefs that the Republican army could be written off as a fighting force. But still the hunt went on.

I had fallen in with Maurice Walshe and Andy Kennedy, and we set out for Newcastle. When we arrived, we found that the place was held by a strong party of Free Staters. We had to remain for two days on the hills, as the Free State troops had brought up large reinforcements to sweep the district. Heavy snow lay on the ground, but we could not venture into any place of shelter. After two days we slipped through the lines and headed for the Glen of Aherlow. We went to ground in my favourite dug-out at a place called Longford. I was so exhausted that I instantly fell into a deep sleep from which I was awakened by the heavy tramp of marching men. I rushed out and found myself covered by several rifles. There was no option but to surrender.

I am not a soft-hearted man. Much hardship had steeled me against tears, but on that day pride alone kept me from crying like a child. For five years I had defied Britain's garrison. I had suffered everything willingly for my country. Now, in my native county, I was a prisoner in the hands of my own countrymen.

180 MY FIGHT FOR IRISH FREEDOM

I was taken first to Galbally where I met Ned O'Brien
my old friend of Knocklong, and also his brother John Joe,
and James Scanlon. They felt the situation just as keenly
as I, but they tried to cheer me up. From Galbally I was
taken under escort to my native town, Tipperary, where
I was put through some form of trial. Next day I was
taken from the Free State headquarters and marched to the
railway station. The humiliation and agony which I endured during that short march I shall never forget. May
the reader never know what it is to be marched, a prisoner,
through his native town for doing what he believed to be
his duty in the cause of his country.

I was taken by passenger-train to Limerick where I was
detained for two months. I have already related my
meeting with McEvoy, Lord French's driver, whom we had
wounded at Ashtown, and now my prison officer. From
Limerick I was taken to Mountjoy jail. In protest against
the treatment meted out to me, I went on hunger-strike.
After twelve days of hunger and six of thirst-strike I was
released.

During my imprisonment the people of Tipperary had
elected me as their Republican Deputy.

L'ENVOI

To conclude, I would like to repeat the words addressed
by President Éamon de Valera to the soldiers of the Republic
on the occasion of the "Cease-fire" order :

Soldiers of the Republic, Legion of the Rearguard . . . .
Your efforts and the sacrifices of your dead comrades in
this forlorn hope will surely bear fruit. . . . You have
saved the nation's honour, preserved the national tradition,
and kept open the road to independence. You have de-
monstrated in a way there is no mistaking that we are
not a nation of willing bondslaves.

May God guard every one of you, and give to the country
in all times of need sons who will love her as dearly and
devotedly as you.

EPILOGUE

Soldier rest! thy warfare o'er,
  Sleep the sleep that knows not breaking!
Dream of battlefields no more,
  Days of danger, nights of waking.

I recalled these lines of Sir Walter Scott some months ago as I knelt at Seán Treacy's grave in Kilfeacle cemetery. It came as a surprise to read on the headstone that Seán was only twenty-five years of age when he was shot down in Talbot Street on 14 October 1920. How apposite for him is that quotation from the *Book of Wisdom*: "Few were his years and yet at the time of his death he had accomplished the work of a full lifetime." Dan Breen has said that Seán seemed to be in a constant hurry. Perhaps some daimon had warned him that his days were numbered. In that short span he set out to perform the heroic feats that have brought him undying fame.

Close to the grave Matt Dwyer, an employee of the County Council, was whetting his scythe. I asked him if he knew Seán Treacy. "Of course I knew him," he replied, "and all the other boys from the neighbourhood that went out to fight." He pointed out a clump of trees about one mile distant. "Dinny Lacey's people lived there. Treacy, Breen, Crowe, Hogan and Lacey came from within a radius of less than three miles. Each one of them had sworn an oath that he would not be taken alive." With these words he bent down to cut a swathe through the rank grass.

From Kilfeacle I went to Soloheadbeg. On the way through the quiet countryside I passed the house where Seán Treacy had lived with his mother and his aunt, Maryanne Allis. The high hedges which line the approach to the limestone quarry bore silent testimony to the animated scene of 21 January 1919. The quarry has fallen into disuse. From it were hewn the stones of the great wall that forms a background to the memorial at Soloheadbeg Cross. In this wall tablets have been inserted, bearing beautifully sculptured designs of the arms of the four provinces of Ireland: the Red Hand of Ulster, the Three Crowns of Munster, the Harp of Leinster, the Eagle and Raised Sword of Connaught. The memorial to the men who took part in the ambush was unveiled by Seán T. O Ceallaig, President of Ireland, on Sunday 20 January 1950.

The official souvenir gives the following details:

OFFICIAL SOUVENIR

of the

SOLOHEADBEG MEMORIAL

Commemorating the Ambush at Soloheadbeg, 21st January, 1919.

Erected at Solohead Cross, Tipperary.

Memorial was designed by P. J. Coffey, B.E., Fethard, executed by Mr. Maguire, Sculptor, Tipperary, and erected in conjunction with Tipperary South Riding County Council Engineer under the guidance of the Seán Treacy Memorial Committee.

Unveiled by the President of Ireland,

SEÁN T. O CEALLAIGH,

On Sunday, 22nd January, 1950.

THE HISTORICAL SIGNIFICANCE OF SOLOHEADBEG

There is a saying: " Where Tipperary leads all Ireland follows." This saying is well borne out by what followed the lead given the country at Soloheadbeg on Tuesday, 21st January, 1919, the day on which the first Dáil Éireann unanimously adopted the Declaration of Irish Independence. On that date an engagement took place between members of the Irish Volunteers and an armed enemy party, resulting in two R.I.C. constables being shot dead and their equipment and arms, and the explosives they were escorting, captured.

It is our proud claim for Soloheadbeg, that it was the first deliberate, planned action by a select party of the Irish Volunteers (shortly to be recognised as the Irish Republican Army) renewing the armed struggle, temporarily suspended, after Easter Week 1916. The period of passive resistance, readjustment and reorganisation which ensued during 1917 and 1918 had ended. The leaders of the Tipperary Volunteers determined to resume the fight. The Soloheadbeg Ambush was conceived and carried through in the full knowledge that the challenge it issued must be backed in arms, and that the fight once embarked upon must be pressed to a successful conclusion, whatever the cost.

The Soloheadbeg encounter was not an accidental one. The ambush position had been occupied on several successive days, involving men from various Tipperary units of the Irish Volunteers, before the fateful 21st of January. It was not known when exactly the escort party conveying the explosives would move out from Tipperary Town, nor could it be known what would be the strength of the escort. This is mentioned to show the deliberateness of the action, and to clinch our claim that the fight against the British was resumed at Soloheadbeg.

To the Volunteers of Tipperary, therefore, must go the credit for carrying out what amounted to a re-declaration of war, involving not alone themselves but the whole country in the consequences. How justified was their action is now a matter of history.

The men who took part in the Solohead Ambush broke so far with tradition that they refused to fly the country after their coup. This course was urged upon them, but they determined to remain and carry on the fight against the enemy wherever and whenever they could, and with ever-increasing intensity. Their lead was an incentive to the rest of the country, and before long the British were finding that they had stirred up a hornet's nest. The rescue of Seán Hogan at the Station of Knocklong in the following May further increased the morale of the I.R.A. by showing what a few ill-armed men could achieve when they were imbued with the determination to do or die. In collaboration with the Dublin Brigade the war was brought into the streets of Dublin, including the abortive attack on the then Lord Lieutenant at Ashtown in December 1919, which had, nevertheless, the effect of further stepping-up the national morale. Barrack attacks, ambushes and raids on enemy communications followed, in all of which the Tipperary Volunteers took a leading part, leading up to the formation of regular Flying Columns in each area. The British now found it impossible to cope with the situation and sought a Truce in 1921. The victory was marred for the Tipperary Volunteers by the death in action in Dublin of the great Seán Treacy, on 14 October 1920, R.I.P.

The Memorial which has now been erected at Solohead Cross in commemoration of the historic action at Soloheadbeg will serve to remind future generations of the events of that stirring time, and of the brave men who fought and died for Ireland's freedom. It was carried out by the Memorial Committee with the co-operation of the Tipperary S.R. County Council. The Memorial comprises a granite shaft supporting a bronze torch, symbolic of the re-kindling of the flame of national resurgence, built upon a limestone base and raised by artistically-finished pedestals bearing an inscription in Irish, as follows:
" I mbuan-chuimne mortasach ar Ath-adhaint Chogadh na Saoirse tareis Seachtmhain na Casca 1916, ag Sulcoid Beag, 21adh Eanair, 1919, Soloheadbeg, January 21st,

1919." The monument proper is erected centrally in a massive limestone wall, in which are incorporated the arms of the Four Provinces, and the names of the eight participants in separate panels: CROWE, RYAN, HOGAN, TREACY, BREEN, McCORMACK, DWYER, ROBINSON—representing the order in which they occupied positions in the engagement.

It may be of interest to mention that the spot where the Memorial is erected was the scene of the Battle of Sulcoit (Solohead) in which Brian Boru defeated the Danes. Here, also, Seán Treacy drilled his first Company of the Irish Volunteers prior to Easter Week, 1916. Truly a suitable site for a National Memorial.

ADDRESS OF WELCOME TO THE PRESIDENT

On the occasion of his first visit to Tipperary Town on 22 January 1950, a number of addresses were presented to Mr. O Ceallaigh at a Reception in the Royal Hotel, before the unveiling ceremony. All the Public Bodies in the County, together with the County Committee of the Gaelic League and the Memorial Committee, were represented.

The Memorial Committee's Address read as follows:

ᴅílᴇᴀ5ʀᴀ ᴅ'á ᴏıʀᴅᴇᴀʀᴄᴀs sᴇán ᴄ. ó ᴄᴇᴀllᴀı5,
uᴀᴄᴄᴀʀán nᴀ ɧéıʀᴇᴀnn

ᴀ ᴏıʀᴅᴇᴀʀᴄᴀıs,

ᴅá ṁıᴀn lınnᴇ, ᴄᴏısᴄᴇ ᴄuıṁnᴇᴀᴄáın sulᴄóıᴅ ᴅᴇᴀ5, ꝼíoʀ-ᴄᴀoın ꝼáılᴄᴇ ᴅ'ꝼᴇᴀʀᴀᴅ ʀoṁᴀᴄ ᴀʀ ᴅo ᴄᴇᴀᴄᴄ 'n áʀ mᴇᴀsᴄ ᴅon ᴄéᴀᴅ uᴀıʀ ıᴅ' uᴀᴄᴄᴀʀán éıʀᴇᴀnn.

ıs ᴇol ᴅúınn ᴀ nᴅᴇᴀʀnᴀ ᴄú ᴀʀ son nᴀ ɧ-éıʀᴇᴀnn ı ʀıᴄ ᴅo sᴀoıl (sᴀol ꝼᴀᴅᴀ bʀuıᴅıuıl, 5nóᴄᴀᴄ) ı sınn ꝼéın, ı 5ᴄonnʀᴀᴅ nᴀ 5ᴀᴇıl5ᴇ, ıᴅ' ᴄᴀıᴅlᴇóıʀ ı ᴅᴄíoʀᴄᴀıᴅ ı 5ᴄéın, mᴀʀ ᴄᴇᴀᴄᴄᴀ ᴅálᴀ; ıs ᴇol ᴅúınn ꝼᴀıʀıs sın ᴀn ᴄ-suím 5níoṁᴀᴄ ᴀ ᴄuıʀᴇᴀnn ᴄú ꝼós ı n5ᴀᴄ 5né ᴅᴇn 5luᴀısᴇᴀᴄᴄ náısıúnᴄᴀ ᴅo ᴄum slánuıᴄᴇ nᴀ ᴄíʀᴇ 'nᴀ náısıún ᴄʀıosᴄᴀí 5ᴀᴇlᴀᴄ, ᴀᴄ 5o ʀó-spᴇısıᴀlᴄᴀ ꝼáılᴄımíᴅ-nᴇ, sᴇᴀn-ᴄompánᴀı5 sᴇáın uí ᴄʀᴇᴀsᴀı5, ꝼáılᴄımíᴅ ʀoṁᴀᴄ mᴀʀ sᴀı5ᴅıúıʀ ᴅ'ᴀʀm nᴀ poblᴀᴄᴄᴀ.

ıs ᴀnnso ı sulᴄóıᴄ ᴅᴇᴀ5 ᴀ ᴄuıʀᴇᴀᴅ ᴀᴄ-ᴄús lᴇ ᴄo5ᴀᴅ nᴀ sᴀoıʀsᴇ ᴀ ᴄosnuı5ᴇᴀᴅ ı 1916, ᴀ5us ıs ᴄuıᴅᴇ 5uʀ sᴇᴀn-sᴀı5ᴅıúıʀ poblᴀᴄᴄᴀᴄ ᴀ ᴅéᴀnꝼᴀᴅ lᴇᴀᴄᴄ ᴅo noᴄᴄᴀᴅ ıns ᴀn ıonᴀᴅ sᴄᴀıʀıúl sᴀn.

ᴄáımíᴅ buíᴅᴇᴀᴄ, ᴄáımíᴅ áᴄᴀsᴀᴄ, ᴄáımíᴅ móʀᴄᴀsᴀᴄ.

ᴄʀᴀosluımíᴅ ᴅo 5ʀᴀᴅᴀm lᴇᴀᴄ ı ᴅ'uᴀᴄᴄᴀʀán, ᴀ5us

ʒuıṁíọ ʒuʀ⁊ ꝼ⁊ọⱥ buⱥn tú ꝼéʼn nʒʀⱥọⱥm sⱥn, ꝼé ṁeⱥs
⁊ʒus ꝼé śⱥınte.

    1s Sınne, ⱥʀ son ⱥn Ċoıste Ċuıṁneⱥċⱥ́ın,

                    ⱥʀt ọe ⱱⱥʀʀlụⱥọ,
                                        Cⱥ́tⱥoıʀleⱥċ.

                    míċeⱥ́l mⱥc ʒıolⱥ pⱥ́ọʀⱥıʒ,
                    seosⱥṁ ó cⱥ́tⱥıl,
                                        Cısteóıʀí.

                    lıⱥm ó conⱥıll,
                                        Rúnⱥıọe Oınıʒ.

KNOCKLONG

Forty-five years have passed since that memorable day
on which Seán Hogan was snatched from the gallows by
his comrades—Treacy, Breen and Robinson—with the
assistance of the gallant men from Galbally. Mrs. Ellen
O'Byrne has a vivid memory of one particular episode.
Her husband, Davey, had returned from the Argentine and
set up a butcher's shop close to the railway-station. On
the evening of 13 May 1919 Davey was attending to a
customer. Some of their children were playing on the
street outside the shop. Mrs. O'Byrne had the youngest
child in her arms. She heard the train steam into the
station and almost instantly the air was rent with sharp
noises. Mrs. O'Byrne's first impression was that some
boy was cracking an Indian whip—quite a favourite pastime
of the young lads. The news soon spread that the Volunteers
were attacking a posse of police who were travelling on the
train. Mrs. O'Byrne promptly called her children into the
house and shepherded them into the kitchen. She laid the
baby in the cradle and had just closed the kitchen-door
when a young man, handcuffed, rushed into the shop. He
was pale and trembling. "Take them off, take them off,"
he pleaded, holding up his hands. Davey jumped to the
conclusion that he was a Volunteer who had escaped from
his escort. With great presence of mind Mrs. O'Byrne bolted
the front door and procured a 7-lb. weight in which there
was a deep groove. She ordered the young man to place
his hands over the centre-bar of the weight and she herself
firmly held them in position. Davey reached for the
cleaver and with one sure and swift blow severed the hand-

cuffs. It was a master-stroke which only a practised hand could administer. The smallest deflection would have resulted in the severing of an artery. Ellen O'Byrne brought Seán Hogan to the rear of the house and guided him through the garden-path which led to open country.

The part which the O'Byrnes played was kept a close secret—even from next-door neighbours—until years had passed. They were never questioned about the matter, although the police had tried to trace Hogan's movements, step by step, from the moment of his escape.

Mrs. O'Byrne recalled the morning of the attack on Kilmallock barracks. " I gave breakfast to twenty-five of the Cork boys who were on their way to Kilmallock. They knew that a butcher's house was a good place to come for a meal," she said with a pleasant smile. When the war was over and people were putting in their claims for compensation, the O'Byrnes did not present their bill. " We didn't want to spoil the memory by looking for money . . . They were the brave boys," she mused to herself, half aloud.

Davey died 16 September 1957. The cleaver is in the Dublin " War of Independence " museum—a souvenir of those exciting days.

" FERNSIDE "

Memories live on from generation to generation in the countryside. There is no such permanence in cities where families frequently change from one district to another. This fact was forcibly impressed on my mind when I tried to locate the house in which Dan Breen and Seán Treacy fought it out with the Crown forces. The shop-attendants in the Drumcondra and Whitehall area had never heard of the famous gun-battle that took place in the early morning of 12 October 1920. An old lady followed me from a provision store and told me that the caretaker of St. Patrick's Training College might be able to give me some information, but when I called at the gate-lodge I learned that this man had died some time ago. A member of the college staff put me in touch with a retired National teacher, Edmond Herbert. During that troubled time Mr. Herbert lived nearly half a mile from the Whitehall area. On the night of the encounter he heard several bursts of firing. He accompanied me to " Fernside " which is the fourth house of the terrace on Drumcondra Road, between the

Training College and Home Farm Road. The present
occupant, Miss McCarron, kindly allowed us to inspect the
premises. The room that was occupied by Breen and Treacy
is immediately to the right at the head of the landing. The
conservatory has been removed, but the outline of its
juncture with the end of the dwellinghouse is clearly defined.
The bullet holes in the bedroom door had been filled with
putty and the panels repainted, but one can still trace the
impressions that had been made in the woodwork by the
bullets.

In those days Miss McCarron lived with her parents a
few doors farther down the terrace. She has a very clear
memory of that night's terror—the incessant shooting, the
crashing of glass and the shouting of orders to the soldiers
who had taken up a position in the laneway at the rear.
The inhabitants of the neighbourhood spent a sleepless
night. When morning came, they spoke to one another in
hushed voices. Rumours were afloat that several soldiers
had been killed and removed by ambulances. A dispute
had arisen between the military and the drivers of the
corporation-owned ambulances. The latter had been ordered
by their authorities to take the corpses to the city-morgue,
but they were compelled at gun-point to drive to King
George V hospital (now St. Bricin's).

When Dan wrote the original version of *My Fight for
Irish Freedom*, he omitted one very striking detail. Having
pursued the soldiers as far as the front door, he took a
grenade from one of the men who was lying mortally
wounded in the hallway and hurled it after the retreating
figures. The soldiers who lined the far side of the road
were thrown into such confusion by the explosion that they
turned their machine-gun against their own men who were
running from the house. In the moonlight it would have
been difficult to distinguish friend from foe. This fatal error
of judgment accounts for the high number of casualties
among the raiding-party.

Dan mentions that he escaped through fields which were
close to the rear of the house. This territory, once open
country, is now the thickly-populated Home Farm area.
It seems almost incredible that a man so grievously
wounded could have scaled the high wall that enclosed
St. Patrick's Training College. In moments of stress a
human being will call on unsuspected reserves of strength.
During the fighting he had been filled with the rage of battle,

and this infusion of spirit helped him to make that super-human spring from the ground to the coping-stone of the high wall. In his youth he had the lithe movement of a panther, and constant hardship kept him in perfect physical trim. He has related how on a previous occasion, loaded down with rifle and knapsack, he had taken a five-barred gate in his stride as he ran from " The Tin House " on the approach of a group of police.

When the smoke of battle had cleared away, and an un-easy peace came to Ireland, the image of Dan Breen emerged from the crucible of war as the typical Irish Volunteer. In his memoirs, *Winter's Tale*, the chief of the Dublin Castle Secret Service, General Sir Ormonde Winter, paid a grudging tribute to " Breen and Treacy, the brave and fearless gunmen from Tipperary." The image was not dimmed with the passage of time. Long after the Civil War Dan was travelling one day on the Dublin-Belfast train. While the Customs inspection was taking place at the border, the B-Specials who were on duty and all the officials crowded round the compartment window to have a close look at the notorious Dan Breen. Down south, a rare tribute was paid to Dan's prowess by an old beggar-woman who travelled from town to town. She was known as " Mary Help " or " Mary the Kettle," because she always carried a capacious kettle into which she transferred the alms that were tendered in kind—tea, sugar, or any comestible. One day she called to a huckster's shop that was owned by an R.I.C. pensioner and his wife. This woman had been twice widowed. Her former husbands had been also members of the R.I.C. In the words of Thomas Moore's melody *Believe Me If All Those Endearing Young Charms* :

> The heart that has truly loved never forgets
> But as dearly loves on to the close.

Her present husband was already in decline. Mary asked for the usual " help." The pensioner was behind the counter, and was about to proffer some alms, when a voice sounded from a room off the shop, " If that's Mary Kettle, send her about her business." Mary shrieked indignantly, " Beware of that woman of yours. If she lives long enough she'll chalk up as many Peelers to her credit as Dan Breen has notches to his gun."

Even at the other side of St. George's Channel his fame had become established. A group of Dublin businessmen got the bright idea of forming a company for the purpose of having George Bernard Shaw's plays filmed in Ireland. Shaw favoured the project and sent Gabriel Pascal to Dublin with specific instructions to bring over Dan Breen as representative of the Company. An Irishwoman who was the wife of a British army officer drove Dan to Ayot St. Laurence. The village policeman directed them to the house of "the bloke who makes his money from writing." The door was opened by a girl from County Mayo. Shaw's flaming red beard, knickerbocker and long stockings reminded Dan of a picture of "Old Nick" that he had seen in his boyhood. G.B.S. entertained his visitor with a pot of black tea and endless conversation. He spoke of his visit to Roger Casement in the Tower of London on the eve of his impeachment for high treason. He advised Casement to dispense with counsel for the defence. "You'll be hanged without a doubt. Plead your own cause. This will give you an opportunity of making your speech for posterity. If you employ a barrister, the presiding judge will congratulate him on his specious arguments and then don the black cap." Shaw expressed surprise that the Volunteers allowed the R.I.C. to function for such a long time. They should have been eliminated with greater ruthlessness. If this had been done, the British Government could not carry on for one day without "their eyes and ears."

The scheme for the filming of the plays fell through because sufficient capital was not forthcoming, but, as a result of the discussions, G.B.S. and Dan became fast friends. Many letters were exchanged. Unfortunately, only one of Shaw's letters has survived. It deserves to be quoted in full.

From Bernard Shaw

4 Whitehall Court

London S.W.

Telegrams—Socialist, Parl, London.

Dear Dan,

Get all this sentimental rubbish out of your blessed old noodle; I have no feeling in business. You can't humbug me; and it grieves me that you have humbugged yourself to the tune of £1,000.

I have given you time to do your damnedest to raise

Irish capital. The result is £40,000. For film purposes it might as well be 40 brass farthings; a million and a half is the least we could start with; and it would barely see us through two big feature films.

The simplest and perhaps the honestest thing for the S.A. Ltd., would be to wind up and pocket its losses. But after the company has been advertised as it has been its failure would be a failure for Ireland. What is the available alternative ? First, to get rid of me and Pascal. The Protestant capitalists will not back me because I am on talking terms with you, and do not believe that you will go to hell when you die. The clergy, now that they know that I will not write up the saints for them, will not back a notorious free-thinker. The Catholic laity will not back a bloody Protestant. The capitalists who have no religion and no politics except money-making rule me out as a highbrow in whom there is no money. All of them object to Pascal because he is a foreigner who throws away millions as if they were threepenny bits. So out we go with our contracts torn up.

Next, S.A. must cut film production out of its program and become a studio building company raising the capital wherever it can get it, from Rank, Korda, Hollywood, Belfast, Ballsbridge, Paddy Murphy, John Bull and Solomon Isacs. It is true that the studios will cost two millions in two years; but when they are ready the company will be an Irish landlord gathering rent from all the producing companies on earth.

I can see no alternative to a winding-up order except this. I have written it all to Dev; so don't try to gammon him about it; but believe me and face it. When (———) turned S.A. down with £10,000, the game was up. You all thought I was your ace of trumps; I knew that I might be your drawback, but thought I might as well have a try. It has been a failure. I apologise and withdraw.

Still, ever the best of friends,

G. Bernard Shaw.

Dan Breen, Esq., M.P.,
Dáil Éireann,
Leinster House,
Dublin.
Éire.

I have written to Arthur Cox to the same effect; but in greater detail as to the agenda on the shareholders' meeting which will be necessary if you change your policy as I suggest.

When Father John Hannon, S.J., was sent by Pope Pius XII cn a special mission to India, Dan provided him with a personal introduction to Gandhi. This proved invaluable to Father Hannon. Gandhi assured him of his own friendly interest in the work, and granted full freedom of movement through the country. On his return from India, Father Hannon emphasised in a special audience with the Holy Father the role that Dan Breen had played. Pius XII showed his appreciation by sending Dan the Apostolic Benediction and a special message of thanks.

Dan's souvenirs of his war against the British will go with him to the grave. He can show several scars received in battle; a splinter of lead still rests on his spinal cord. He deserves well of his country. He was one of that noble band of Irishmen who risked everything for the freedom of their native land.

Editor—Anvil Books.

POSTSCRIPT

Portion of Professor Carolan's statement made at the Mater Hospital in the presence of witnesses:

I admitted the raiding party on the morning of 12th October. They asked me about Dick (Mulcahy) and I replied that he had not been here for some time.

A gun was pressed to my temple. "What do you know of the men who have fired at our Forces?" "Nothing." I was taken to the landing. Several minutes had elapsed since I had heard the crash of glass in the greenhouse. I hoped that by this time the two men had got away. A shot was fired at me point-blank. I felt a searing pain in my throat. I fell over a corpse that was lying on the corridor. I was carried to Enright's room (Enright was a harbour pilot who lodged in our house) and placed on a bed. Doctor Murray bandaged my wound.

They cross-examined me about the identity of the two men. I said that I did not know them. "Who recommended them?" I did not answer. They threatened to set fire to the house. To save my wife and young son, I said that they told me that they came from Fleming's but that Mr. Fleming had not personally recommended them. This was quite true. When they called to me on the first occasion, I was reluctant about taking them in. They looked so crestfallen and seemed to be such decent young fellows that I decided to admit them to the house.

The military said that they found a letter in the mackintosh which was hanging on the hall-stand. This letter was addressed to The Quartermaster, Third Tipperary Brigade. The military stated that I told them that the mackintosh belonged to Ryan. I never made this statement. I was asked whether the mackintosh was mine. I replied that it did not belong to me. I singled out my coat from the others that were hanging on the hall-stand. I did not enter into any discussion with the military concerning the identity of the man called Ryan.